**Ejidos and Regions
of Refuge in
Northwestern Mexico**

ANTHROPOLOGICAL PAPERS OF
THE UNIVERSITY OF ARIZONA
NUMBER 46

Ejidos and Regions of Refuge in Northwestern Mexico

N. Ross Crumrine
Phil C. Weigand
EDITORS

THE UNIVERSITY OF ARIZONA PRESS
TUCSON
1987

About the Editors

N. ROSS CRUMRINE, one of the few outsiders able to communicate in the Mayo language, spent several years in resident field research among the Mayo of southern Sonora. His major focus has been on the relationship between rapid economic and technological change and cultural stability and dynamics. He has conducted comparative field research in the Catacaos area of Piura, the northwest coast region of Peru, which provides a broad basis for the analysis and understanding of the northwestern Mexican data. Crumrine received a doctoral degree from the University of Arizona in 1968, and is a Professor of Anthropology at the University of Victoria in Canada. Among his numerous publications are *The Mayo Indians of Sonora: A People Who Refuse to Die* and *The Power of Symbols: Masks and Masquerade in the Americas,* edited with Marjorie Halpin.

PHIL C. WEIGAND has specialized in the archaeology and ethnography of western and northwestern Mexico. His primary interests are in economic and social organization in an archaeological and historical perspective, and he has done fieldwork throughout the American Southwest and Mexico. He holds a Bachelor of Arts degree in History from Indiana University and a doctoral degree in Anthropology from Southern Illinois University. Dr. Weigand is a member of the faculty at the State University of New York, Stony Brook and is Chairman of that Department of Anthropology. Recent publications include *Mining and Mining Techniques in Ancient Mesoamerica,* edited with Gretchen Gwynne, and *The Archaeology of Western and Northwestern Mesoamerica,* edited with Michael Foster.

Cover: A Mayo home, located just above and north of the Fuerte River Valley.

THE UNIVERSITY OF ARIZONA PRESS
Copyright © 1987
The Arizona Board of Regents
All Rights Reserved
This book was set in 10/12 Linotron Times Roman.
Manufactured in the U.S.A.
Library of Congress Cataloging-in-Publication Data

Ejidos and regions of refuge in northwestern Mexico.
  (Anthropological papers of the University of
Arizona; no. 46)
    Bibliography: p.
    Includes index.
    1. Indians of Mexico—Cultural assimilation.
2. Indians of Mexico—Ethnic identity. 3. Mayo
Indians—Cultural assimilation. 4. Mayo Indians—
Ethnic identity. 5. Yaqui Indians—Cultural assimilation. 6. Yaqui Indians—Ethnic identity. I. Crumrine,
N. Ross. II. Weigand, Phil C. III. Series.
F1219.3.C85E37 1987   305.8'97   86-24978
ISBN 0-8165-1002-4
British Library Cataloguing in Publication data are available.

In Memory
of
Ralph L. Beals

Contents

Preface	ix
1. Reflections, Contrasts, and Directions Ralph L. Beals and N. Ross Crumrine	1
2. Yaqui Indian Enclavement: The Effects of an Experimental Indian Policy in Northwestern Mexico Steven V. Lutes	11
3. Mechanisms of Enclavement Maintenance and Sociocultural Blocking of Modernization Among the Mayo of Southern Sonora N. Ross Crumrine	21
4. Enclavement Processes, State Policies, and Cultural Identity Among the Mayo Indians of Sinaloa, Mexico Manuel L. Carlos	33
5. Production, Social Identity, and Agrarian Struggle Among the Tepecano Indians of Northern Jalisco Robert D. Shadow	39
6. The Marginalization of the Ejidos of the Magdalena-Etzatlán Unidad de Riego, Jalisco Phil C. Weigand and Francisco Ron Siordia	47
7. Families from Tarascan Villages Mary Lee Nolan	57
8. Insistence and Persistence in Cultural Enclavement: Villages That Progress Chose? George Castile	73
9. Old World Diseases and the Dynamics of Indian and Jesuit Relations in Northwestern New Spain, 1520–1660 Daniel T. Reff	85
10. The Renaissance of Anthropological Studies in Northwestern Mexico Ralph L. Beals	95
References	103
Index	111

FIGURES

1.1. Location of the major indigenous and mestizo groups in northwestern Mexico	xii
1.2. The modern town hall in Navojoa	4
1.3. Mayo corn drying, with the home owner's wheat field beyond	5
1.4. Traditional Mayo coffee-making in the cooking jacal	6
1.5. A traditional Mayo baker	7
2.1. The former Yaqui church in Bacom as now reconstructed	16
3.1. A gathering at a Mayo home for the 8 Day Ritual after death	26
3.2. Circling (konti) of the grave after the prayers during the 8 Day Ritual	27
6.1. The Magdalena-Etzatlán Irrigation District, Jalisco	46
6.2. View to the north of the Etzatlán Valley, with Etzatlán in the foreground and the Ejido of San Pedro in the background	53
6.3. The ejido lands of San Juanito, Santiago, and La Joya, showing the fragmentation of these plots	54
7.1. San Juan fiesta dancers	60
7.2. Elementary school graduation in Zacan, 1971	62
7.3. Secondary school graduation in San Juan, 1971	62
7.4. Angahuan child and girls from urban Mexico	71
8.1. Modern transportation to Cherán	77
8.2. The coordinating center of I.N.I. in Cherán	78
8.3. The procession of the *panaleros*	79
8.4. One example of "modernization"	80
8.5. The town council and the local school teachers taking part in the "Day of the Flag"	82

TABLES

2.1.	Policy and lifestyle variables	19
6.1.	Land tenure according to type of legal possession	48
6.2.	Area cultivated by season and harvests	49
6.3.	Sorghum-maize and wheat-garbanzo contrasts in ejido-pequeña propiedad	50
6.4.	Average income in pesos per hectare	51
6.5.	Mechanization	52
6.6.	Points of equilibrium: 1974–1975 season	55
7.1.	Ancestral couples and descendants by town of origin	61
7.2.	Residence of descendants	64
7.3.	Location by generation	64
7.4.	Occupations of adult descendants	65
7.5.	Occupation groups of adult descendants	65
7.6.	Occupation of descendants by residence	66
7.7.	Occupation by generation	67
7.8.	Generational change in terms of Cosio's socioeconomic categories	68
7.9.	Traditional and modern occupations by generation	68
7.10.	Ancestor ethnicity and descendant occupations	69
7.11.	Socioeconomic status of parents and offspring	69

Preface

This volume explores two interrelated concepts and specific types of socioculture change and continuity: enclavement and the region of refuge. We believe these concepts, as developed in the two seminal volumes *Regiones de Refugio* by Gonzalo Aguirre Beltrán and *Cycles of Conquest* by Edward H. Spicer, provide a firm basis for continued analysis of technological, economic, and political patterns of culture contact and change. We realize that, perhaps in part because of the complexity of the arguments, these concepts and volumes may not continue to receive the attention and consideration that they merit. Because our area interests are northwestern and western Mexico, it is productive to reanalyze the enclavement and region of refuge models in terms of modern data being collected by anthropologists working in this region.

Thomas Hinton and Phil Weigand organized one of the first symposiums focusing on this general area, "Themes of Indigenous Acculturation in Northwest Mexico"; it was held during the 69th Annual Meeting of the American Anthropological Association in San Diego in 1970 (Hinton and Weigand 1981). That symposium of papers provided the first step toward this volume. Eight years later the 77th Annual Meeting of the Association was held in Los Angeles, providing a central location close to northwestern Mexico for our subsequent symposium, "Social Enclavement in Northwestern and Western Mexico." We invited papers dealing with either Indian, mestizo, or mixed communities.

Within this general geographic region, certain communities have undergone intensive periods of culture contact yet remain marginal in many ways, whereas other communities are still quite isolated. Nevertheless, certain patterns of change and of resistance to change, patterns of enclavement and "regiones de refugio," characterize the area. Our aim in the symposium was to focus on the presentation of specific case studies in terms of these models of culture contact. The work of Aguirre Beltrán on regions of refuge was examined from a more northerly perspective, and the enclavement model of Edward Spicer was extended to the more southerly areas of the study region. The technological, economic, and political variables became major orientations, although we did not exclude papers that also examined modern technological innovations or ethnic and ideological aspects when these variables were linked with the former ones. Our ultimate goal involved the clarification, reexamination, and analysis of major variables and processes associated with enclavement and regions of refuge within the general theory of culture change.

The papers, discussions, and general development of the 1978 symposium indicated that recent years represent a most crucial period in the development of indigenous traditions in northwestern and western Mexico, and also in our thinking about and analysis of the changes in process. Many of the papers presented in the original Hinton and Weigand 1970 symposium (published in 1981) do not portray the more recent broad dynamic modernization taking place in the area. Conceptually, however, they proved most useful in assessing changes in enclavement and regions of refuge responding to modernization, in some cases breaking down, yet in others retaining a striking and dynamic adaptation to change. It became clear that specific changes on the coastal plain in the Yaqui-Mayo area were formally different yet structurally quite similar to processes taking place in the Huichol region and in the Tarascan area.

On the coastal plain of southern Sonora and northern Sinaloa, we observe Yaqui and Sonoran and Sinaloan Mayo groups. Ecologically fantastically varied, this region is now characterized by intense modernization and agricultural business developments alongside discouraging poverty and culturally diverse perceptions of and reactions toward the area. That the most modern region of Mexico is characterized by certain elements of enclavement and of a region of refuge at first appears inconsistent and unbelievable. However, the three chapters dealing with these peoples and this region clarify and develop models and explanations of this perplexing problem. These analyses focus on modern conditions and dip into reconstruction and early explorer and missionary documents for a precontact and mission period base line. Of course, in contrast to the completely assimilated Opata, the Yaqui and Mayo represent surviving indigenous groups.

In Chapter 2, Steven Lutes describes the conditions of modern Yaqui enclavement in part by contrasting the Yaqui with the Mayo and mestizos of the region. He touches on the question of recent Yaqui and Mayo divergences, a problem first examined by Beals (1945) and later discussed by Erasmus (1961, 1967), Spicer (1970), and Crumrine (1981). Lutes also points out that traits that contrast the Yaqui with the mestizo tend to take on high symbolic value in the Yaqui perception of the modern world, for example, Yaqui and Mayo masked dancing complexes that are unique in southern Sonora and northern Sinaloa (Lutes 1983, Crumrine 1983). In strong contrast to the Yaqui, revitalization movements characterize modern Mayo religion, a divergence that has challenged anthropological interpretation (Spicer 1970, Crumrine 1981). Also in contrast to Yaqui behavior, the Mayo supported both verbally and physically the recent land invasions in southern Sonora that took place during the last months of the Etcheverría Presidency.

Agreeing with Lute's distinction between the Yaqui and the Mayo, N. Ross Crumrine (Chapter 3) focuses on the niche that the Mayo both have generated and into which they have been forced. In contrast to the following chapter by Carlos, Crumrine tends to examine the perception of and response to modernization by individual Sonoran Mayo and their development of an opposition cultural tradition. Thus, the modern Mayo do not reflect a classic enclaved society nor a region of refuge but rather a group embedded within contemporary Mexico. Continuing to analyze Cáhitan data, the Mayo of Sinaloa, Manuel Carlos shifts the point of view to a more general level and in so doing diverges theoretically from Lutes and Crumrine. As author (Carlos 1974) of a previous volume on the Sinaloa Mayo, Carlos draws on a broad data base. He analyzes Sinaloan Mayo culture change in terms of the Mayo reflection of their own dependency on Mexican society. Although the points of view of the chapters are somewhat different, the structural patterns of embedding and dependency developed in each prove strikingly similar. The three chapters supplement each other and provide a useful single picture of modern Mayo-Yaqui patterns of change and adaptation in these three adjacent coastal river regions.

The following chapters turn to processes of enclavement and assimilation among indigenous and mestizo groups of western and southern northwestern Mexico. Robert Shadow (Chapter 5) develops the relationship between production as an independent variable and identity as a dependent variable among the Tepecano Indians of northern Jalisco. Although culturally and ideologically assimilated to local peasant mestizo culture, the Tepecano maintain a concept of their separate Indian identity and support their colonial corporate communal land structure. In Chapter 6, Phil Weigand and Francisco Ron Siordia discuss the relationship between the concepts of marginalization and enclavement, using an analysis of their research among the mestizo ejidos of the Magdalena-Etzatlán basin of central west Jalisco.

Shifting to the Tarascan region of western Mexico, Mary Lee Nolan (Chapter 7) provides a graphic example of the migration and adaptation of families and communities to a drastic environmental change, the appearance and eruptions of the volcano Parícutin. In the analysis not only of local adjustment to enclavement and to assimilation but also of patterns of migrations and occupational change, Nolan follows up numerous suggestions concerning migration from regions of refuge discussed by Aguirre Beltrán (1967) in his classic work. In Chapter 8, George Castile develops his original role as one of the symposium discussants into a broad commentary of the models of enclavement and of regions of refuge. He couples this discussion with a specific analysis of the Tarascan community of Cherán, which he studied in 1969 and 1970. In Chapter 9 Daniel Reff has expanded his general interest in the role of disease in northwestern Mexico in relation to enclavement. In his original symposium paper, Reff documented the devastating spread of European diseases to northern Sinaloa and southern Sonora that occurred 30 years before the arrival of the Jesuit missionaries. He argued that these diseases also ravished central and northern Sonora, disrupting Opata village life and forcing the populace to abandon villages and settle in dispersed communities. Thus, the Opata conceived of the mission pueblos as a partial reestablishment of the old and traditional order.

The volume is summarized and concluded by the fascinating chapter by Ralph Beals. He provides a broad historical perspective of the development of research in this general region and an analysis of the theories and models that stimulated anthropological thought concerning northwestern and western Mexico. Not only does his account make exciting reading but his assessment of historical changes, continuities, and progress provides a most thoughtful and useful contribution to the volume. After outlining the history of research in the region, Beals discusses the chapters, adding his mature vision to a meaningful and well-founded critique, and appeals for an examination of the connections between the concepts and theories of enclavement and ethnicity. In the sense that the research and publications of Professor Beals have stimulated essentially all the contributing authors, it is especially fitting and an honor that he was kind enough to write this concluding chapter.

The data presented in this volume emphasize the dynamic nature of the relations of various peoples to cultural and natural ecological conditions, and the importance of a close examination of specific time periods and sociocultural dynamics. One of the aims of this volume is to record the structures of culture contact and the dynamics of adjustment that characterize the indigenous groups of northwestern and western Mexico. Other events also suggest that this volume is most timely. *Regiones de Refugio* (originally published by Gonzalo Aguirre Beltrán in 1967) was translated into English and published by the Society for Applied Anthropology in 1980. In addition, that year represented the 50th anniversary of the initial field research of Ralph Beals in northwestern Mexico and the year of publication of *The Yaquis: A Cultural History* by Edward Spicer, and Spicer's *Cycles of Conquest* was reprinted in 1986. On a much sadder note, 1983 and 1985 mark the deaths of Edward Spicer and Ralph Beals. Their loss as active anthropologists leaves an irreplaceable void in the group of northwestern Mexico scholars. Clearly this volume builds on their pioneering research and stimulus as teachers and colleagues. This is an appropriate time, indeed, to reexamine our field research in northwestern and western Mexico both in terms of intense modernization and of enclavement and regions of refuge as analytical explanatory models.

N. Ross Crumrine
Phil C. Weigand

**Ejidos and Regions
of Refuge in
Northwestern Mexico**

Figure 1.1. Location of the major indigenous and mestizo groups in northwestern Mexico. (Drawing by Barbara Dashwood.)

CHAPTER ONE

Reflections, Contrasts, and Directions

Ralph Beals (University of California, Los Angeles)
N. Ross Crumrine (University of Victoria, Victoria, Canada)

The chapters in this book reveal sweeping economic and technological changes that occurred in northwestern and western Mexico both in the early years of Spanish domination and colonization and in the years following the Second World War. The authors describe the persistence and revitalization of indigenous cultures and societies and the continued exploitation and manipulation of the local indigenous groups by national, state, and regional economic and political interests. Their perceptions are based on field research in that region of Mexico (Fig. 1.1), and it is appropriate and informative to review the significant changes in the conditions of the fieldwork itself. In describing his initial field research experiences, Ralph Beals emphasizes the physical hardships involved in traveling and living in that area in the 1930s. Those conditions provide a striking contrast to field research among the Mayo forty years later.

REFLECTIONS
(Ralph Beals)

My interest in Mexico began during a visit of nearly a year in Sonora and Sinaloa long before I had heard of anthropology. The personal reasons for the trip are irrelevant here as are many of the details. It was good preparation for my later interests, for I came to know very well many classes of the local society. As a result I formed a deep affection for the country and its people, even the poorest of whom were mostly friendly and often shared with me their meager rations and gave me shelter. I saw some of the effects of the long period of Revolution, the burned haciendas and destroyed houses in towns, the effects of disease and starvation as well as the actual ravages of the influenza epidemic of 1918 and 1919, here accompanied by a smallpox epidemic that sometimes depopulated whole villages. I also heard many stories of the Yaqui wars.

In Sonora, travel outside the settlements was extremely hazardous except with an armed party of some size. The thrice weekly trains of the Sud Pacífico de México included two steel gondolas with two mounted machine guns, each manned by 20 or 30 soldiers. And near Cajeme (now Ciudad Obregón), I hid under a bush while a large mounted Yaqui war party crossed the cart track nearby, the leaders with their coyote skin and parrot feather headdresses, some men armed only with bows and arrows, the war drums tapping at each end of the extended skirmish line. Even before I learned about anthropology, I was intensely curious about these people, their apparent preservation of indigenous culture, and their long and fierce battles for independence.

Even in 1930, Mexico had not completely recovered from the devastating effects of the Revolution and public order was often precarious. The last Yaqui uprising in Sonora was in 1928, and in 1930 some rebels still hid out in the Sierra de Bacatete. The Yaqui area was under martial law during the period of my fieldwork there and access was restricted. I recently found a folder with the documents I had carried in the field; there were nine, including letters from the Governor of Sonora; the Ministers of Education, both national and state; letters from Ramón Beteta and Moisés Saenz, both prominent political figures of the time; José Manuel Puig Cassauranc, Mexico's ambassador to the United States; and a letter of safe conduct, written in Yaqui, by General Angel Flores, a Yaqui war chief living in Pascua Village near Tucson, Arizona. The letter recommended me to all Yaqui, and was intended to introduce me to the rebels in the Sierra. More important, it turned out, were personal contacts. One was an introduction to Arthur Hofmann and his wife, Mona, from Max Rosenberg, a friend of Kroeber's and an amateur armchair anthropologist with an extensive private library. Hofmann was manager of the largest rice mill in Mexico. It was located in Ciudad Obregón (then still called Cajeme after a famous Yaqui war chief), and was one of the worldwide enterprises of Rosenberg Brothers, dealers in dried foods. Important in a different way was an introduction provided by Carl Sauer to Gus Dingfelder, a German-American for many years resident in Mexico.

Dingfelder had fought on both sides in the Yaqui wars and had gruesome photographs to back up his stories of atrocities committed by both sides. At the time he was developing a large tomato farm on the south side of the Yaqui river close to Potam, the westernmost of the Yaqui towns later to be studied by Edward Spicer (1954). Potam could be reached from Dingfelder's ranch by a ford across the Yaqui River if water was low. The crossing was somewhat chancy for the river was still uncontrolled and could rise rapidly. I once was stalled in the middle and the rising waters had reached the top of the seat before Dingfelder, notified by a passing horseman, sent a team of mules to rescue me.

Dingfelder introduced me to the officials at Potam and gained me permission to stay. He helped me find an unused corner of a storeroom in which to sleep and a primitive *fonda* where I could buy meals. I thus entered the Yaqui territory through a "back door" unbeknownst to the military. Potam lacked a garrison, for it was a new establishment settled by "neutral" Yaqui who had been sitting out the wars near Guaymas. It also boasted such amenities as a post office.

Unfortunately I soon came down with malaria, although one was supposedly safe from contracting this disease during winter. Most probably I was infected during a few days spent in Hermosillo, the capital, while gaining clearance from state government officials. I was forced to return to Ciudad Obregón, where Arthur Hofmann and Mona took me into their home. Arthur had warned me against the local medicos and undertook treatment himself, drawing on his long experience not only in Mexico but also in the Argentine Chaco, where for some nine years he managed a Rosenberg cattle ranch. He was a shrewd manipulator of the local social and political structure, an ability he used later in my behalf.

After recovering from malaria, I attempted to return to the Yaqui villages, but was turned back by Mexican army officials because the area was under martial law and I lacked proper credentials. For the remainder of the season I consequently devoted all my time to the Mayo, establishing headquarters in Navojoa. Living in Mayo towns seemed impractical because of official attitudes, the negativism of the Mayo toward strangers, lack of housing, and real or fancied health hazards. Normally I drove to a Mayo settlement each day, observed, took what notes I could, and talked with anyone who would respond. During ceremonials I sometimes stayed the night. Note taking at ceremonies was nearly impossible for lack of light and the hostility note taking evoked. Consequently I worked hard at developing my memory, when possible later going over my recollections of observed events with an informant. In the following year when Elsie Clews Parsons spent some weeks with me, we practiced writing independent accounts and then comparing them to check our accuracy, which was rather high.

I also reconnoitered all the major settlements on not only the Mayo, but the Fuerte and Sinaloa rivers, penetrating the Sierra foothills as far as the towns of Alamos, El Fuerte, and Sinaloa. One purpose was to identify the settlements with Mayo speech and to seek traces of other Cáhita groups such as the Ahome, Sinaloa, Tehueco, and Nios. All these groups apparently had vanished, either being replaced by Mayo or being Mayoized (the alternatives probably can never be determined barring the discovery of documents for the 18th-century period).

The following year I tried to follow protocol and operate through channels—a formal letter from the President of the University to the State Department, thence through the Foreign Office in Mexico City (seeking clearance to enter Yaqui territory). After three months I left for the field without any response to the official request. In Cajeme, Arthur Hofmann took me to the General commanding the military district and urged my case for visiting the Yaqui. The General improved my opinion of Mexican army intelligence considerably. He knew about my visit in Pascua village near Tucson, including the names of all the people I had talked with, and requested that I tell him about our discussions. I was able to satisfy him with some rather general and nonincriminating statements and he issued me a permit to enter and reside in the villages under martial law, subject to conditions established by the officers on the spot. I was required to live in Estación Vicam, a new settlement on the railroad, staying in the only inn within Yaqui territory. For the first month or so of my stay I also was forbidden to leave the inn unless accompanied by a Lieutenant of the Army, a young man who fortunately spoke fluent Cáhita. He was more or less favorably known to the Yaqui and at times interpreted for me. With him I was able to visit various towns and to observe ceremonies. I also was able to persuade a few Yaqui to visit and talk with me at the inn. I was also visited secretly by a representative of the rebels who wanted me to visit them in the Sierra de Bacatete, an invitation I declined not from fear of the Yaqui but of the certainty that I would land in a Mexican jail on my return. The army restrictions were intended to protect me and avoid any "incident."

After about a month, the army decided I was able to get on with the Yaqui sufficiently well not to get into trouble and removed all restrictions on my movement. Ironically, after my return from the field a denial of my original request came through the same elaborate channels, stating that because of the remoteness of the Yaqui area from centers of control the government of Mexico could not guarantee my safety.

The concerns of Mexican authorities were not entirely baseless. The last major attempt at an armed revolt against the government had occurred only two years before my field trip, and one of the important campaigns had been fought along the Pacific Coast from the U.S. border to Mazatlan. A major battle had occurred just south of the Mayo River. The Yaqui had staged a general uprising at the same time. A peace treaty had been signed with them in 1929 under which adult males were enrolled as a special militia, paid one peso a day by the government, with payment dependent on presence at a roll call morning and evening. Nevertheless, many Yaqui had refused to sign the peace accords and either had fled to the United States or were living as "outlaws" in the Sierra de Bacatete only a few hours away from the settlements along the railway skirting the mountains. While no recent attacks on trains had occurred, travelers on the road paralleling the railroad were frequently attacked and robbed, and one or more killings a week occurred. Army posts were located every fifteen miles or so. Travelers were checked at each point and information telephoned ahead; if they did not show up at the next check point in a reasonable time, a patrol was sent out to look for them or their remains. In addition, motorized patrols covered the road two or more times a day. Interestingly enough, in response to extensive criticism in regional newspapers, the army insisted the attacks and murders on the road were not the work of Yaqui Indians but of mestizo bandits.

Unrest in northwestern Mexico was not confined to Yaqui territory or just to rural areas. Development of the south bank of the Yaqui River had begun and Cajeme was a typical "boom" town, attracting undesirables from all over Mexico. Brawls occurred nightly in the west side cantinas and there was about one murder a night. Robbery was common and the *ley fuga* reputedly was commonly invoked. Prisoners were advised to run away and then were shot "while escaping." The region around Navojoa, a more peaceful town, was terrorized by a bandit called Manos Arriba. Although he had been captured in 1930, banditry was still common and I was advised to stop for no one on the roads between settlements. Later in Nayarit, in 1933, when I sought to travel to Jesús María, the nearest Cora settlement five or six days into the mountains from Tepic, I was told I would have to have a military escort. About the same time, Isabel Kelly had to have a military escort when she did her archaeological survey in the regions west and south of Tepic.

Physical conditions were also difficult. Rail travel was poor. In 1930 only three *mixtos* (mixed freight and passenger trains) were scheduled each week, but they soon were augmented by two *rapidos* (all passenger trains) a week. The trains, especially the mixtos, were slow and often ran hours, or after heavy storms, days late. In winter and spring refrigerated vegetable trains ran much faster and on tighter schedules, and it was possible to bribe the conductor to ride in the caboose.

Automobile travel was possible to most places but there were no paved roads. Indeed, the only paving in towns was in older settlements still maintaining colonial cobbled streets. In Sinaloa there were some graded roads, but most roads were simply tracks cut through the thorn forests or, in the north, the steppe or desert vegetation. Roads along the coastal plain often were deep in fine alluvial dust. All were impassable, often for days, after heavy rains.

Living accommodations were minimal. Rawhide string beds covered with a tanned cow hide were usual even in towns. Better accommodations were available in a few towns. In any case, one did not sleep on the ground because of swarming centipedes, scorpions, and tarantulas. Boots and britches seemed essential unless one were immune to flea bites. In warmer weather enormous cockroaches swarmed in many places; in the Inn at Yaqui Estación Vicam, setting bedposts in water kept them out of bed, but otherwise I took action only when they ran across the table where I wrote. Muslin canopies were hung over beds in warm weather to catch scorpions falling from the ceiling.

Sanitation was primitive. The best hotel in Navojoa had one flush toilet, often not functioning, and a single cold shower. At my favorite restaurant in Navojoa I soon learned not to complain of flies in soup; the waitress simply went out of sight, removed the flies with her forefinger, and returned the plate. Not surprisingly, recurrent diarrhea plagued everyone. Malaria was rife in the warm season when mosquitoes swarmed in incredible numbers. Health facilities were minimal. Doctors were few and ill-trained and there were no real hospitals. The best medical service in the area by far was provided by a clinic near Cajeme (Ciudad Obregón) operated by two Seventh Day Adventist medical missionaries from Loma Linda University Medical School. One exception was a young doctor from Mexico City I met socially in the town of Sinaloa. He would not subject his family to the living conditions there but he hoped, with the lack of competition, to make enough money in a few years to be able to return permanently to "civilization." During the hot season from early May to October, when daily temperature maxima ranged well above 100 degrees F., dehydration posed an additional peril; probably not more than one out of five infants born during this period survived.

Food likewise was limited. The staples were tortillas, beans, and some form of meat—biftek, carne picado (chopped beef) often with chile, stewed or fried chicken, or in a *mole* sauce were the most common forms. Potatoes were a rarity and tomatoes and other vegetables in cooked form were sparingly mixed with various meat dishes; raw, of course, they were unsafe. Some fruits were available, particularly citrus, bananas, and papaya, but were not served normally except if demanded by regular gringo customers. Tortillas served with every meal in towns were supplemented often by hard "French" rolls. In ranchos and small settlements, food was much simpler.

This emphasis on fieldwork difficulties may seem to offer inadequate obstacles to field research, especially when compared with other areas of the world. But in Mexico there were no colonial administrators or officials to guide the novice field worker in the path of survival as there then were in much of Oceania and Africa or Asia. Few grants allowed for field expenses and safari guides were unknown. While Bennett and Zingg faced equal or more difficult problems among the Tarahumara and Huichol, many others avoided them. Elsie Clews Parsons began her Mexican work in Mitla; although an almost wholly Zapotec town, it has a mild climate and was a common weekend vacation spot for officials and upper class Oaxacans from the city. In the same area, Paul Radin collected his folk tales and linguistic data from a room in the best hotel in Oaxaca City, and even Redfield was within a few hours of Mexico City. Leslie White visited Mexico not long after returning from a long stay in China. When shortly after he visited me in 1937 in Los Angeles, he mainly wanted to know how I could do fieldwork under the appalling sanitation and food conditions, compared with those in China.

CONTRASTS
(N. Ross Crumrine)

Today, in striking contrast, even a long weekend can provide enough time for a brief visit to southern Sonora, considerable chatting with the Mayo, and the observation of a traditional ritual. From as far away as Victoria, British Columbia, I can reach the Mayo area within a day. Leaving on the 7:00 A.M. flight from Victoria to Vancouver, I connect with a flight to Los Angeles, and take a short commuter flight to San Diego in the early afternoon. I ride the local bus downtown and the trolley to the border at Tijuana, and a taxi carries me to the Tijuana airport. After receiving a boarding pass from Aero-Mexico, presenting to immigration my passport and a Mexican

Figure 1.2. The modern town hall in Navojoa. (Photograph by N. Ross Crumrine.)

tourist card that is easily obtained from either the airline or my travel agent, and opening my luggage for customs, I board the 7:00 P.M. flight for Ciudad Obregón in the Yaqui region. In the Ciudad Obregón airport there is a car rental desk where my reservation for a VW sedan is waiting, and soon I am on the highway south to Navojoa (Fig. 1.2). About an hour later I arrive in Navojoa, where there is a choice of two first class motels or several more modest ones nearer the highway down the Mayo River Valley. Thus by 9:00 or 10:00 P.M. I am settling into a modest yet pleasant motel room with an air conditioner, hot and cold running water, and a private bath and shower.

Early the next morning, I stop by the supermarket and select a large steak packaged on a styrofoam plate and wrapped in clear plastic and several pounds of green bean coffee for my friends. Although this is the first Friday of Lent, the Mayo enjoy meat whenever it is available, except during Thursday and Good Friday of Easter Week when it is prohibited. Driving down the Mayo River Valley, I pass by several blocks of modern elegant family homes, many with satellite receiving dishes. The scenery reminds one of the mid-west, with green wheat fields stretching in all directions as far as one can see. The winter corn crop has been harvested and most farmers have rejected planting more expensive cotton or safflower in favor of the most recent hybrid wheats (Fig. 1.3). Passing through Etchojoa, I detour one block off the main street to observe the Etchojoa Mayo church and see the first *pahkome* (fiesta hosts) drifting toward it in preparation for the first Friday procession, one of the few that actually takes place in Etchojoa. After leaving Etchojoa, I turn off the highway to the right and soon dip into the Mayo River bed, crossing over a cement culvert with the remaining water that has not been drawn off for irrigation flowing beneath.

After a short drive down a narrow path bordering a canal, I see an older man working in a green wheat field, wave to him, and stop several hundred meters on down the canal. Crossing a neighbor's narrow wheat field, I approach José's earthen roofed home, with his several-hectare wheat field stretching beyond. After the traditional set of Mayo greetings with his wife, I hand her the steak, which she accepts. Several years ago she showed surprise when she noticed the styrofoam plate; however, now she recognizes it as part of the packaging of meat in many of the larger grocery stores of the region. After chatting for a few minutes, her husband arrives from his field and we greet each other again, using the formal Mayo conventions.

"The road of work never ends," he says laughing and responding to my question, "Am I disturbing you, are you too busy to stop work?" At over 85 years of age, he continues to farm his ejido parcel. We sit down in the shade of the ramada in front of his house and his wife moves into the cooking jacal (thatch room) in order to light the wood fire in her mud hearth to boil water for coffee, which is always offered by Mayo hosts to their visitors (Fig. 1.4). He inquires about my family and about acquaintances in Victoria, where he accompanied me for a visit several years ago, and I ask about the health of my Mayo friends hoping that nobody is seriously ill or has died since my last visit. We shift to a discussion of his crops, which

Figure 1.3. Mayo corn drying, with the home owner's wheat field beyond. (Photograph by N. Ross Crumrine.)

he explains are excellent but financed by the agrarian bank. Several years ago his fields were leveled with heavy equipment available in the region. He appears most successful with his crops and realizes the importance of fertilizers and insecticides. He explains that he is no longer able to finance even a small plot himself because a year ago, after receiving his payment for his crop, he placed several thousand dollars worth of pesos in his shirt pocket. When he arrived home the money was gone, lost somewhere between Huatabampo and his home, a tragedy for a rural ejido farmer. When it did not appear, he sought the aid of a diviner in Navojoa, who reported "seeing" somebody picking it up from the canal road; however, to date he has not recovered anything.

A neighbor arrives and José drifts into a complex discussion of the construction of adobe bricks. His wife, meanwhile, brings the water to a boil, pours it through a cloth strainer containing finely ground coffee powder, and serves us steaming cups of coffee with a large plastic container of sugar, since the Mayo always drink their coffee with about three teaspoons of sugar.

Soon the neighbor drifts off and José tells me about a big "program" that was recently sponsored at the Júpare church by the National Indian Institute. He continues explaining that mestizo Mexicans do not like Mayo *pahkom* (fiestas) because they are a "waste of money"; however, he argues that they represent a Mayo duty, a responsibility, and a debt to God and therefore must be completed. Soon he is telling me about the serpents who live under the ground and would eat up all humanity without the protection of God. When the serpents rise to the surface the power of God destroys them. "Today, many people no longer believe in God and the Saints; however, they protect us." As his wife finishes patting and toasting corn tortillas and turns on their new propane range to cook the meat, he commences a long explanation of the Mayo Easter ritual, since this is the first Friday *konti* (procession) of Lent.

Living at the edge of his fields and in contrast to many Mayo families, José and his wife do not have running water nor electricity, but the small propane range placed inside one of their substantial adobe rooms is new since my last visit. José describes how the rich families denied Mary lodging before the birth of Jesus and how the Pariseros pursued and killed him, relating this to the Mayo Lenten rituals and to the origin of death. We move to a small wooden table and his wife serves a stack of corn tortillas and two bowls of heavy soup consisting of large pieces of meat, squash, onion, and tomato, and a side dish of refried beans, followed by another cup of coffee with sugar.

Figure 1.4. Traditional Mayo coffee-making in the cooking jacal. (Photograph by N. Ross Crumrine.)

Figure 1.5. A traditional Mayo baker. (Photograph by N. Ross Crumrine.)

After lunch, which is the Mayo main meal, his wife begins to dress their granddaughter as one of the *Bahi Mariam* (Three Marys) for the Friday konti. I indicate that I also wish to go to the konti and ask José if he is going and if they would like a ride. He again remarks that the road of work never ends but he wants to attend the konti. Soon they are ready and we drive the few kilometers to Júpare, one of the Mayo church centers where the Easter ritual takes place.

As we enter Júpare, I stop at the home of another friend, Juana, where I am welcome to leave the car. After the formal Mayo greetings, José and his family drift off toward the church and I give Juana a pound of green coffee beans and remain to chat for a few minutes. Because they all are busy preparing for the konti (Fig. 1.5), and many neighbors, relatives, and friends are arriving, I say goodby for the moment and drift off toward the church.

This Friday was a good choice for a visit as the crowd is large and many Pariserom as well as the church officials are participating. Within the church the *Bahi Mariam* (little girls) and the *Bahi Reyesim* (small boys, Three Kings) are resting in two long lines with their mothers or godmothers standing behind them. In the late afternoon, the *maestrom* (lay ministers) read the service, the Parisero officers enter the church, and the procession with the large crucifix and the image of the Virgin Mary forms. As we leave the church two long lines of masked Pariserom are standing in front. When the procession is beyond the church door they thunder in to steal flowers from the altar and carry them in the procession. The procession stops at the 14 stations, each marked by a cross, participants kneel, and the maestrom read a set of prayers while the masked Pariserom either make sure everyone within the center of the procession kneels properly or burlesque the ritual and poke fun at the men and children standing at the fringes of the ritual. After lengthy prayers at Kalbario, the midpoint, the procession re-forms and returns to the church as the sun is setting in the west. After concluding prayers in the church, the participants begin to return home.

While watching the final groups of participants leaving the church, I see José, who helped carry the large crucifix in the procession. Before leaving I ask if he and his family would like a ride home, which he gratefully accepts. I drift back to Juana's home where the car is parked and bid goodby to everyone there. José and his family load into the car, and answer several of my questions about aspects of the ritual on the ride home. After the return drive, I arrive at the motel around 9:00 P.M.

The next morning I drive to the airport in Ciudad Obregón in time for the mid-morning flight to Tijuana, and, reversing the route down, I arrive home around midnight, after taking the late flight to Victoria. Although not really desirable in terms of the short time available for actual contact with Mayo friends, it is possible today to visit several Mayo communities and observe a complex ritual within the short period of three days. It is necessary, of course, to have acquired considerable knowledge of the area and developed contacts with individuals of the indigenous society.

In any case, this description provides a dramatic contrast with the conditions under which Ralph Beals initiated his field research in the area. It also emphasizes the intense degree of change and modernization, coupled with a retention of certain traditional beliefs and rituals, that has taken place in northwestern Mexico over the last 30 or 40 years. These modern data suggest that, rather than enclaved in a region of refuge, modern indigenous groups of northwestern Mexico are embedded, encapsulated (Howard 1982: 164), and enclosed (Yoneyama 1967: 214) within modern Mexico.

DIRECTIONS
(N. Ross Crumrine)

Cultural retention and change has been a popular area of study and research among anthropologists since at least the time of Edward Tylor and Franz Boas. One early attempt to codify this general interest can be traced to the 1936 Memorandum assembled by Robert Redfield, Melville Herskovits, and Ralph Linton, supported by the Social Science Research Council, and published in the *American Anthropologist* (Redfield and others 1936). In England, the International Institute of African Languages and Cultures initiated a program for the study of culture change in 1931 that was discussed by Malinowski (1938) and others. Responding especially to the 1936 Memorandum, Herskovits (1938) published a study of culture change and developed his theory of cultural focus (Herskovits 1938: 542–560), Malinowski (1945) elaborated on "contact institutions," Redfield's model of cultural change was perfected by the Wilsons (1945), Beals (1953a) published a summary article on acculturation, Keesing (1953) collected his bibliographic summary on culture change, and Broom, Siegel, Vogt, and Watson (1954) published the results of the 1954 SSRC Seminar on Acculturation.

The crucial underlying innovation resulting from the 1936 Memorandum was a methodological one rather than a solution to the culture change process. The Memorandum drew the attention of the above anthropologists to the role of process and the range of crucial factors in culture contact situations. However, in the development of Spicer's model of culture change, the resulting work of Linton (1940) on acculturative types and processes played a major and lasting role. Perceiving differences in contact situations, Linton developed his basic awareness of directed as opposed to nondirected contact. This distinction or typology of contact situations became the major and basic tool in Spicer's framework for the analysis of the social structure of contact and the resulting types of culture change. Depending on additional contact conditions, differing sets of dominant integrational types followed from either the directed or nondirected contact types (Spicer 1961: 539–541). After an initial phase of additive integration, "the honeymoon of contact," characterizing both directed and nondirected contact, the nondirected contact type tends to develop incorporative integration. In contrast, a directed contact situation produces fusional integration or isolative integration, depending on the contact conditions. Isolative integration tends to resist further culture change whereas fusional integration, again depending on contact conditions, may shift toward either assimilation or incorporative integration (Spicer 1961: 540). In a 1969 publication, Spicer (1969a) labeled four types of integration resulting from differing colonial programs and conditions of directed contact: an alienating process characteristic of central Aztec Mexico, a militant separatism exemplified by Yaqui history, accommodating adjustment of the Pueblos of the Southwest, and individual assimilation with associated disintegration of indigenous communities in the Bajío and adjacent areas of Mexico.

In an article entitled "Procesos de aculturación más importantes," Spicer (1964: 8) develops the concept of enclavement and the cultural enclave:

> . . . By "enclave" we mean the process by which the groups within a society maintain a sense of separate identity from the members of the principal society of which they form a part; nevertheless we mean something more than this. We also imply the maintenance of a separate territory in some way, from the members of the principal society. . . . We also include in our definition of enclave the implication of distinctive cultural differences between the groups of the enclave and the components of the major society. Thus, we are able to define an enclave as a group of individuals, territorially restricted, within a principal society, which maintains cultural differences and a characteristic sense of identity with respect to the members of the principal society within which it is politically incorporated. [The translations of this quotation and those that follow are by N.R.C.]

This process of enclavement or "differentiation" also requires two additional sets of conditions: a feeling of difference or hostility on the part of the dominated group, and an ability to maintain intergroup unity and intergroup boundaries (Spicer 1964: 9):

> . . . one of the societies refuses to be submerged and to become assimilated within the other. There has to be, in a word, a certain level of hostility or sense of vital difference among the members of the societies, in such a way that there might be resistance to the fusion of identities . . . one of the societies, even in spite of hostility or resistance, might be capable of maintaining the boundaries between itself and the other society or societies with which it has contact.

As Spicer was elaborating his concept of enclavement and the cultural enclave in the early 1960s, a second anthropologist, Gonzalo Aguirre Beltrán, was revealing the power of a twin concept, the *región de refugio,* region of refuge. The seminal thinking and analyses of both anthropologists converge closely in these beginning years of the 1960s. Early work in medicine lead Aguirre Beltrán to develop interests in racial as well as sociocultural patterns. As early as 1942 and 1946 he had published major contributions concerning Mexican negro populations. In his monograph outlining the culture of an isolated Pacific coast black village, Aguirre Beltrán (1958: 10) developed concepts of cultural persistence, isolation, and enclavement (cloister) both of dominant and dominated groups:

> It dictated all those laws and dispositions which authorized the support of a situation of hegemony over the principal groups of the population, and tried to cloister its own group conserving it "uncontaminated" both biologically and culturally . . . the negro, considered tainted by his blood and degraded by his condition of slavery, remained cloistered within his caste.

In his classic volume, *Regiones de Refugio,* the notion of cloister, which represents a close parallel to Spicer's enclave (1964), is refined, expanded, and elaborated into an analytical model and used as the major methodological basis for applied anthropology and for the programs of the Instituto Nacional Indigenista (Aguirre Beltrán 1967: xv):

> . . . Because of their conception and by their manner of operation, the coordinating centers are the Mexican version of community development projects implemented in the underdeveloped regions of a country. We have assigned to those regions the suggestive name of regions of refuge because within them, characterized by the inherited structure of the Colonial period and of the ancient culture of clearly pre-industrial content, they have encountered shelter against the sudden attacks of modern civilization.

Thus it would appear that during the 1960s, the analyses of Spicer treating enclavement and of Aguirre Beltrán clarifying the development and maintenance of regions of refuge were in close agreement. In the early 1970s, both anthropologists wrote ground-breaking seminal articles treating the symbolism of cultural identity systems (Spicer 1971, Aguirre Beltrán 1970b). However, since that time both men developed their ideas in response to more recent research and theoretical and political innovations in their respective areas. Spicer continued to refine his analysis of the differing types of conditions of contact and their associated culture change types and patterns, especially in terms of ethnographic and ethnohistorical data. The concepts of enduring peoples and persistent identity systems have become focal points in the development of his analysis, stimulating Spicer's research to move considerably beyond a concept as general as the enclave. Although retaining the concept of region of refuge, Aguirre Beltrán's analysis has increasingly come under serious criticism by younger and opposed Mexican social scientists. He has spent considerable work and effort both in his attempts to refute his academic critics (Aguirre Beltrán 1970b) and in his applied leadership roles.

In a balanced discussion of this criticism, Bernardo Berdichewsky (1979), a former Chilean and presently Canadian anthropologist, has written a most informative article, "Anthropolgy and the Peasant Mode of Production." Instead of isolation, enclavement, and regions of refuge, he presents an opposing argument that distinguishes a single society with only one socioeconomic formation but with diverse modes of production. The modern northwestern and western Mexican Indian groups are not really isolated or enclaved but represent the broken communal-tribe mode of production. Overexploited groups that have been reduced to a peasant class are constantly being drained of their meager surplus by the capitalist national systems of which they are a part. As Berdichewsky (1979: 25) explains: ". . . This successive decomposition, from tribal community to peasant community, and from this to family economy, and finally to diverse relations of production, changes the peasantry into different classes which are structured in a new social stratification." Thus the real problems are not isolation, enclavement, and regions of refuge, but the conflict between social classes—a social problem—and the retention of sufficient land holdings to ensure a reasonable standard of living for the peasant farmers and their families. As Huizer (1973), Berdichewsky (1979), and others have argued, peasant organizations, militance, rebellions, and revolutions are in great part motivated by land reform rationale. Roger Bartra (1974), S. Eckstein (1966), Edmond Flores (1961), González Casanova (1967), Stavenhagen (1970a, 1970b, 1975), Warman (1976, 1978) and others have all contributed to the development of aspects of this position.

It is not necessary to take sides in this discussion, but it is important to indicate the various points of view. In response to his critics, Aguirre Beltrán (1970a, 1970b, 1977) has adapted and explicated his analysis in several differing contexts. He (Aguirre Beltrán 1977: 8) has emphasized that modern Indians represent the end product of a social condition of submission: "Today the term Indian, as in the period in which it was invented, does not designate an ethnic category but a social condition: that of colonized, that of the subjected." He also has recognized that Indians are integrated in the class system but has argued that this does not necessarily mean a loss of distinctive identity: "In those countries the destiny of the Indian is more and more his proletarization and conscious entry into the battle of the classes; which does not necessarily imply the loss of his ethnic identity but its expansion" (Aguirre Beltrán 1977: 9). He has concluded that the modern indigenismo theory and practice does not necessarily represent the destruction of Indian identity nor an extension of modern aggressive capitalism:

> . . . When de-tribalization results in anomia there is true ethnocide; if it achieves a new integration ethnicity is not extinguished, it is expanded and incorporated into a more comprehensive awareness of cohesion. The national formations of the mestizo-American countries are con-

structed on a base of de-tribalization . . . The religious missions, the Indian institutes, other integrative agencies, and even the anthropologists who work in programs of development have been accused now and then of commiting ethnocide. The accusations come from other anthropologists and social scientists who, as Rousseau requested, desire to preserve the pristine purity of the Indian cultures, disillusioned as they are by all the evils which our capitalist, aggressive, and alienated civilization entails (Aguirre Beltrán 1977: 10).

Thus in terms of this lively discussion between anthropologists holding divergent points of view, it is most crucial to reexamine older materials and present newer information and analyses based on our understanding of ongoing processes of culture change. The chapters in this volume directly address these points and questions, and they explore data concerning conditions of culture contact and culture change. The authors describe and analyze enclavement and culture change among the Yaqui, the Mayo, and the protohistoric Opata in northwestern Mexico, and then discuss regions of refuge and indigenous groups in western Mexico. Rather than enclaved societies or regions of refuge, these indigenous groups might better be described as encapsulated, enclosed, and embedded communities, which reflect yet differ from the national Mexican society. In fact, Robert Hunt (1979: 2), in his introduction to the English translation of *Regions of Refuge,* uses the term embedded: "a major anthropological concern in Mestizo America is the evolution of the social structure in which the Indian is embedded (the most modern phase of which is discussed as modernization and economic development) . . ." The following chapters reveal the depth of penetration of national patterns and structures into the embedded units and the conditions associated with this type of integration. These embedded communities maintain their own posture of opposition to complete assimilation into modern Mexican society, an opposition that dissolved under specific contact conditions only in the case of the Opata.

Aguirre Beltrán 1942, 1946, 1958, 1967, 1970a, 1970b, 1977
Bartra 1974
Beals 1953a
Berdichewsky 1979
Broom and others 1954
Eckstein 1966
Flores 1961
González Casanova 1967
Herskovits 1938
Howard 1982
Huizer 1973
Hunt 1979
Keesing 1953
Linton 1940
Malinowski 1938, 1945
Redfield and others 1936
Spicer 1961, 1964, 1969a, 1971
Stavenhagen 1970a, 1970b, 1975
Warman 1976, 1978
Wilson and Wilson 1945
Yoneyama 1967

CHAPTER TWO

Yaqui Indian Enclavement: The Effects of an Experimental Indian Policy in Northwestern Mexico

Steven V. Lutes (San Francisco)

Instances of enclavement always share some traits in common. By the simplest definition, enclavement is a state within a state, a condition wherein a territory, its people, and their institutions are surrounded by a second and similar entity. If the definition is extended to cover the encirclement of *tribal* groups by a *modern* state, additional traits may be included in the definition. As in the case of the readings offered in this book, additional components cluster around the concept of inequality, and there are institutional and human disparities in the relations characterizing the two groups.

Enclaved ethnic and tribal populations do appear to regularly suffer from socially patterned marginality with respect to economic activities, social and political power, and a host of related items such as access to education and health care. The plight of enclaved peoples is often in the news (consider the Basques, Kurds, Muslim Filipinos, and Palestinians) and likely will remain an issue of international concern for a long while. The question is, must the growth of the nation state always be associated with large scale human tragedies? If not, it should be possible to locate examples where the usual problems have been avoided or greatly diminished.

Northern Mexico, the state of Sonora in particular, contains examples of several significantly different state policies toward enclaved native societies. For this area it is possible to document some of the processes that result in integration, assimilation, and continued boundary maintenance.

Integration is often a goal of policy makers. It usually refers to something vaguely understood as the development of interdependency between the peoples, regions, and institutions of a nation. In modern times, and with regard to cultural minorities, integration is usually thought to increase proportionately with assimilation. In some cases, assimilation may be actively sought by both parties, but, more often, rapid changes in the traditional lifeways of a group are resisted. One result is that the dominant society employs strategies of coercive assimilation against the minority group.

One alternative to coercive assimilation is a policy of accommodation to ethnic, tribal, or religious pluralism. It is especially attractive in instances where large segments of a population do not exist within the mainstream of national life or social organization. This chapter assesses one such example of accommodation and contrasts its fruits with those yielded by a more Draconian policy applied to an almost identical minority population. I also discuss how both approaches affect integrational tendencies, and their relative costs in terms of economic and social development goals.

The primary topic is the enclavement of the Yaqui Indians, an indigenous people of southwestern Sonora, Mexico. Because of the comparative scope employed, the nearby and kindred Mayo are considered also. In a number of instances, it is convenient to compare conditions in the native groups to like conditions among surrounding mestizos. By so doing, we can identify and discriminate between processes that are linked to integration, assimilation, and boundary maintenance.

The following seven trait variables link each separate aspect of the chapter. Changes in their value over time, separately and covariantly, are indicative of the integrative, assimilative, and isolationist forces at work.

1. The status of Indian authorities in relation to mestizo authorities.
2. Formal means of conflict resolution between the Indians and mestizos.
3. The nature of land tenure.
4. Mestizo responses to Indian culture and lifeways.
5. Indian and mestizo living standards; access to opportunities for social and economic mobility.
6. Traits indicative of the nature of psychosocial stability: alcohol use, theft, violent crime, cultism.
7. Group differentials in the propensity to engage in violent conflict patterned along ethnic or socioeconomic class lines.

It is assumed that policies of accommodation yield different associated trends than do policies of coercive assimilation. Such trends should be easy to document. It is unfortunate that "good" indicator data do not exist for the region, a problem that is not uncommon in the Third World (Hackenberg 1970: 343). Nevertheless, the use of ethnographic descriptions is a partial remedy for the problem.

BACKGROUND OF YAQUI ENCLAVEMENT

Few of the historical indigenous peoples of Sonora have endured to modern times. Northern Mexico was not densely settled when the Spanish arrived. War, the use of forced labor, and disease must have taken a tremendous toll during the colonial era (see Chapter 9). Of the surviving groups, the Yaqui perhaps are the best known and are second in size only to the nearby Mayo. The isolation of the Yaqui and Mayo within Sonora is nearly complete. Other indigenous groups, the Seri and Pima Bajo for example, have few contacts with either tribe. Yaqui tribal lands are centered in the southwestern portion of the state. In the north, they extend nearly to the modern cities of Guaymas and Empalme. To the south, the boundaries are drawn around the town of Bacum, not far from Ciudad Obregón.

Population data for the area are both scarce and imprecise. It is estimated that between 18,000 and 20,000 Yaqui reside on tribal lands (Lutes 1977: 40; Vargas Montero 1978: 41). Crumrine (1977: 15) suggests that there are from 30,000 to 60,000 Mayo living in an area from Navojoa, south to the Río Fuerte, which serves as a boundary line between Sonora and Sinaloa. The population estimate is broad, in part because various sources available to Crumrine used conflicting criteria concerning mixed marriages for ascribing ethnicity. The Yaqui and Mayo speak nearly identical dialects of the Cáhitan language and share many other traits of cultural and social organization.

Both of the Indian groups are surrounded by a mestizo population that far exceeds their own, a situation more pronounced for the Yaqui than the Mayo. The population of Ciudad Obregón was estimated in 1975 to be between 150,000 and 200,000. The Guaymas-Empalme area is roughly the same size. Both urban areas are characterized by high growth rates and each has hinterlands with additional inhabitants.

The Yaqui and Mayo engage in a variety of exchanges; the one involving ritual specialists and ceremonial goods probably is the most common. Substantial numbers of Mayo have migrated to Yaqui territory in recent years. Many Mayo can be found in the mestizo town of Vicam Estación, an enclave within an enclave and the site of Mexican government and military headquarters in Yaqui country. The migrants take on roles appropriate to either mestizos or Indians, the choice depending on individual social preference and the relative advantages of being one or the other. Yaqui-Mayo intermarriage is a common occurrence within Yaqui territory.

Before treating the modern situation in greater detail, some history is given about the Yaqui prior to their enclavement. The Yaqui lived in small rancherías before the advent of the Spanish in 1533. Such small settlements, probably based on kinship groupings, were found along the banks of the now diverted Yaqui River. The river was of crucial importance to life. Its flood waters nourished Yaqui crops, and the dense plant growth along its sides provided food and shelter for local game animals. Although they were mostly farmers and hunters, the Yaqui also engaged in limited fishing and shellfish collecting in coastal *bahías*.

Precontact political organization centered on the principles of age seniority and kinship. In the rancherías the eldest male kinsmen provided leadership (Beals 1943), and it is likely that a council of senior authorities met to decide questions of importance to all Yaqui. During military encounters with the Spanish, Yaqui forces were assembled on short notice and fought under a unified command. Accounts of the tribe's organizational capabilities appear as early as 1645 in the memoirs of Andres Pérez de Ribas (1968).

During the colonial era, Spanish influence led to a major reshaping of Yaqui life. The tribe had great success in resisting early attempts at military conquest. They were impressed, however, by Spanish might and cultural practices; in 1617 the Jesuit Order entered the tribe's territory at the Indians' request. They stayed until the Order was expelled from the New World in 1767. The Jesuits introduced new domestic plants and animals and farming techniques were improved. The Yaqui were converted to the Catholic faith. They began to take Spanish names and reckon kinship in terms of the Hispanic variant of the Eskimo system. The Jesuits also implemented the *reducción*, whereby the dispersed population was unified and brought together in eight church-centered towns. A familiar style of Hispanic colonial civil government was established and staffed by Yaqui officials working in conjunction with the Jesuit fathers.

Periodic conflicts caused some problems during the colonial era. The Jesuits themselves were at times objects of Yaqui hostilities. Following the exodus of the Jesuits and, later, the Mexican war of independence, fighting became more frequent and intense. The Yaqui are notoriously sensitive about the issue of autonomy, even today, and have shown a continuous will to resist the encroachments of alien colonists and authority. The colonial and early national governments were equally convinced of the need to open new areas to colonization and bring their native inhabitants into the Hispanic social and cultural fold. For more than a century, the result of the disagreement was bloody conflict and misery for all concerned.

During the last two decades of the 19th century, life became more disruptive for the Yaqui. Their kindred and sometime allies, the Mayo, were finally repressed around 1880 and showed little desire for more fighting. The Yaqui fought on, but the superior arms and numbers of the mestizos took a terrible toll. In the face of continued resistance, the Sonoran government engaged in an openly genocidal campaign against the tribe. Cultural, if not biological, extinction surely would have followed had it not been for the eruption of the civil war during the regime of Porfirio Díaz. In the murky events of the national conflict, the Yaqui were less likely to be singled out as objects of hostility.

When the fighting ended, Indian policies were examined in more humanitarian terms. The Yaqui seemed to merit special attention, perhaps because of the notoriety their long struggle had brought them. President Lázaro Cárdenas, commencing in 1936, issued a set of decrees that drastically restructured the formal relations of the Yaqui with the mestizo state and national governments. If there is any mestizo whom the Yaqui regard as a tribal hero, it is certainly Lázaro Cárdenas. By his efforts, the Indians gained a measure of autonomy and protection against outside forces. The date 1936, then, is the time when the Yaqui first became an enclaved people, the time when they were officially designated as a people apart from the others.

The Cárdenas decrees established an area of 485,000 hectares as the Yaqui Indigenous Community (Vargas Montero

1978: 8). The tribe had collective and inalienable rights to the land, meaning that it could not be reexpropriated through a subsequent series of private agreements between individual Indians and mestizos. Unlike ejidos, the territory was Yaqui and only Yaqui could enjoy its bounties. The authority of tribal officials was established in local affairs, water rights were granted, and aid in such areas as agriculture, health care, and education was promised. Texts of the Cárdenas decrees are in Dabdoub (1965: 222–235) and Fabila (1940: 295–313).

The Mayo enjoyed no such benefits. The coming of peace signaled the state of rapid growth in Sonora's cities and in economic output. Huge tracts of land were opened to large scale commercial agriculture. The Mayo country, perhaps better endowed in terms of resources, soon was in non-Indian hands. The Mayo received no aid, no recognition, and continued to be persecuted whenever they showed any signs of collective identity or unrest. For the first time in their intimately related histories, the contrast between the Yaqui and the Mayo became pronounced. Subsequent trends toward social divergence are at least associated with the abrupt alteration in the status of the two groups with respect to mestizo institutions and authority.

YAQUI-MESTIZO INTEGRATIVE LINKAGES

The unfolding of Yaqui-mestizo relations after 1936 has produced a number of trends, and those of an integrative nature link the Yaqui and their social order with that of the outsiders. Such trends occur in two relatively distinct domains of social organization: (1) the area of formal articulation covered by legally binding agreements between Yaqui and mestizo political authorities, and (2) less formal types of linkage that arise from the day-to-day dealings between individual members of each group.

Prior to 1936, treaties between the Yaqui and the mestizos are most notable for their failure to achieve any positive, lasting results. The two sides pursued completely different goals. The Yaqui wanted the mestizos to remain outsiders. The mestizos, however, were convinced of the necessity to open Yaqui lands to colonization and to bring the Indians within the framework of state and national government. To complicate matters further, neither side understood the other's form of political or social organization.

Political power is dispersed in Yaqui society. The legacy of the Jesuits was eight separate pueblos, each having its own civil government ruling with the help of church officials. After the Jesuits left, subsequent Yaqui modifications of the system actually created additional checks and balances. Each pueblo maintained a civil government ruling in conjunction with the church leaders, who were then exclusively Yaqui. However, all binding judgements had to be endorsed at a public gathering attended by the senior representatives of each household as well as by the representatives of the pueblo's military organization. There were probably interpueblo meetings, as before, but no pan-tribal, formal scheme of government applying to all Yaqui pueblos. As the mestizos soon discovered, a pact with the leaders of one settlement might be meaningless to other settlements. Some accounts of Yaqui treachery seem to have been based on these kinds of misunderstandings of the Indian political organization.

Leadership among mestizos tends to be concentrated in the hands of powerful individuals who govern until they are ousted because of popular discontent and the desertion of their allies. Only since the fall of the Díaz government has the role of the strongman diminished in the higher level state and national offices. Leadership of this type contrasts sharply with that of the Yaqui.

The structure of Yaqui-mestizo relationships, as developed in the 1936 accords, reflects a maturation in the political system of both groups. Mexico entered a period characterized by increased continuity in policy affairs between successive administrations. On their part, the Yaqui were compelled to forge a political system capable of reaching agreements with mestizos on behalf of the entire tribe. The Unified Yaqui Tribe (TYU) is the result of their efforts.

Vicam Pueblo is held in esteem by all Yaqui. It has figured prominently in tribal legend and myths. The ranking governor *(primer gobernador)* of Vicam Pueblo is considered to be the chief authority in the territory's civil affairs. With the coming of a lasting peace and the need for centralized decision-making, Vicam Pueblo and its primer gobernador were logical choices as centerpieces in the political apparatus of the TYU. The tribal hierarchy is mirrored in the documents of the TYU and each decree is signed by the leaders of the eight Yaqui pueblos. Vicam always appears first, followed by Potam. The two settlements are often called the first and second seats of government.

Nevertheless, the old tendency toward the dispersion of power is retained. All binding issues must be agreed on by the leadership of all pueblos, acting in accord with the decisions of their own village governments. Following traditional patterns of broad community representation, pending issues are thoroughly aired in each pueblo. The designated spokesmen of each village then convene at Vicam Pueblo at a meeting chaired by that pueblo's first governor. Binding agreements must be ratified by unanimous consent. Several conclaves are frequently necessary to arrive at a consensus and the first governor of Vicam Pueblo may not act in a unilateral manner in any affair concerning TYU business with the mestizos. Despite the drawbacks of such a system, it does provide resolutions that are respected by all Yaqui and required by the mestizo scheme of negotiation and consultation.

The uses to which the tribal organization are put mostly concern relations between the Yaqui and the federal government, the implementation of government programs on the Indians' land, and a number of essentially economic matters. However, since the time of Cárdenas, the Yaqui have come to regard the federal government and especially the office of president as their patron and protector against infractions of the treaty agreements by mestizos. (In recent years the governor of Sonora often has replaced the president as a source of appeal in local issues.) It is said that local and state authorities frequently disregard the decrees or seek to undermine them in a number of ways. During my stay in Potam, no less than seven delegations were sent to Mexico City in order to discuss problems thought to involve the tribe's rights under the 1936 decrees.

Such grievances usually center around land disputes. After peace was established, government survey teams mapped the boundaries of the Indigenous Community's territory. For a number of reasons, and there are many colorful accounts of the survey party, the maps are vague in certain respects. The result is that there is much room for maneuvering and litigation among Yaqui and mestizo claimants to disputed parcels of land. The Yaqui expect fair treatment when such cases are mediated by federal authorities. Most of the cases involving violations of the tribe's treaty rights do appear to have been settled in a way that is satisfactory to them.

There are additional signs of accommodation and flexibility on both sides, particularly in cases involving the organization of government agricultural projects on the Indians' land. One means of retaining control over the uses of land brought into production at government expense is by establishing cooperatives run under federal supervision. The ejido provides a model for such undertakings on Yaqui land, but special circumstances have resulted in some adjustments to the typical ejido form, as at Potam.

There are three types of agricultural occupation, based on land tenure, in Potam. *Particulares* are independent farmers who have land-use rights granted to them by tribal authorities in the pueblo where the land is situated. There is also a small group of landless agricultural wage workers *(obreros)* hired by kin and compadres to assist on their farms. Usually, the obreros are younger men. The largest group of farmers is that composed of men called *socios,* who belong to government sponsored and regulated *sociedades.* In 1976, Potam contained about half the male labor force in agriculture, working roughly 10,000 hectares of land. It was estimated that 60 percent of the land was being farmed by members of sociedades and that 600 adult men qualified as socios, about 43 percent of the adult male labor force.

According to mestizo officials, the sociedades are organized like ejidos. Although the members are exclusively Yaqui, each of the groups must adhere to rules established by outsiders. Sociedad officers include a president, treasurer, and secretary, plus a council of vigilance that hears and settles disputes within each cooperative. The officers are responsible for record keeping and maintaining proper ties with rural bank personnel. In theory, the officers are to be elected by all members in a session characterized by secret ballot. So long as the appearance of compliance to this Mexican way of doing things persists, they interfere little in the affairs of the cooperatives.

In actuality, the socios operate according to rules that are rooted in Yaqui traditions. The results are given the appearance of ejido practices such that the mestizos are satisfied. The mestizo-designed charter says little about the composition of Yaqui sociedades. The Yaqui preference is to form cooperatives around a set of real and ritual kin. Propriety and tradition then suggest that the officers should be the senior male kinsmen of the group. One new criterion is that the officers must have minimal skills in literacy and arithmetic, which are required for filing reports on the cooperatives' activities with bank officials. In effect, the senior kinsmen are confirmed in office by a vote that reaffirms the cardinal principles of Yaqui society: loyalty within the bilateral kindred and network of compadres, plus respect for age seniority.

The incongruities between the real and ideal must be visible to both sides. However, the spirit of accommodation established in 1936 allows them to ignore minor inconsistencies so long as the goal of agricultural production does not suffer. Similar arrangements probably characterize activities in the government sponsored cattle and fishing cooperative.

At times, accommodation is associated with both integrative processes and assimilation. More than 40 years ago Beals (1932a: 28–33) noted that among surviving Cáhitan peoples the borrowing of traits from surrounding mestizo populations was quite evident. Today that is even more true, and a comparison of Cáhitan and rural mestizo traits, especially traits of material culture, certainly yields more similarities than differences.

Given a reliable and lucrative demand for their produce, the assimilation of the Yaqui into Mexico's market economy depends on further development of their land-based resources and only supportive developments in the regional infrastructure. An expanded cash economy and economic integration are likely only in association with improved agriculture, cattle raising, and fishing (Bartell 1964). These, in turn, only flourish with the construction of roads, canals, storage facilities, and the extension of rural electrification and transportation services.

For a variety of reasons, the ability of the Yaqui to purchase modern goods is limited. They are wealthy in terms of land resources and produce but they are cash poor. Credit is available from the banks and local merchants, but the Yaqui are reluctant to avail themselves of borrowing. Usually, it seems, they fear gross usury. Instead, other means of access to goods and services have developed.

Only Yaqui may hold rights to and cultivate land within the confines of the Indigenous Community. As a consequence there are few, if any, mestizo *campesinos* in the territory. In addition to bank and government personnel, mestizos on Yaqui land include merchants, professionals, and skilled workers. The last two groups are hired and paid by the banks and other government agencies that oversee official projects on tribal land. The mestizos generally are well paid but are resource poor.

Some mestizos like to augment their income by acting as middlemen for Yaqui produce. Particulares, for example, often have a surplus of crops but lack arrangements to market them through the banks. Mestizos buy the surplus and resell it at a profit in Ciudad Obregón. Both barter and purchase are common, and usually the buyer-seller relationship is cast in personalized terms rather than in impersonal market transactions. The cementing of individual Yaqui-mestizo trade relationships is one of the most frequent bases for interethnic *compadrazgo* ties. In the hope of buying surplus produce, local merchants often cultivate personal ties with particular Indians by giving small gifts or informally extending credit. Both types of ties are brittle, however, and if one or the other party is displeased with a series of transactions, the bond is quickly severed.

Intermarriage between the Yaqui and mestizos does not occur frequently. Therefore, the political and economic ties described above constitute the primary points of articulation between the two societies. In most respects, they live in different worlds and discussed below are those areas of life in which marked contrasts occur. If a majority of traits are shared, it is equally certain that those traits that are not held in common are of crucial importance in the eyes of the Yaqui and their mestizo neighbors.

CONTRASTS IN YAQUI AND MESTIZO LIFEWAYS

Two basic levels of contrast are evident when the Yaqui and the local mestizos are compared. The most obvious diversity is the display by one group of a trait or trait complex that does not occur in the other, for example, the masked dancers associated with Yaqui ritual and ceremonial life. Local mestizos do not have analogous elements in their own lifeways. Less obviously there are shared traits, which, as Spicer (1954: 54) notes, are organized into different complexes and take on divergent meaning and functions in the two social contexts.

Social and cultural traits may involve both the structuring of human activities and an associated set of dispositions regarding how such activities ought to be organized and to what purpose (the normative component of social organization). The differences and the feelings they provoke may exert influence on subsequent trends of assimilation, integration, or continued boundary maintenance.

The Yaqui and mestizos share similar ideas about who their kin are. For both, the bilateral kindred is the field of persons with whom one may claim ties of kinship. However, such things as residential patterning and the moral force thought to characterize such ties are not identical in practice. Among mestizos, the basic social unit is the neolocal, nuclear family. It frequently may be augmented by the presence of additional generational or collateral relatives, but the tendency is clearly toward a unit composed of a single couple and their unmarried children. The Yaqui exhibit a preference for the extended family household. Although a strict residential rule is lacking, it is strongly felt that aggregates of related nuclear families ought to share a common residential site. Neolocal choices are not encouraged but sometimes occur under limited circumstances.

Variability in the patterning of residential practices and the importance of the kindred are associated with differences in economic organization. Sonora is not one of Mexico's so-called backward states. The major economic activities are in agriculture and related endeavors, but these are increasingly carried on as large scale, commercial ventures. Enterprises of this nature require an impressive array of sophisticated technology and management skills. The state's economy is based on an organic rather than mechanical type division of labor, because the success of the total undertaking is dependent on people performing specialized and interrelated tasks. The complex division of labor itself is embedded in an impersonal market economy where shifting patterns of demand for labor are conducive to residential mobility.

The Yaqui economy is less complex, involving little task specialization. There is an emphasis on self-sufficiency in the production of subsistence goods. The extended family is the basic unit of economic production and is bolstered by its constituents' bilateral kindreds, which are called on for support in times of household need. Given the concentrated nature of Yaqui settlement patterns, the kindred and compadrazgo network also are common avenues of interhousehold exchange. In contrast, mestizos are more likely to rely on occupational and class peers for help and comradeship. A relative abundance of land in relation to Yaqui population size currently minimizes the need or impetus for migration away from Yaqui territory. Consequently, while residential change is not uncommon, it usually is restricted to within a village or between nearby villages and almost always involves going from one group of kin to another.

For many Yaqui, commercial farming takes second place to subsistence agriculture. The two activities are kept separate and it is easy to see the difference between commercial and subsistence plots. The former show clear evidence of exploitation using modern techniques. Large tracts are planted in a single crop and the arrangement is planned for machine cultivation and harvesting. In contrast, the subsistence plots are smaller, more crowded, contain many species of plant life, and are obviously tended and harvested exclusively through the use of manual labor.

Regardless of how income is earned, Yaqui and mestizo societies differ greatly in how earnings are used and distributed. As might be expected, the mestizo nuclear families tend to spend their money for their own needs. There is an ideal that members of the same kindred ought to help each other, but kin are often separated by so many years and miles that the realization of the ideal suffers in actual practice. The style of development encountered in Sonora fragments family bonds by increasing the distance and decreasing the personal exchanges between kin, and by increasing reliance on the impersonal market place rather than on familiar economic arrangements.

The kinship based solidarity of the Yaqui is reflected clearly in their ritual and religious life. It is in such areas that the most pronounced visual contrasts between Yaqui and mestizos occur. Mestizos typically say that they are devoted Catholics. In day-to-day life, however, their faith usually requires little time and few resources. The Yaqui, in contrast, are reluctant to say much about religion or their rituals, but they devote prodigal amounts of their time and resources to the supernaturals (Fig. 2.1). Interpersonal competition is not highly prized among the Yaqui, nor is self-aggrandizement in the realm of material wealth. The

Figure 2.1. The former Yaqui church in Bacom as now reconstructed. (Photograph by N. Ross Crumrine.)

only obvious competition in ritual life is centered on who can give the most goods and enjoyment to the community. At the same time, the fiesta is not an opportunity merely for personal indulgence, but rather it requires careful cooperation and onerous labor among both the sponsors and onlookers.

Mestizo cultural events, the *fiestas patrias* for example, are clearly opportunities to turn a profit and engage in personal excess. Mestizos often have reservations about their own festivities in terms of the violence and philandering that always seem to mar such events. The observant visitor to Yaqui and mestizo fiestas soon realizes that the similarities are superficial. This is not to say that mestizos do not cooperate or that Yaqui do not philander; the difference is the striking degree to which the two groups vary in the importance they attach to these aspects of their respective cultural performances.

The Yaqui and mestizos themselves are aware of some of these contrasts. Although conclusive evidence is lacking, I feel Yaqui insight into mestizo life is more acute than the reverse. The Yaqui consistently pointed out that there are winners and losers in mestizo society, that the latter grossly outnumber the former, and that the more fortunate mestizos seem to care little about what happens to the others. To the Yaqui way of thinking, this kind of situation is intolerable and an abomination to be avoided at all cost.

The role of rational calculation in resistance to social and cultural change is often ignored or understated. Among educated local mestizos, especially those critical of their own social order, accommodations such as those between the Yaqui and the Mexican government are said to do no more than create a servile and cheap labor force in the countryside. They sometimes would suggest that assimilation was being deterred by cynical mestizo powers rather than being resisted by the Indians. Although the available data are limited, a general description of average income, standard of living, and access to life-enhancing opportunities are given below for the Yaqui, the Mayo, and the mestizo population that enclaves them. From a comparison and discussion of such observations, the extent to which Yaqui enclavement is atypical and exceptional may be better understood.

CONFLICT AND OPPORTUNITY IN THREE SONORAN GROUPS

Sonora is a relatively affluent state, and prosperous looking, middle class mestizos are much in evidence. A comparison with the easily observable Indian dwellings along the International Highway between Guaymas and Navojoa suggests then that the Indians are greatly disadvantaged. An increasing familiarity with the fringe areas of the cities and the rural countryside, however, soon demonstrates that the vast majority of mestizos are not so fortunate either. While it is true that Mexico's economy has grown at impressive rates at various times in this century, it also appears that income concentration has multiplied such that few of the benefits of increased productivity ever reach the average Mexican (Navarrete 1970). Because a large majority of the mestizos live in impoverished conditions, it seems reasonable to designate such people as a reference population in this discussion of Indians in general and the Yaqui in particular.

In a pluralistic setting, whether it is characterized by accommodation or not, opportunity and conflict can be a result either of conditions internal to one subgroup or of relationships between subgroups. Mestizo society is characterized by competition for an extremely limited array of resources and opportunities. The avenue to increased prestige and life-enhancing opportunities is largely defined in terms of those things that denote socioeconomic status in the developed countries: occupation, education, and income.

The normative goal of attaining material well-being and leading the "good life" is coupled with a generalized incapacity for most mestizos to achieve even modest success by their own standards. A situation of this type is conducive to discontent and the use of normatively prohibited means for realizing culturally valued goals. At the economic margins of mestizo life, where simple survival is a day-to-day struggle, the potential for explosive violence is always highly visible.

Many, if not most, Sonoran Indian populations were forcefully integrated into the state political and economic mainstream by use of the military and by land expropriation. The process has been furthered through a denial of the legitimacy of Indian collective leadership and the necessity of dislocated native peoples to engage in wage labor. Indians suffer an additional disadvantage of differing from mestizos in language skills and other social and cultural traits. Barriers such as these make it even less likely that Indians can find wage work in any but the least rewarding occupational areas.

Even with the strictures imposed on native mobility in the market economy, it would be difficult to show that Indians and poor mestizos differ much with respect to meaningful social and economic opportunities in the national and state system. Middle class occupations are not numerous and taken as a fraction of total job possibilities, they do not expand rapidly enough to allow significant gains in their share of the labor force. Differences in educational opportunity and socialization are likely to ensure that middle class occupations and incomes will go to the children of the already affluent population, thus continuing patterns of income concentration.

The Yaqui occupy a transitional position in this economic scheme and are viewed as the affluent poor of Sonora. While staying there, I was often told by mestizos and the Mayo that the Yaqui were "rich Indians." Many were openly envious of the tribe's economic standing. Even so, the Yaqui have few opportunities to join the middle classes. I met only a small number of younger Yaqui who had completed more than three years of schooling. School attendance is frustrated by many sentiments, on both sides of the ethnic divide, and so is the desire for occupational specialization.

In theory the Yaqui own their land, but the 1936 treaty was clearly dependent on the willingness of the Yaqui to allow the introduction of commercial farming within the tribal territory. The advantages that accrue to the tribe from cash cropping are not clear-cut and have problematic aspects. Commercial farming in the Indigenous Community uses high technology in planting, tending, and harvesting the crops. Some of the skilled and semiskilled positions in agricultural work are well paid by local standards. However, very few Yaqui work at such jobs as truck and tractor drivers, combine operators, fumigators, or mechanics. They enter into cash cropping only as manual laborers, providing the work force for land clearing, weeding, and some irrigation tasks. The bank hires outsiders for the more specialized work.

The bank also determines the choice of crops to be planted, the charges for bank-provided supplies and contract labor, and the amount paid for the harvest. In 1975 and 1976, a 10 hectare plot of wheat was said to yield a gross return of 52,000 pesos (the prevailing rate of exchange was P12.5 to $1.00 U.S.). Of the total, the Yaqui farmer might realize as much as 11,000 pesos, after costs. A second harvest, usually corn or *cártamo*, could increase the yearly income from the plot by another 4,000 to 9,000 pesos.

Because many Yaqui also tend subsistence gardens, the profits from cash crops need not be used exclusively for basic food needs. Housing costs are also minimal because the tribe promises that all Yaqui shall have land for housing. Serviceable dwellings can be built with inexpensive material and free labor supplied by kin and compadres. Still, the average cash income is meager when compared to the monthly salaries reported by mestizos working on tribal land: 3,500 pesos for a pump tender, 5,500 pesos for an equipment mechanic, and up to 15,000 pesos a month for a high ranking secondary school teacher or administrator. Consequently, some Yaqui feel cheated. They say they are little more than campesinos on their own land. There is a good case for saying that the mestizos are the main beneficiaries of Yaqui cash cropping.

There are other contrasts in the utilization of income when the Yaqui and mestizos living on tribal land are compared. Mestizo expenditures tend to cluster about the needs of the nuclear family. A Yaqui is expected to share income not only within the extended household, but also to honor reasonable requests for financial help from other members of his or her kindred, compadres, and in-laws.

It is clear that the well-paid mestizos enjoy more luxurious goods and, in general, a higher level of material comfort than do the Yaqui. Part of the difference is due to earning levels. The mestizos' cash income is at least twice that of most Yaqui and commonly even five or six times higher. The additional demands on Yaqui earnings made by kin are not easy to estimate, but certainly they make the gap between Yaqui and mestizo disposable income even greater.

A more striking contrast emerges when the relatively affluent mestizos and Yaqui within the tribal territory are compared with poor mestizos and other Indians. In 1975, the minimum wage in the state was set by the Comisión Nacional de los Salarios Mínimos at 75 pesos per full day employment. The workers I encountered reported that when work was available, 50 pesos was the best pay given. Women, who tend soda stands or work as clerks, fare much worse, and many of them reported no more than 12 pesos a day for their labor. A husband and wife working continuously for an entire year usually earn less than 15,000 pesos.

The peso buys less in Sonora than in some parts of the country. Close proximity to the United States and the relatively large number of middle class workers tend to inflate prices. Moving southward, the cost of basic goods usually declines. Unlike the Yaqui, most poor mestizos cannot grow adequate subsistence crops. Because many of them live in urban areas where prices are dearer yet, basic needs take up nearly all their earnings. This economic outlook for the poor mestizos applies with equal force to the Mayo. I asked some Mayo why they had come to live in the Yaqui territory. They uniformly replied that they could not find work on their former lands, their children were sick and hungry, and the mestizos abused them and cheated them.

It is suggested therefore, that although the Yaqui are poor, they do not fit into the pattern of complete social and economic marginality shared by the majority of mestizos and nearly all of the Mayo. Thus, if it is an error to say that enclavement has freed the Yaqui from exploitation, it is equally incorrect to assert that enclavement has caused disadvantages for them in comparison to the average mestizo.

As noted, the Mayo were defeated by a superior military force in the 1880s. Their defeat was attended by the final breakup of the tribe's territory and traditional political system. Ejidos were introduced after the civil war, but they benefited only a fraction of the Mayo population. When the Mayo received special notice from mestizo authorities, it was nearly always negative and aimed at repressing such things as expressions of indigenous political complaints and traditional ceremonial events (Crumrine 1977: 18). Because Mayo enclavement differs so much from the Yaqui experience, it is reasonable to expect the two peoples to display equally divergent trends associated with their respective treatment at the hands of mestizo policy makers.

Ingroup violence occurs at low levels of frequency and intensity in Yaqui society. They are generally calm people. There are notorious individual exceptions, but such people are rare. What is notable is the degree to which social custom prohibits and controls aggressiveness and displays of wrath. Theft generally involves products of agriculture and basic food items, and the Yaqui attribute it largely to mestizos. The Yaqui perception of abuse localizes problems outside the tribe; for instance, the Yaqui believe in witchcraft but are inclined to ascribe it to the practices of outsiders who wish them ill.

Violent, antisocial behavior is easier to assess. Yaqui seldom come to blows with each other, even during large events attended by many drunken males. The Yaqui believe that they fight among themselves but little compared to mestizo fighting. When Yaqui violence did occur, it was limited to the use of hands and feet. At mestizo fiestas, fighting was common and it often degenerated when one or both parties resorted to the use of weapons. Mayo individuals claimed that little violence occurred in the confines of their own group, a statement that Crumrine has endorsed in personal communications.

Mestizos appear to differ from the two Indian groups in terms of stealing, wife beating, and child abuse. Such activities seldom occur among the Yaqui. It is likely that theft among the Yaqui and Mayo is lessened by the generalized poverty they share—few of them have anything that their fellows lack. Poverty, however, does not seem to impede stealing among poor mestizos. The Yaqui say that punishment for serious ingroup infractions is severe. I tried to discuss comparative punishment with some of them, noting that in the United States severe punishment was thought to have little effect in deterring violent crime. Most were amused or skeptical, saying that punishment was not for things in the future but for deeds already done. As one man said, "If an evil doer is not punished, the heart of the community becomes heavy with anger." Yaqui theory seems to stress the need for public revenge rather than to expect an inhibitive effect on future misdeeds.

The abusive use of alcohol is another trait that is thought to indicate the state of social order. Because Yaqui men frequently are seen in pronounced states of intoxication, mestizos view the Yaqui as chronic drunkards. Nevertheless, patterns of consumption rather than mere frequency of drunkenness are probably more effective indicators of abuse (Seevers 1971: 102). Habitual consumption is one of the most reliable indices for alcohol dependency and alcohol-linked physical maladies. Using inability to abstain as a criterion for problem drinking, only 0.25 percent of the Yaqui men in Potam show signs of dependency; another 1.0 percent have behavioral and social problems due to their alcohol consumption (Lutes 1977: 219–225, 268). By way of comparison, Fromm and Maccoby (1970: 157–158) cite figures of 3.5 percent (Mexico), 4.5 percent (U.S.), and 5.2 percent (France) as indicative of the alcohol problem rates in those countries. Martínez (1963: 70–85) has described a high correlation between drunkenness and crime in mestizo Mexico, a correlation that is not evident in Yaqui society. The Yaqui are episodic binge drinkers; local mestizos often drink a few beers each day. The same contrast is likely among the Mayo and the local mestizos in their area, at least in those parts of Mayo country where a semblance of traditional life has survived.

The Yaqui are also little prone to revitalization movements, which are often linked to profound periods of social disintegration and unrest. Among the Mayo, Crumrine (1977) has provided an excellent account of such cultic phenomena and they appear to thrive in association with coercive mestizo Indian policies. Crumrine ascribes the impetus for Mayo revitalization

Table 2.1. Policy and Lifestyle Variables

Variable	Ethnicity		
	Yaqui	Mayo	Mestizo
Type of local group	Pueblo civic and religious leaders	Pueblo civic and religious leaders	Elected officials, Syndicate, ejido leaders
Position of local group authorities to the higher level mestizo authorities	Recognized as local authorities	Not recognized	Recognized, but often have little effective power
Type of land tenure	Land-use rights by tribal fiat, inalienable from tribe	No tribal rights, ejido or small privately owned plots only	Individual land ownership of various sized plots, ejidos
Mestizo response to Indian social and cultural expressions	Tolerance	Lack of tolerance	
Standard of living, by own assessment	Generally adequate, but little cash	Minimal, with chronic shortages of goods and cash	Varies widely with class stratum, but generally is similar to Mayo
Psychological stability	Pronounced and conservative	Weak, cultic movements and social disintegration	Varied, but with high rates of ingroup violence and alcoholism
Propensity for class-ethnic oriented conflict	Low	Present and increasing, shift to class from ethnic orientation	High, especially among poor and dislocated classes

movements to patterns of stress that arise from mestizo colonization and policies. The Yaqui, too, are surrounded by a large mestizo population, but apparently their insulated condition provides some immunity to the forces of chaotic disintegration and cultic movements.

Beyond expressions of discontent contained in social phenomena centered around the supernatural realm, there is the possibility of open violence in this world. Until recent times both the Yaqui and Mayo resisted, with force, the usurpation of their lands and society. However, after the Indian problems were partially resolved, class-linked violence centered around land continued to erupt and has never been eliminated in any satisfactory manner.

In 1976 and 1977, land-centered conflicts were issues of much social concern in Sonora and Sinaloa. One particularly nasty episode occurred while I was living in Potam. It involved the Yaqui, rural squatters (including dislocated Mayo), plus state, municipal, and national armed forces. At issue were large tracts of land near Ciudad Obregón that the government had long promised but failed to expropriate from their former owners and redistribute among the landless poor.

Led by a local "professor," several hundred campesinos moved onto the disputed land and vowed that they would resist all attempts to dislodge them. At the same time, the squatters announced plans to extend their activities to additional land to the north. This brought the Yaqui into the picture, since they, too, were disputing ownership of the contested area. Guns began appearing in Yaqui territory and the Indians were prepared to confront the "invaders" if they tried to enter the area that the Yaqui felt was theirs under the terms of the 1936 peace agreement.

The Yaqui threat was not taken lightly by the leaders of the campesinos. In interviews with local reporters they said that they had no quarrel with the Yaqui and would not provoke them. The Yaqui themselves expressed little sympathy for the owners, the state government, or the squatters. They did tell of Mayo who were with the landless elements, saying that "before, they did not resist the *Yorim* [mestizos] to the end, now they have nothing of their own."

Shortly thereafter, police and military units advanced on the squatter positions. Shots were fired. At least 17 of the campesinos were killed (some say more died), including the leader. Pictures of the slain men appeared in all of the papers, and the event at San Ignacio Río Muerte became the occasion of heated debate. The furor resulted in the resignation of Sonora's governor and a large number of lesser state and municipal authorities.

Similar land-related violence flared in Sinaloa the following year. The most unfortunate implication of such events is that their likelihood seems to increase rather than decrease with time. The national government is not in an enviable position. It generally is supportive of more humanitarian policies, but the realities of regional power blocks and alliances often preclude government action.

A comparison of the policies and policy implications as they pertain to the Yaqui, Mayo, and poor mestizos clearly shows various key distinctions. The differences are summarized in Table 2.1 in terms of the trait variables introduced at the beginning of the chapter.

POLICY COMPARISONS AND CONCLUSIONS

Policies toward cultural minorities often seem to be based on dreams and not reality. The economic integration of a nation's various subgroups is rightfully of high priority, but officials seem to pursue it with the belief that only assimilation and cultural homogeneity will produce the right effect. It is in this perspective that attempts to formulate alternate models of social development have attracted the attention of anthropologists and others whose goal is to understand and clarify the large-scale trends that occur in human social life. One excellent avenue for describing some of those social trends is the study of enclavement.

When countries as diverse as the United States, China, Mexico, and the Philippines begin a shift toward accommodation to pluralism rather than enforce heavy-handed policies of assimilation, we are faced with some interesting hypotheses. The shift could represent a temporary digression in an irreversible process or a fundamental turning point in development trends themselves, for reasons not thoroughly understood. In either case, what has happened and what will happen in northern Mexico is not an isolated curiosity in the annals of humankind.

The assumption herein is that different policy approaches are clearly linked to the subsequent differences in social development and collective behavior that have been described throughout this chapter. One crucial dimension is the suggestion that coercive policies aimed at integration through assimilation have yielded dubious rewards. The Mayo continue to exist as a group, but one that is victimized by social policy. When Mayo do begin to act in terms of class rather than ethnicity, their behavior typically takes the form of violence directed against those powers that are viewed as thwarting the poor and their minimal ability to provide for life's needs.

Support for Draconian measures in southwestern Sonora is usually based on two premises: (1) the cost of alternative strategies is high and impedes the rapid modernization of the state and its economy; (2) based on current theoretical notions, kinship based societies are in conflict with the requirements of the modern state, which must inevitably replace the former. It is not uncommon to find Sonorans who believe that the cost of Indian enclaves, and ejidos, is measured in lower productivity and profits. Private agrobusiness, they say, yields more substantial returns that are in line with the area's development goals. This viewpoint is probably true when cost and profit are defined only in narrow terms and not put into broader social perspective.

What is usually not clearly analyzed is the manner in which the increased profits are used. In most cases it appears that in private agrobusiness extravagant sums are diverted for the principal owners' material well-being. Taxation is easily avoided, and in the case of several large landholders I encountered, significant amounts of their total income are invested outside of Mexico. "It is safer in the U.S.," as one man noted. Some income becomes investment capital, to be used in improving productive capabilities. Little income is left to trickle down to the less fortunate, and as noted above, income concentration in Mexico has increased along with growth in the nation's Gross National Product.

It is evident, too, that landless agricultural workers are a politically volatile group and are prone to violence. Large expenditures are required for maintaining peace and order. In addition to the national troops and state and municipal forces, landowners also maintain armies of *"pistoleros,"* who pursue the goals of their private employers. The total social and economic cost of lapses in peace and order is difficult to assess, largely because of the very conditions associated with and existing prior to the unrest itself. The pursuit of policies such as those directed at the Mayo will do little but contribute to problems that already detract from claims of economic and social growth.

The circumstances of Yaqui enclavement are less than perfect, but they display certain characteristics that hold the promise of more gradual development with fewer attendant risks to all concerned. It is evident that the Yaqui are able to realize their own minimal needs in a way that satisfies most of them. At the same time, the tribe's territory provides a support base for the labor of a relatively large and skilled mestizo work force. Material improvements in the land's productive capacities and infrastructure have been realized and continue to be upgraded. Completed projects include roads, canals, electrification, potable water delivery systems, public schools, and public health clinics. The role and presence of the military on Yaqui land has been greatly reduced in recent years and there is little for the territory's small police force to do. The status quo, with its openness to negotiation and change, is accepted by the majority of Yaqui and mestizos.

Yaqui authorities tend to be respected by their constituents. The authorities feel that they have a vested interest in dealing with the national government. Both sides practice give-and-take rather than seek to impose unilateral decisions by force. As a consequence, the Yaqui generally are supportive of federal authority in a way that few mestizos are. The quality of these social and political conditions reflects the balance achieved through accommodation, and in the Yaqui case, it is tempting to say that enclavement enhanced integration.

Note. The data presented are mainly from my fieldwork in and around the Yaqui pueblo of Potam during 1975 and 1976. Additional published sources are cited in the text. I am particularly indebted to N. Ross Crumrine, whose written work and comments on the Mayo have been extensively used for comparative purposes.

Alisky 1971
Bartell 1965
Beals 1932a, 1943
Crumrine 1977
Dabdoub 1965
Fabila 1940
Fromm and Maccoby 1970
Hackenberg 1970
Lutes 1977
Martínez 1963
Navarrette 1970
Pérez de Ribas 1968
Seevers 1971
Spicer 1954
Vargas Montero 1978

CHAPTER THREE

Mechanisms of Enclavement Maintenance and Sociocultural Blocking of Modernization Among the Mayo of Southern Sonora

N. Ross Crumrine (University of Victoria, Canada)

Living in a high-yield irrigation agricultural zone, the modern Mayo of southern Sonora are characterized by dramatic agricultural modernization and technological and economic assimilation. As members of ejidos, many Mayo Indians farm small areas of parceled land (four to six hectares) that must be worked and may not be rented or sold. The hydraulic commission and the ejido banks essentially control the times, amounts, and crops of planting. Modern technological advances, such as insecticides and spray planes, fertilizers, salting clouds to produce rain, and the latest hybrid crops, are part of everyday Mayo existence but are not well integrated into their traditional way of life. However, modern Mayo values, mythology, ceremonialism, use of the Mayo language, and perception of the world stand in complete contrast to this dramatic modernization in southern Sonora. Mayo identity, insofar as it represents a separate system from that of mestizo Mexico, is linked with this ritual system and unique view of the world.

A number of the characteristics of "Regiones de Refugio," as developed by Gonzalo Aguirre Beltrán (1967), are not present in the Mayo case. Today, the concept of geographical isolation in a hostile environment makes little sense for the Mayo. Their isolation is real, but it is rather one of intellectual and educational background than of deserts, mountains, and great distances. Traditionally, demographically speaking, the Mayo death rate appears high and life expectancy low in contrast to those rates for middle and upper class mestizos; however, many of the Mayo today have easy access to modern medicine, clinics, and hospitals. Yet Aguirre Beltrán's concepts regarding regions of refuge and their dual economies prove useful in the case of the modern Mayo. Their lack of real political power and inability to advance successfully within the mestizo class system due to lack of educational and intellectual background suggests certain remnants of a region of refuge. Mayo response has focused on the creation of an "opposition culture," of a "culture" of enclavement. This unique embedded culture symbolizes the Mayo as a separate people, *Yoremem*, in contrast to mestizos, *Yorim*.

The persistent Mayo opposition culture has been developed through a history of interaction with and adaptation to changing patterns of social contact between Mayos and broader, more dominant societies. In the early 1600s the Mayos were missionized by the Jesuits, who were successful in converting and reeducating them, in introducing new crops such as wheat, and in increasing Mayo productivity. In the late 1700s, the Jesuits were removed from the area and the Mayo experienced a period of relative autonomy. Since that time they have gradually lost autonomy, assimilating in the economic and political arenas, and being forced into the lowest status positions within these systems. Through dynamic adaptation of their traditional culture, they have maintained linguistic and ceremonial isolation. Modern Mayo religious movements revitalize Mayo ceremonialism in opposition to technological and economic assimilation. These movements focus on an intense fear of the anger of God and the possibility that He may choose to destroy mankind if they do not make the appropriate ceremonies, that is, Mayo type rituals. Members argue that their past ceremonies have saved humanity, including the Mayo and mestizos, from inevitable destruction (Crumrine 1975 and 1981). Thus, modern Mayo are not geographically isolated but are embedded within modern mestizo society and have developed an opposition culture, a culture of enclavement (Spicer 1961, 1962, 1971, and 1980). This chapter discusses and explains the development of this Mayo perception of opposition.

MODERN MAYO TECHNOLOGICAL AND ECONOMIC ASSIMILATION

The natural and cultural ecologies of northwestern Mexico are without doubt some of the most interesting in the world. The two most striking sets of modern oppositions exist between the commercial irrigated agricultural areas versus the desert thorn forest, and between the urban towns and smaller, more dispersed villages versus the wild desert forests. Often visible from the lower river valley, the Sierra Madre Mountains stand out on the eastern horizon in contrast to the huge sand dunes and broad beaches of the Gulf of California to the west, just beyond the last villages. Along the coastal plain, some 60 kilometers to the north, runs the Yaqui River, while some 160 kilometers to the south flows the Fuerte River, a second area of Mayo homes and villages. Even though they are visible from the lower river valley, extensive mountainous areas only commence some 60 to 80 kilometers east of the lower Mayo River valley, contrasting with the Yaqui area to the north where extensive mountainous areas are much closer to the villages. The Yaqui River produces considerably more water than the Mayo River and the Yaqui dam is larger than the Mayo one; these features are ecologically significant because the planting of a second yearly crop has been greatly restricted in the last few years in the Mayo area due to scarcity of water. Much of the irrigation water used in the Mayo area is pumped from wells rather than drawn from the Mocuzari or Adolfo Ruiz Cortines dam, making irrigation more expensive. The period of late December 1984 and early January 1985, however, was characterized by broad spread flooding due to the heaviest winter rains in the last 60 years, which filled and overflowed the dams, ". . . leaving sufficient water for the agricultural tasks of the fall-winter cycle. . . ." (Pesquiera Olea 1985: 27).

In terms of natural resources, the area produces fish and sea foods in the coastal areas; fire wood, building materials, and wild nuts and cactus fruits in the coastal plain; and additional hardwoods, wild animals, and nuts and fruits in the foothills of the Sierra Madre Mountains. With the exception of firewood for cooking, some building materials, and seafoods, the wild natural resources are relatively unimportant in the lives of the modern Mayo. Medicines are an exception, because many Mayos still retain a comprehensive knowledge of wild plant and animal medicines that they may utilize on occasion. Fishing is important, even for individuals who conceive of themselves as farmers, partly because of the abundant sea life in the Gulf of Georgia. Farmers living in the lower river valley construct casting nets to use from the beach, or they block small coastal inlets with long nets and pick up the fish stranded by the falling tide (Crumrine 1977). A whole range of edible fish, plus shrimp, are caught in these ways. Clams are collected and eaten by the fishermen, who often must camp for the night near the beach. The fish are salted and dried, and either eaten by the family or sold or exchanged with neighbors.

Other Mayos, less involved in farming, conceive of themselves as commercial fishermen. Many are members of fishing cooperatives and are able to obtain loans for large flat-ended canoes with outboard motors. These men also use casting nets in fishing for shrimp and other fish from canoes or larger boats. The farmer who fishes occasionally would be afraid to spend much time in the canoes and fishes only from the shore. Commercial shrimping is closely supervised and controlled by the government. Members of the cooperatives fish only during a certain season and take their catch to a centralized ice plant where it is processed and shipped to the large urban centers of Mexico and foreign countries. Using a line and hooks, they also fish for small sharks that are sold as fish food in the local markets. In the past the livers were used in the manufacture of vitamin D, but today they are discarded. Membership in a cooperative and its commercial fishing activity is an excellent occupation for a young man who does not have land for farming or is not a member of a farming ejido. Obviously, this type of fishing is fully commercial and controlled by the Mexican government and the economy of the Mexican and worldwide market systems. Mayos who farm will eat fish during Easter week and if nothing else is available, but fish is not a preferred food and is not well liked. Shrimp are acceptable but are expensive and usually not readily available to most Mayos.

The main production in the Mayo area is commercial agriculture. Legally the area is classified as agricultural, and Mayos are chiefly involved in agricultural wage labor. Most families also care for a few chickens and perhaps several pigs. Chicken eggs and the chickens themselves are eaten; however, the pigs are often sold to neighbors or dealers in the villages and towns. A number of large chicken and pig ranches flourish in the area, but none of them are owned by Mayos. All households have several thin, sickly, shaggy dogs. Turkeys, domestic ducks, geese, and house cats are known, but owned by few Mayo families. The government has tried to introduce domestic rabbits, but I know of no Mayo family with rabbits. Cattle, goats, and sheep are more popular but far too expensive for most central valley Mayo families, because feed is difficult to obtain. Families living in peripheral areas have more goats, sheep, and cattle, which they graze in the desert areas beyond the irrigation zone. The women of some of these families still weave Mayo blankets from sheep wool. But large animals are increasingly difficult to maintain, especially since the area now has been declared an agricultural zone. Most central areas are cropped, and when cattle break into a field their owner may be taken to court and fined for damages. Cattle, or goats and sheep, may be used for a fiesta or sold; however, with increasing feed costs and decreasing wild pasturage the profit is considerably reduced for a Mayo family, which may own only several cattle. As in the case of chickens and pigs, large cattle ranches do flourish in the area, but these are not owned by Mayos and tend to be concentrated in nonagricultural areas. At the present time Sonoran large cattle-ranging companies are in direct competition with small-scale farmers for lands, creating a problem much broader than just in the Mayo area and a tense situation for the state government. As small-scale farmers, Mayos look to the government for support and petition for grants of land in the form of ejidos. Thus, animal husbandry in the river valley is controlled by the government and by large ranching interests, and is but a small part of Mayo productivity. Even a farm animal such as the horse has almost disappeared from the river valley, and only occasionally is a horse used for field work. For example, in seeking an elderly Mayo friend, his son told me that his father was out in the bush taking care of his horse. I asked the son if he used the horse in the fields and he replied, "No, he never uses the horse in the fields. It does no work. All it does is eat." I asked why the old man had the horse. The son said, "He likes the horse. It is a pet." As a boy, this man did a lot of herding in the bush and had developed an affection for horses. Today he is farming an ejido plot and clearing other lands, yet he still keeps a horse although it is productively useless. I mention this case only to stress the fact that today the Mayo area is legally, culturally, and productively an agricultural zone, and it is becoming more so each day as new lands are cleared and transformed into fields.

From the Mayo point of view the only honorable work, the only real profession, is that of agriculturist. Many Mayos have memberships in ejidos, working ejido lands, while others own small plots of land. Since ejido and private plots often are small and many individuals do not hold any farm lands, most Mayos also must engage in wage labor. In the 1970s, individuals working in the fields were lucky if they were paid 100 pesos per day's work (about $5.00 per day). They might irrigate the crops, pick peas, tomatoes, or other vegetables, or hand weed young *cártamo* (safflower), cotton, or other crops. Cotton, which was a key crop in the early 1970s and required a great deal of wage labor, was reduced to some 247 hectares in 1976 due to low cotton prices and overproduction in the past. For the 1977 cycle the farmers had permission to plant some 6,000 hectares, which required additional wage labor. The availability of wage labor relates directly to the types of crops planted, which, in turn, depend on governmental quotas and water supply. For instance, cotton requires 56 *jornales* (day's labor) per hectare in contrast to wheat requiring only six jornales.

The Mayo produce for commercial markets not only as wage labor in the fields, but also as *etlerom* (planters or agriculturists). After the Mexican Revolution of 1910, President Cárdenas, among others, expropriated lands from large land holders and, supplementing these with government-owned lands, donated large blocks of lands in the form of ejidos to peasant farmers. Many Mayos received ejido membership and the right to work ejido lands, often four hectares in irrigated lands and four hectares in uncleared lands, although the amounts of land granted varied depending on the size of the ejido and the type of land under consideration. Most of the ejidos in the Mayo area are parceled, that is, the individual members are assigned plots and are free to work those plots until they retire or die. At the time of death the plot can be inherited by the deceased member's descendants. The plot must be worked and may not be rented or sold. The ejido organization, consisting of a president, vice-president, secretary, and other officers, and a vigilance committee that acts as a check on the officers and members, was a creation of the Revolutionary Government and was imposed on the traditional Mayo socioeconomic organization. Thus the Mayo had no control over the organizational structure of the ejidos. Today the organizations own tractors and plowing, sowing, and leveling machinery as well as excavating equipment. When the members' needs have been served, the equipment with operators may be rented or loaned to other farmers.

Agricultural advisers recommend certain crops and Ejido Bank inspectors examine fields and also make recommendations. Water levels in the dam, reservoirs, and wells are taken into account and crop quotas are set. In terms of this advice and these restrictions, ejido members decide which crops to plant. Members wishing to plant the same crop are grouped together and ejido officers apply to the Ejido Bank, financed and operated by the government, for loans to cover the cost of seed, water, and fertilizer. The 1977 interest rate for loans under a year was six percent and over a year, eight percent. Individual farmers request irrigation water, and the plowing, sowing, and fertilizing is a mechanized procedure utilizing the ejido tractor and equipment. Additional fertilizer, insecticide, weeding, and irrigation water are supplied by the individual farmer. The crop is harvested either with ejido equipment or with wage labor. Government agronomists set the range of dates within which the crop may be planted and indicate when it should be ready for harvest. As mentioned earlier, the national and international markets play an important role in the number of hectares that is allocated to a specific crop.

These Mayo also carry insurance on their crops and many are members of the Social Security medical plan. Sick members and their immediate family are treated at local clinics, or at the hospitals in Huatabampo, Navojoa, or Ciudad Obregón. When Hurricane Liza struck the Mayo area in October 1976, bank officials examined crop damage and often refused to accept damaged crops. The insurance then paid the costs of the crop and it was left for the farmer to plow under and replant the field. By mid-December one of my friends was gathering ripe corn from his damaged field. He explained that the bank had rejected the crop but many plants had recovered and it was worth his while to harvest the ripe corn for his own use.

In the spring of 1977, because of cloudy weather, a bad wheat rust *(chahuixtle)* attacked many hectares of the Jupateco variety of wheat and many farmers were forced to harrow their crops and replant cártamo. Large areas were sprayed with fungicides from the air and some fields were saved. In contrast, unusually heavy August 1980 rains encouraged Río Mayo farmers to plant corn that many then harvested several months later without requiring artificial irrigation.

Set amounts of money are advanced on the crop so families will be able to buy food. Most families also plant small gardens of vegetables and flowers around their homes for their own use. Typical fall-winter crops are sesame, corn, peas, and assorted vegetables and spring-summer crops are wheat, cártamo, linseed, and cotton. Throughout the entire year small spray airplanes daily swoop low over one or another field. Orchards of oranges, papaya, and mangoes as well as fields of tomatoes, chilis, and other vegetables exist but are seldom owned by Mayos. Since the spring of 1977 when marigolds were introduced on a wider scale, large fields of this crop have been planted, although not usually by the Mayo. Corn and peas are used by the Mayo, but the other crops are grown simply for their commercial value. Often Mayos have little idea even how the crops are used.

I present the preceding data to demonstrate in a dramatic way that modern Mayo technological and economic systems are completely structured and dominated by the broader mestizo society and government. New crops such as marigolds, or new techniques, are absolutely foreign to their realm of knowledge and understanding, completely imposed on their traditional way of life, and often are not well received by highly successful yet traditionally oriented Mayo.

In summary, the history of Mayo technological and economic development has been one of gradual assimilation, loss of autonomy, and incorporation into the modern world economy. Modern Mayo farming practices reflect a fragile adjustment of a difficult ecology with modern banking and agricultural business institutions in which the Mayo often appear to act as the lowest ranking members. In addition, within this context unresolved opposition and tension, especially regarding land ownership, still exist. Most Mayos have been deprived of their aboriginal lands, and even those who hold some lands (either as members of an ejido or as small property owners) usually have no more than eight or ten hectares. The children of these individual land holders receive even smaller parcels as their "inheritance" is divided among brothers and sisters. Yet the Mayo continue to idealize the *etlero* (agriculturist) and the farming way of life as the true Mayo vocation. They remain closed to other possibilities and either reject innovation and modernization whenever possible, or play the passive role of helpless tools in the modern agribusiness domination of the Mayo River valley. In the following section this Mayo rejection of modernization and domination by external events and processes is explicated.

MAYO AUTONOMY AND ACCEPTANCE OF EXTERNAL INNOVATION

The following legend, as told by the Mayo, forcefully reveals an important aspect of Mayo world view.

In the past, before 1926, the Mayo church was available to everyone, Mayos and mestizos. The doors were open and never locked. One day Juan Pacheco, a mestizo under orders from the state government, entered and set fire to the Mayo church in Júpare, a small Mayo pueblo near Huatabampo, Sonora, Mexico. He carried off the saint, *ili usim,* the Little Children. As they crossed the Mayo river, San Juan, one saint saved himself by jumping into the water, even though Pacheco shot at him. Then Pacheco took the rest of the saints part of the way to Huatabampo and burned them.

Today, marking this spot, stand several crosses that Mayos continuously decorate. The rebuilt Mayo church in Júpare was closed, *pattiak,* as is its modern replacement. When the new church is not in use its door is locked. Only Mayos are truly welcome at any time. If anyone attempted to burn the church today I believe that person would be killed before he or she could leave Júpare. I feel that this legend is symbolic of the closing of Mayo culture to certain external innovation, and that the loss of Mayo autonomy and resulting decline of Mayo incentive for modernization serve as mechanisms in promoting and maintaining nonreceptivity to otherwise available aspects of modernization. Among lower river Mayos a process of revival of traditional Mayo culture and society, in fact, is now taking place. This discussion is based on an examination of the relevant facts of Mayo history and of present day Mayo and mestizo value systems as these relate to the loss of Mayo autonomy, of ability to integrate value systems, and of the incentive for modernization.

The following historical data consist of a description of the history of culture contact, or more specifically of contact communities and the types of change linked with types of contact communities. With a few important differences, Mayo history closely parallels that of the Yaqui as reported by Spicer (1961: 8, Table 1; 1980) and Hu-DeHart (1981, 1984).

Ranchería Period

In period one the Yaqui and Mayo practiced some floodwater farming and hunting and gathering in their river valleys, relying on about forty percent wild food resources. The level of sociopolitical organization for peace-time was the local group, the ranchería, which consisted of no more than 400 persons. The local group was exogamous and the present day kinship terminology indicates the absence of lineages and the presence of a bilateral extended family as the basic social unit (Spicer 1961: 14, which was probably also true for the Mayo). Economically, each ranchería was a self-sufficient farming settlement. The ceremonial activity included warfare, initiation rites, hunting and curing, ritual techniques emphasizing "the individual as a source of supernatural power and . . . a variety of group and individual dances often connected with animal representation either in the dance or in ground paintings" (Spicer 1961: 19).

Mission Pueblo Period

In the second period the first contacts were made with Spanish expeditions. Both peoples, Mayo and Yaqui, had seen or heard of Jesuit innovations in the river valleys to the south such as new crops, methods of agriculture, and huge elaborate churches. They were so anxious for Jesuit missionaries that they sent requests for them. The missionaries were required to come without the army in the Yaqui case, whereas the Mayo took advantage of the opportunity to ally themselves with the Spanish forces against their traditional enemies, the Yaqui and Tehueco. During this period the Mayo and Yaqui were open to the Jesuit teachings and the Jesuits in turn learned the Yaqui-Mayo language, lived with the people, taught Christianity by employing the Indian power structure, trained Mayo and Yaqui leaders as teachers, and instead of destroying indigenous ritual attempted to give it Christian meanings. Under these terms the people readily accepted and gradually modified Jesuit teachings. Their autonomy had not been seriously threatened and they were free to accept what fit their value system or to modify their value system to fit what the Jesuits taught. The type of culture characterizing this period is that of acceptance of Spanish innovation.

Autonomous Pueblo Period

In the third period Spanish settlers began to move into the Yaqui-Mayo country, which has caused increasing conflict even to the present time. Two events happened in this period at about the same time. First, in 1767 the Spanish Crown decreed the expulsion of the complete Jesuit Order from Spanish colonies in America. The Jesuit withdrawal from the Yaqui-Mayo area took place without difficulties (Hu-DeHart 1981: 95), and they have never been replaced successfully for the Mayo. Second, Spanish power was being broken, and mestizo authority was not strong enough until the late 1800s to completely control the Mayo and Yaqui. The year 1740 marked a generalized Indian revolt in northwest Mexico, especially among the Yaqui and Mayo.

During this period both the contact communities were broken and the "autonomous river towns" were under constant physical and cultural attack, resulting in a process of cultural resynthesis or fusion. It most probably was during this time that, to take an example from Mayo religious belief, a precontact concept of the sun as a divinity and an old man was fused with the Christian concept of God and Christ. This fusion is restated each year during Lent when an old man representing Christ is chased around the Way of the Cross. In this period, with Spanish and mestizo settlers beginning to represent a real threat to Mayo autonomy, the system closed to outside innovation and fused Jesuit teaching and indigenous belief into a tighter system.

Destruction and Revitalization Period

In the fourth period the Mayo were fighting a constant battle with mestizos to retain their lands. In the late 1800s Mayo religious and political leaders were more systematically destroyed than were those of the Yaqui. Mestizos settled more successfully in Mayo communities, yielding somewhat different modern contact communities than among the Yaqui, who live on a type of reservation and retain a more obvious system of political control over their own destinies than do the Mayo. Finally in the late 1800s and early 1900s, when mestizo control became strong enough, the Mayo and Yaqui were defeated. All Yaqui and many Mayo were deported from their river valleys to plantations in Yucatan or they fled to other towns in Sonora, Sinaloa, and the United States, where they were given political asylum. In the United States the Yaqui and some intermixed Mayo soon revived parts of their culture. In Arizona economic assimilation was necessary, whereas the traditional religious customs were encouraged by friendly Anglo-Americans. The Mayo joined the Mexican Revolution of 1910 en masse. Often not knowing which side they were fighting for, they believed that they were fighting to get their land back because the Díaz government had reduced them to landless peons. After the Revolution, both the Mayo and Yaqui returned to their river valleys and attempted to the best of their ability to reestablish the old ways. This period is characterized by contact communities of the relocated town type in Sonora and urban segment type in Arizona, and by culture change of the cultural revival type in Sonora groups and assimilation in Arizona groups. At this time there is not a predominance of cultural fusion but an attempt to recreate the autonomous period culture. To the present time, some Mayo communities have remained in this state of cultural revival, especially in the domains of religious belief and ritual (Crumrine 1981).

This historical reconstruction illustrates a developmental sequence in the creation of a folk culture from a fusion of indigenous Mayo culture with Spanish-Jesuit culture of an early time period, with the subsequent dispersion of the society and the resettlement of the original Mayo country. The result was a revival of the folk culture and an increasing rigidity in that way of life. What variables may be isolated from this process of increasing closure to innovation from the outside? Loss of political and religious autonomy and loss of the land base, or economic autonomy, represent aspects of a general independent variable, the loss of Mayo autonomy, acting within this system. This loss of Mayo autonomy is considered as one of two possible mechanisms illuminating both the conflict between mestizo modernization and traditional Mayo folk culture and between society and Mayo enclavement within modern Mexico.

CONTRASTS IN MAYO AND MESTIZO VALUES AS FACTORS IN MODERNIZATION

The preceding section introduced a consideration of the degree of Mayo autonomy as one of the variables in Mayo acceptance or rejection of modernization and assimilation. In that analytic description Mayo sociocultural development was examined. This section, a summary of Mayo and mestizo values, shifts to a synchronic study of present day value systems in the Mayo River area. The heuristic descriptive framework used to present the two value systems was inspired by the earlier research of Clyde and Florence Kluckhohn (Clyde Kluckhohn 1951, Florence Kluckhohn 1950); however, its present form includes my own modifications. The social facts, which have been isolated from life along the Mayo River, provide the basis for describing Mayo and mestizo value orientations. This chapter focuses on the Mayo as a group in contrast to Mayo River valley mestizos. Clearly the mestizos are a heterogeneous group and should be divided into classes, and the Mayo and rural mestizos actually share many traits and patterns of interaction (Erasmus 1961, 1967). Although the following value profile is more pronounced among traditional Mayo, it is more broadly present in diffuse and fragmented forms among many less traditional Mayo. Mary O'Connor (1980) clearly emphasizes and discusses some of these complexities and divergences of ethnic identity within the modern populations inhabiting the Mayo region. For the purposes of this chapter, however, I accept that mestizos in the area share sufficient general cultural and social patterns to be considered a group when contrasted with other groups such as the Yaqui and Mayo, and that except for physical appearance, material culture, and certain social patterns, the Mayo represent an enduring people separated from mestizos by a range of symbolic and ritual patterns and social interaction that are shared by other Mayos (Crumrine 1964, 1977, 1981).

Relationships to Nature

Mayos have a tendency to see humanity as a part of a natural and supernatural world, whereas mestizos perceive humanity in contrast to nature or as holding a rational mastery over nature. A deep love for the land, the plant growth, and the animals of the bush is a characteristic of most Mayo individuals. The only truly traditional Mayo occupation and the mark of a good person is to work the land. As an initial priority, most Mayos desire sufficient land on which to grow food to feed themselves and their families, to have a small surplus for ceremonial giving, and to sell for enough money to buy clothes, perhaps a radio,

Figure 3.1. A gathering at a Mayo home for the 8 Day Ritual after death. (Photograph by N. Ross Crumrine.)

electric lights, and a bicycle. They feel sad to see all the bush being cleared, for it is an area of natural resources (wood, food, and medicine) as well as the world of the animals. The Mayo language includes a long list of words for the animals and plants of the bush that people not only talk about frequently, but that come to their minds immediately as one begins to elicit words in a study of the Mayo language. Many Mayos also know a range of wild plant and animal medicines. Mayo ceremonial dancers, the paskolas and deer dancers, are said to go to the bush to learn how to dance well. Although the individuals themselves deny this, it is generally known that the musicians of these dancers also learn their tunes and songs from the bush world, *huya anía,* in return for the promise of their souls after death. The bush and the deer singers also provide the setting for at least one type of curing. Religious processions take place on the land, as Mayo dead not only are buried in the land but at one time walked and worked on it (Figs. 3.1, 3.2). Thus the land itself, as well as the bush and the animals and plants in the bush, is sacred and is unified with the Mayo. The Mayo proverb "the earth will eat us up" refers to the contract with the land, in which "our bodies will be consumed as we consume" the products of the earth.

For mestizos this relation of humanity to nature is different, for they perceive the world rather as an object to be used or to gain mastery over it. Mestizos build a dam on the upper Mayo River to control the flooding and provide irrigation water, and are constantly clearing the bush and bringing new land under irrigation. In addition, working the land is not considered as a desirable occupation but as rather lowly. Many mestizos even dislike getting their hands dirty and wash them compulsively if they are forced to get them muddy. Although Mayos manipulate machinery, their real expertise is in actual dirt farming. Thus there is a clear difference in the Mayo and mestizo view of nature and the relation between humanity and nature; Mayos perceive of themselves more as an integrated part of nature while mestizos see humans in a position of rational mastery over nature. This constitutes a difference that would not cause conflict between the two groups unless they were both attempting to act in their own ways on the same geographic area.

Time Orientations

There is also a difference in the time orientations of Mayos and mestizos. Mayos are relatively past oriented, with emphasis also on the present, and mestizos are more future oriented. The

Figure 3.2. Circling (konti) of the grave after the prayers during the 8 Day Ritual. (Photograph by N. Ross Crumrine.)

mestizo family is working for a better life in the future, not only for themselves but for their children, so that the next generation will have something. Often when mestizos discuss death someone will say that life is short but it is given meaning in their work on behalf of the children. Their fulfillment is in their children getting ahead. For a Mayo, working and giving has no connection in particular with the future generations, but he or she is fulfilling a promise made in the past to God or one of the saints. If the individual or a family member should be cured from an illness, the individual would work for the divinity, paying for the cure. For Mayos, giving has some bearing on the future life in that one gives at a ceremony in order to receive that "Holy Flower" in Heaven, but it has little to do with improving one's lot on this earth. Another example of the differences in these two time orientations is the mestizo desire for their children to learn English whereas mature Mayos want to learn it themselves. Older Mayos have no fear of attacking a learning problem such as this because they are older and thus feel they have more accumulated power to learn. Mestizos of equal age say they are too old to learn a new language, but want their children to learn English, which is a useful language in getting jobs in this part of Mexico.

The Mayo value for age may be seen also in the fact that the greatest saint or the most respected person is generally the oldest. A Mayo family is considered truly poor if it does not have an old person. Initially Mayos believed I was rich because my parents were still living when I undertook research in their communities. If you are Mayo, no matter how old you are, you still consider it a great loss if your parents are dead; when they die you feel you are an orphan. In a sense you never really expect them to die. Also old persons are ceremonially important; on Thursday of Holy Week it is an old man who represents Christ, and old people portray the Apostles on the day of San Ignacio in the summer.

Mayo and mestizo attitudes toward money also reflect this difference in time orientation. Mestizos view money as the road to a bright future, whereas Mayos perceive it as a corrupting influence in Mayo life. For Mayos, a great deal of money means that the possessor in all probability has sold himself to the Devil or at least has been in league with non-Christian powers. As one of my Mayo friends said in referring to a large pueblo ceremony exploited by hundreds of mestizo vendors in the churchyard, "Much money fell within the four corners of that holy church ground, and it will not come out right for those who sold there. That is the place to give" (that is, not to sell). Thus in terms of attitudes toward money, education, work, ceremonial exchange, and old people and children, a definite value orientation for each group may be abstracted, showing Mayos to be generally past and present oriented and mestizos present and future oriented.

Personality Values

The ideal personality types fall into three categories: being, being-in-becoming, and doing-achieving. They represent "the personality component type which releases and indulges existing desires," the "personality component type which is self-contained and controls itself through a meditation and detachment that brings understanding" (F. Kluckhohn 1950: 379), and the active striving type. In terms of Mayo and mestizo values, the type of personality most valued by the Mayo is the being-in-becoming, whereas the mestizos value the doing-achieving type. There is a tendency toward aggressiveness in the mestizo group. Often when a crisis occurred among my mestizo neighbors, the guilty party had not been aggressive enough in a business deal and had been cheated. When Mayo behavior is examined this tendency is quite reversed. Mayos generally prefer to be polite and be cheated, rather than become involved in an argument. A Mayo person among his own group of friends and compadres may be very aggressive but in a subtle way, not ordering, but suggesting with firm words, backed up by sanctions of duty and tradition. Mayo children are never struck, it is said, but when they do wrong they are corrected with good words and made to kneel on garbanzos (chickpeas) in front of the house cross, a wooden cross placed in the ground about twenty feet in front of the front door (Crumrine 1964). Physical punishment is said and observed to be a common mestizo method of discipline. The mestizo value for the doing component of the personality is evident in the game of "get ahead," which may be played either in the bank, at a stop street, or in other public places. The idea is to "fake out" the other person by not recognizing his or her existence. In the bank or market one goes to the head of the line and tries to reach over everyone else's head. This sort of behavior is not typical of Mayos, who will allow themselves to be pushed out of a line by an aggressive mestizo. It should be mentioned, however, that within Mayo culture and society, roles exist for individuals with doing-achieving personalities (see Lutes 1983, whose argument is also true for the Mayo). These native Mayo achievers such as paskolas, deer dancers, curers, church specialists, and consistent ceremonial givers have a central place in their society. Without more specific testing it would be difficult to say if these persons have high "need achievement" in McClelland's (1961) sense of the concept, but certainly they appear to have more need to excel than do many other Mayos. Because these persons are so deeply involved in traditional Mayo culture, however, they do not tend to be innovators for modernization for revivalists.

Human Relationships

The dominant modality of the relationship of individuals to other human beings in northwestern Mexican mestizo values is individualistic with lineal and collateral aspects. They do stress compadres and parents and thus place some emphasis on the lineal and collateral aspects, but their adult children often do not live with their parents, residence is neolocal, and the compadres are not as integral a part of life as they are for Mayos. The dominant type of relationship a mestizo feels toward other humans is individualistic. As stated above, Mayo parents not only are important but usually live with their children. Mayos expect daughters to remain in the home while sons are more mobile. After their deaths, parents must be given a set of special ceremonies and remembered and prayed for each November on All Saints Day. In addition, some Mayo families have preserved books of the dead in which the names of the deceased family members are written. Within the family the old people have nearly absolute control and are highly respected. Thus the lineal principle is of great importance in Mayo life. Good compadres are also extremely important for Mayos, as compadres help finance them in the fulfillment of their promises to give ceremonies. This ceremony-giving group, the *kompānia,* is the basis of Mayo social and ceremonial life and illustrates the collateral principle in Mayo value orientations.

A contrast is evident also in two patterns of the dance, *baile.* Mestizo bailes are given by social clubs, individuals, or families. They present an opportunity for a mestizo family to maneuver its child as an individual into the mestizo social system. Much care is taken and money spent to ensure the child is properly dressed. Mayo bailes are the result of a *manda,* a promise, and involve the organization of a kompānia and the attendance of a saint, in addition to the social event of the dance. Mestizos tend to see a person's relation to others as individualistic, whereas Mayos tend to see it as both lineal and collateral.

Innate Predispositions

It appears that the value orientation of mestizo culture is one of viewing humanity as good but corruptible. Mestizos are both optimistic and realistic in their evaluations of human nature. They realize that individuals can be bribed and that one person will take advantage of another if possible, but they also perceive humanity as good and improvable. This is clear in their attitude toward Mayos. Mestizos tend to feel that Mayos live at an extremely poor level, "like dogs," but that if they would stop ceremonial giving and would concentrate on raising their standard of living, they would improve and become a full part of mestizo society. In other words, Mayos are basically good and they could easily become mestizos like themselves if they would just give up being Mayos. Thus there is little idea of innate racial inferiority or innate evil in being Mayo, but rather a sort of sadness that Mayos will not let go of their extreme ceremonialism and become solid members of the mestizo community.

For Mayos the innate predisposition of humanity is neither good nor evil but power-seeking. Power is intrinsically neither good nor evil but may be used to cure or harm others. For example, *gracia*, a gift from God, may be used to cure certain diseases but the same curer may cause disease, although not by means of a God-sent gracia. Curers always and repeatedly state that their power is a gift from God and is not their own. The people who crucify Christ during Lent are not said to be evil but it is explained that they wished to rule, to command. Since ultimately their power is not as great as Christ's, He returns and they must die, must be burned up by God's power. The paskolas, deer dancers, and musicians who receive their dancing and singing power through a contract with the bush world for their souls, are not considered necessarily evil persons, but rather as people serving a different master. Excellence in curing, dancing, singing, gambling, money-making or in any other characteristic that sets one off from the rest of the community, is considered as a gift of power from God or as resulting from the promise of the person's soul to the bush world or, as some suggest, to the Devil, and thus excellence is not necessarily innately evil nor good.

Relationships to God and the Saints

Most mestizos have little relation with God and the Saints except for confirmation, marriage, and death. Insofar as it exists, this pattern contains more emphasis on submission to an uncontrollable, unpredictable God than becoming one with or controlling God through ritual. The Mayo relation to God, on the other hand, is contractual. God is a powerful curer who can send illness as well as cure. No Mayo can cure a God-sent illness, but can only appeal to God to remove the illness. However, one may and will work for God and the Saints by giving a ceremony or decorating the house cross or the church cross or altar. As one of my Mayo friends noted, even the fireworks and the fiesta food served at a Mayo ceremony symbolize flowers given to God. Mayo religion is a complex system of controlling and repaying God and the Saints. Mestizos also make promises to God or the Saints but their promises involve much simpler acts such as one-night vigils in the church, crawling to the altar, or sprinkling water in front of an image in a procession, whereas Mayo promises involve days, weeks, even three or six years, or a lifetime of service. All of the Mayos I know have promised themselves or have been promised for many weeks of service at least once during their lives, and many are constantly working off promises. The Mayo relation to God and the Saints is a contractual system focusing on the control of illness and death. In contrast, the Mestizo relation ranges from submission to an uncontrollable God to a complete lack of interest in God and the Saints.

Summary

The description of mestizo and Mayo values has revealed that the systems vary on many points: Mayos perceive humanity within and as a part of nature and mestizos view human society as above nature; Mayos hold a past-present time orientation and mestizos a present-future one; Mayos value a being-in-becoming personality for the ordinary individual and in some instances a doing personality, while mestizos value a doing personality for everyone; Mayos' modality of relationship is lineal and collateral, while the mestizo pattern is relatively individualistic; Mayos' concept of innate human nature is power-seeking, whereas mestizos view humanity as good but corruptible; Mayos' relation to God and the Saints is a contractual system, while mestizos show either submission or lack of interest. Clearly the two systems are opposed at many points.

If the Mayo had sufficient autonomy and increased incentive for change they would feel the need to adapt their value system in order to improve its fit with the mestizo system and to minimize the conflict between the two systems. The data presented above indicated that this type of development took place during earlier periods in Mayo history. Such variables as autonomy and incentive for modernization are examined below in order to suggest mechanisms partially responsible in the blocking of value adaptation and of increasing modernization.

MECHANISMS IN THE BLOCKING OF MAYO MODERNIZATION

One of the best ways to examine the problem of blocks in the process of Mayo modernization is to focus on the question: just what does modernization involve for the present day Mayo? In the analysis of Mayo history it was shown that the Mayo had periods of amazingly rapid and thorough culture change. During the Mission Period they accepted new crops and agricultural techniques, new settlement patterns, and new political and religious systems, including new concepts of the world, of authority, and of ceremony-giving. During the later periods, however, they became closed to outside innovation except for some new items of material culture. Therefore, analysis of the present slow rate of development in Mayo modernization should be based on a discussion of the mechanisms involved in this closure to general outside innovation, two of which were suggested at the conclusion of the last section: (1) loss of Mayo autonomy and thus loss of hope that Mayos will be capable as Mayos of revising their value system and culture as a whole to fit a modernized life pattern in northwestern Mexico; and thus, (2) loss of any Mayo incentive towards modernization. The second point will be discussed first.

Loss of Incentive for Modernization

The loss of the incentive of the Mayo toward modernization may be considered in terms of our initial question, what does modernization entail for the present day Mayo? To state it in a more limited way, through what channels is modernization presented to the Mayo or how and by whom is it introduced? What is the structure of the social organization of contact or of the contact community?

Clearly the social structure of contact today limits Mayo modernization to one single channel, that of individual Mayos becoming mestizos. Several logically possible alternatives exist for Mayos and Mayo culture and society: (1) individual Mayos become mestizos and eventually Mayo culture and society simply disappear, (2) Mayos adapt Mayo culture and society in terms of modernization, and lastly, (3) Mayos resist change, revitalize, and adapt the Autonomous Period culture and society as much as possible. The present dominant process among many Mayos in the lower river valley is a resistance to mestization and thus a rejection of modernization insofar as it is linked with mestizo culture and society. This Mayo rejection of modernization, however, is a rejection of mestizo culture and society and not a lack of interest in modernization itself. Mayos blame mestizos for their loss of autonomy, and likely would adapt their value system and culture as they have done in the past if they retained the autonomy to achieve these modifications. However, many Mayos have no desire or incentive for modernization if this signifies becoming a mestizo, because they must not only give up all Mayo ritual and cultural wealth and security but also must enter mestizo society at the bottom. This position represents no obvious social or economic gain as rural lower class mestizos have much the same standard of living as do Mayos.

In northwestern Mexico, modernization is intimately linked with mestizo society and culture, to the disadvantage of the Mayo. The school teachers are nearly all mestizos and teach the children only Spanish, laughing at the Mayo "dialect" or "tongue," and there is a lack of understanding between Mayo families and the school. As a result, Mayo children attend poorly and are not encouraged to study at home. Mayo business experience is limited to buying from a mestizo in the market, borrowing money for seed and other necessities from the mestizo bank, or working as a peon for a mestizo patron for whom one may have toiled all his life. The bank, a Mayo will say, cheats him, taking two crops and paying for one, and in the market Mayos often pay more than they should. Mayos have neither what they consider a fair entrepreneurial pattern to follow nor a situation in which to learn how to be a successful businessman. Thus it is not surprising that for the Mayo, mestizo entrepreneurship in itself has become both unattainable and undesirable. For example, the presence of vendors at Mayo ceremonies has come to symbolize the money world, while the hoarding of money or accumulating capital represent great disruptive forces and, therefore, an evil process encroaching on Mayo culture. A new road built near a Mayo community by mestizos was viewed by the Mayo not as an aid in their trips to market and to ceremonies but simply as another mestizo technique in their continued exploitation of the Mayo. The Mayo have confused modernization with becoming mestizo, and all who elect to remain Mayo naturally have little or no incentive toward modernization.

Yet many Mayo families enjoy modernization in terms of material culture. They desire mestizo goods and services, electricity, radios, and bicycles, and find their ways into communities where land is more easily available or redistribution is promised. These families still participate in Mayo society and may give even more ceremonies because they have more goods to distribute. On the basis of other criteria of modernization, however, these families must be considered as traditional rather than modern, even though they appear to have a higher need achievement than many other Mayo. If the Mayo were open to innovation, these perhaps would be the families that would achieve a workable modification of Mayo values in terms of modernization. This group might then provide a Mayo example of the small innovating group mentioned by Hagen (1962), although they do not appear to show the social status deprivation that he feels is important in the formation of such a group. A modification of values that could originate in such a group would be a most satisfactory solution for the majority of Mayos; however, the number of these families are few and they are blocked in their ability to adapt traditional Mayo values by their loss of autonomy and their confusion of modernization with mestizo culture. Because the Mayo who elect to become mestizos are no longer Mayo, and because few families find a broad enough basis for fusion and involvement in modernization while remaining Mayo, the remaining Mayo of the lower Mayo River valley are revitalizing traditional Mayo culture and resisting mestization. They have little incentive for modernization both because they confuse it with mestization and because no other modernization process except mestization appears open to them.

Loss of Mayo Autonomy

The loss of Mayo autonomy is the basis for Mayo dislike of mestizos and mestizo ways. Today the Mayo have lost their land, their right to select what they plant, their ceremonial centers in the original mission centers, the right to govern themselves, their right to the use of river water without paying for it and of the bush and its resources, the right to hold ceremonies in certain areas and only under permit in other areas, and even in the recent past the right to have a church of their own. Today they are considered a minority in their own river valley.

Mayo history has been a constant process of land loss, from nearly complete autonomy during the Mission Period to nearly complete loss of autonomy during the Profirio Díaz government from about 1870 to 1910, when the Mayos were reduced to peons working on the haciendas. At the time of the 1910 Revolution, the Mayo joined the battles carrying bows and arrows in order to force the return of their own lands, which very few in actuality achieved. However, since that time many have received some land in the form of ejido parcels, often four hectares irrigable and four hectares in bush.

Land is such an emotion-producing subject that Mayo men will tremble and sweat profusely when talking of their land. The loss of Mayo ceremonial centers is an important aspect of the loss of control of the river valley and of the present messianic discourse concerning the "Eight Pueblos." For example, Huatabampo used to be a Mayo ceremonial center, but the Mayo were driven out and now Huatabampo is a mestizo center. Mayo also do not have the right to select the crops they plant, for when they go to the bank to borrow money for seed the bank tells them what to plant. In 1961 they grew predominantly cotton, although by 1981 cotton was of little importance. Such decisions make the Mayo unhappy, for they would rather plant corn, beans, and squash. The river water, which the Mayo believe is theirs, is taxed, and the bush is being cut so that both their natural resources are diminishing—firewood, building materials, herbs for curing, deer for hunting—and the *huya anía,* forest world, is being destroyed. These, obviously, are other reasons for Mayo association of modernization with mestizos and a rejection of both.

The Mayo have also lost the right to govern themselves, for mestizos occupy all the local offices. Everyone votes but no Mayo is allowed to run for office. The Mayo complain bitterly that they have no chance for political office and no voice in the government. Even the right to hold certain home ceremonies in Huatabampo has been forbidden by law and in other areas permits must be secured. Mayo ceremonies may be broken up by police on the pretext that too many persons are becoming drunk and disorderly. In 1926 the worst conceivable atrocity was committed by a mestizo, the churches were burned and the Saints destroyed.

To summarize, the following historical processes and events provided the major blows dealt to Mayo receptivity to economic growth and modernization: encroachments on Mayo land; Mayo militaristic revolts defeated; reduction of the Mayo to peons by the Díaz government; Mayo nativistic reaction with leaders systematically short; deportation during the 1910 Revolution, leading to Mayo dispersion and even further loss of land; and the church burning. These successive blows constitute the history of the loss of Mayo autonomy at the hands of mestizos. Loss of autonomy and control of culture change, in addition to loss of incentive for modernization linked to mestizos, provide mechanisms that explain the retention of a traditional Mayo value system. Without some modification, the structure of this system not only makes modernization difficult but it also intensifies the mismatch between its orientations and those of the mestizo value system.

CONCLUSION

Because Mayo culture and society are not dominantly characterized by ontological uncertainty, by high prestige awarded to economic innovators, by a social system that readily absorbs and uses new tested knowledge diffused from mestizo society, by high need achievement personality types who have the autonomy needed to act, by specific occupational roles and corporate specialties, and by a procedural value system rather than a substantive one, they must be considered traditional rather than modern. Although accepting that the Mayo retain scant economic and political power in southern Sonora, the point of view of the analysis in this chapter is a Mayo one. If the Mayo had a greater degree of autonomy and fewer blocked incentives for modernization, some individuals and their families would modify and adapt the traditional value system, yielding a system more compatible with modernization, and then other families would accept these modifications. This creative process is exemplified in the cases of the Arizona Yaqui and the Guatemalan Indian inhabitants of Cantel. In Spicer's publications describing Pascua (1940, 1961, 1980), he analyzes the modifications in Arizona Yaqui culture and society that were necessary to enable the Yaqui to participate both in Yaqui society and in the modern American economic system. In this case, Yaqui autonomy and creativity were encouraged by Anglo-Americans rather than blocked by hate and fear on the part of both groups. Also in Cantel, Guatemala, as reported by Manning Nash (1955, 1958), a similar process developed in one period of Cantel's historical evolution. Although a factory was constructed near Cantel, the autonomy of the local people was encouraged by the management. Factory decisions concerning the town were made by the management after first consulting the village elders. Persons were given leaves of absence so they could fulfill ceremonial and political obligations in the village. In this way the peasants of Cantel were free to modify their traditional values and the factory management adjusted their operation so that neither lost autonomy. Through adaptation conflict was minimized between the two systems and they were able to work together with a certain degree of harmony. In conclusion, a minimal level of autonomy coupled with an incentive for modernization function as mechanisms in the adaptive evolution of value systems, and these modified systems then contribute to the modernization process. On the other hand, in their absence, the traditional value system and culture are revived and maintained as long as the group retains a minimal membership to carry on their way of life. The people may be isolated in a region of refuge or in an enclaved condition or they may continue to exist embedded within modern society as do the Mayo of southern Sonora.

Aguirre Beltrán 1967
Crumrine 1964, 1975, 1977, 1981
Erasmus 1961, 1967
Hagen 1962
Hu-DeHart 1981, 1984
Kluckhohn, C. 1951
Kluckhohn, F. 1950
Lutes 1983
McClelland 1961
Nash 1955, 1958
O'Connor 1980
Pesqueira Olea 1985
Spicer 1940, 1961, 1962, 1971, 1980, 1984

CHAPTER FOUR

Enclavement Processes, State Policies, and Cultural Identity Among the Mayo Indians of Sinaloa, Mexico

Manuel L. Carlos (University of California, Santa Barbara)

Enclavement processes and resultant patterns of sociocultural, economic, and political encroachment and marginalization among the Mayo Indians of Sinaloa, Mexico are analyzed in this chapter. The sources of ethnic cleavage, socioeconomic status of the Mayo, and the accrued relative disadvantages of Mayo, as compared to non-Mayo, segments of society are examined also. The purpose is to explain how and why certain State policies of encroachment and domination and State-inspired cultural and economic expansionist policies of non-Mayo society have converged to produce a culturally marginalized and socioeconomically dependent and subordinate ethnic group. As part of this analysis of enclavement and marginalization, I discuss the differential effects of these processes on the assimilation of different Mayo groups and communities.

Most aspects of ethnic enclavement among the Mayo I view as a purposive externally induced marginalization process. The subordination of Mayo society to which I refer is in relation to outside society, and more directly and recently to local culturally dominant segments of the Mexican population or mestizo society in adjacent as well as the same rural villages, towns, and urban centers. Mestizo society is the common name given by anthropologists to local-level segments of national Mexican culture. Most mestizos and Mayo in the Fuerte Valley tend to be commercial or subsistence farmers and either day or seasonal farm workers. On the whole, the Mayo are poorer, have smaller land holdings, and proportionately greater numbers of them are landless farm workers and subsistence farmers.

The enclavement of Indian groups in Mexico has a long history. Enclavement is defined in the present study as a sociocultural and economic encroachment and containment process. It involves both historical and contemporary dimensions. More specifically, enclavement involves cultural, economic, and political encroachment by a dominant culture and subsequent retreat, confinement, and dependency by a subordinate culture. It is a process through which dominant economic and cultural segments in a society combine with the State in order to encapsulate, marginalize, and subordinate ethnic groups. Excluded, dominated, and encapsulated ethnic groups such as the Mayo in turn develop parallel rituals and belief systems that are used to intensify their cultural and ethnic identities and thus guarantee for themselves some degree of cultural integrity and continuity. As I explain, however, there is a considerable range of cultural adaptations to enclavement in Mayo society that is revealed in differences in the sociocultural structure and the nature of specific communities and groups within Mayo society.

The Sinaloan Mayo live in the Fuerte River area of the northwestern Mexican state of Sinaloa, an area of much wealth and State developmental activity. I have labeled them Sinaloan Mayo to distinguish them from their better known neighbors the Mayo, who live in the adjacent northern state of Sonora (Crumrine 1977).

THEORETICAL FRAMEWORK AND APPROACH

The theoretical framework and approach to Mayo enclavement I have used are derived, in part, from Gonzalo Aguirre Beltrán's ideas about the role of "domination processes" and the creation of culturally dominated "refuge" enclaves (Aguirre Beltrán 1967). The main difference is that I assert that the formation of such enclaves cannot be fully explained without an analysis of State and State-induced policies. Enclavement involves more than cultural encroachment and subjugation. My view is that enclavement expressed as domination and dependency is a political and economic as well as a sociocultural process.

In this sense my approach conforms more closely to the works of such marginalization and internal colonialism theorists as Rodolfo Stavenhagen and Arturo Warman, particularly their writings on the political control and economic and cultural domination of ethnic groups and rural lower classes in Mexico (Stavenhagen 1970a, Warman 1976). This approach to marginalization and containment emphasizes extra community and group factors and the role of the State as an instrument of support and inspiration for unleashing local-level processes of domination and enclavement. The Stavenhagen–Warman approach stands in contrast to the ethnic identity and boundary maintenance processes paradigm of certain scholars who have focused on intragroup inspired identity and enclavement activities in analyzing Mexican Indian societies (Crumrine 1977; Iwánska 1971). In my own analysis I incorporate this perspective to explain the contribution of intragroup dynamics and factors to the persistence of ethnic loyalties and identities. All three perspectives in understanding enclavement among Mexican Indian populations are necessary: namely, the Aguirre Beltrán formation of refuge areas thesis, the Stavenhagen–

Warman marginalization-subordination model, and the Crumrine–Iwánska boundary maintenance and cultural reinforcement thesis of ethnic group formation subsistence and entrenchment.

ROLE OF THE STATE AND ITS POLICIES IN THE ENCLAVEMENT OF MAYO SOCIETY

The State has played a vital and important role in the enclavement of Mayo society. State policies regarding Mayo society, starting with those of the Spanish crown and Mexico's postindependence governments (throughout the 16th–19th and early 20th centuries), either condoned, supported, or actively promoted cultural, economic, and political encroachment, marginalization, and containment.

The Spanish crown used its military forces and administrative authority to gain initial control of Mayo society and its territory as a means of acquiring tribute and new lands for settlers, who, in turn, increased the tax base and economic trade wealth for the crown. They, and the Mexican government that followed them, claimed large areas of Mayo land, which supported the establishment of haciendas, cattle stations, and new trade and commerce centers. For its part, the Mexican government of the 19th and early 20th centuries maintained a policy of territorial expansion by non-Mayo farmers and hacienda owners that included military protection against Mayo opposition. In the late 19th and early 20th centuries, the government promoted an explicitly official policy of creating and maintaining large labor pools and entire villages of Mayo indebted farm workers for supplying the labor needs of local mestizo farm and hacienda owners. Local officials of the Mexican State also allowed Mayo village land areas and claims to be nullified and superseded by the expansionist policies of haciendas. In the late 19th century, control over the water of the Fuerte River was claimed by the Mexican State and used for the economic advantage of non-Mayo society.

This control allowed the Mexican government to promote the development of non-Mayo farming activities, including the growth of the hacienda system, and to render certain Mayo farm lands useless by depriving them of water. All these State policies had the collective effect of territorially reducing, and socially, culturally, and economically marginalizing, Mayo society. The present geographic distribution, cultural adaptations, economic activities, and political dependency of Mayo society are directly related to these earlier State policies. This period of aggressive encroachment and containment supported by the State continued through the period of the land reforms in the late 1930s, when only a few Mayo settlements were granted permanently protected lands as ejidos (land grant communities).

Other Mayo communities lost some of their lands to adjacent mestizo villages that were granted ejido lands. To reiterate, the land reforms aided some Mayo, but on the whole most Mayo, in contrast to mestizos, were left with overparceled lands of the poorest quality. Again, State policies, intentional or not, worked against Mayo interests and created a permanent basis, in terms of agricultural wealth, for continued inequality between Mayo and non-Mayo society.

More recently, in the years since the late 1950s when the area became a target of massive State-financed irrigation and agricultural development projects, Mayo communities and populations, on the whole, have continued to receive minimum benefits as opposed to local mestizo communities. This relative disadvantage may be measured in terms of such variables as farm loans, numbers of schools, and the presence or absence of public services among Mayo, as compared to non-Mayo, communities.

Currently, Mayo society is more dependent than ever on the State, and as a result of numerous government activities in the area, the State, in turn, is more directly involved in the lives of the Mayo than ever before.

HISTORY OF ENCLAVEMENT IN SINALOAN MAYO SOCIETY

The history of enclavement in Sinaloan Mayo society involves more than 300 years of political, military, sociocultural, and economic encroachment by outside society. This historical process produced a gradual retreat and encapsulation or marginalization of Mayo society into narrow territorial and residential areas. Encroachment has also produced resistance and led to increasing control by, and political and economic dependency on, outside society. Political dependency develops as a result of the role of the State in enclavement of the kind that exists between the Mayo and outside society. For its part, economic dependency is the result of the dominant or outside society gaining control over the economy.

Mayo society once controlled all the geographic areas of the Fuerte River valley from the ocean to the foothills of the Sierra Madre. Enclavement and territorial containment processes began among the Sinaloa Mayo late in the 16th century with the arrival of officials and soldiers of the Spanish crown and the Catholic clergy who accompanied them. The Spanish crown established and for over 200 years maintained its administrative and military headquarters for the entire area in the town of El Fuerte, which is some 20 miles up river from the centers of Mayo society settlement. The town that was founded in the year 1564 quickly became one of the most important administrative centers in the Northwest. It was purposefully founded at a distance from Mayo communities because of contact resistance from the Mayo population, which was the most numerous Indian group in the area and controlled all of the coastal areas below the foothills. The town, El Fuerte, took its name from the fort (*fuerte*) and garrisoned town, which the Spaniards built to protect themselves from armed raids that were periodically launched against them by the Mayo throughout the colonial period.

The Spaniards attempted to spread their religious doctrines and tribute-collecting authority down river to Mayo society and achieved some considerable success. Mayo religious ceremonies acquired Catholic traits. Mayo villages began paying some tribute in goods, and the Mayo began allowing churches and towns to be built in their territory. This period of initial contact lasted from the 16th to the 18th century.

As a result of ceaseless efforts to acculturate and colonize Mayo society forcefully, satellite Spanish settlements were established in the territorial heartland of Mayo society by the mid-18th century in the Mayo pueblos of San Blas and San Miguel. By the late 18th and early 19th centuries, following Mexican independence from Spain, new waves of settlers arrived in the area as part of Mexico's attempt to protect and settle its northern provinces. With the arrival of these settlers, who came in increasingly large numbers, the competition for control over Mayo territory was intensified. By the mid-19th century new settlements of colonists were established still further down river and on the coast itself. These included the old Mayo pueblos of Ahome and Mochicahui. On the coast itself settlements were established in Agiabampo and Topolobampo, where primitive shipping ports were developed in old Mayo fishing villages. During the 19th century all of these towns, with the exception of the ports, became important administrative centers of the Mexican government and areas where wealthy *criollo* (Spanish-mestizo) families built churches, homes, and trading businesses.

From the start of the 18th century to the late 19th century, the heartland of Mayo territory and Mayo farming, hunting, and gathering country was increasingly invaded and settled by outsiders. Cattle raising *estancias* were established in areas where bountiful numbers of deer and other food supply animals once roamed. Many of the small areas farmed by the Mayo along the river banks (in naturally occurring river floodwater channels and flatlands) were taken over by settlers. In other instances, rudimentary irrigation systems were built and the farmed areas were increased, thus further reducing the natural resources available to the Mayo. Important monocrop and market-oriented haciendas developed on the newly taken Mayo lands, which began to draw on an indebted labor force of dependent Mayo villagers who had lost their traditional means of livelihood.

Between the late 19th and early 20th centuries the only remaining independent or "free" Mayo communities were on the river banks in areas that were at a distance from major areas of Mexican settlement and farming activity. In addition, these communities had farm land that, because of its uneven terrain and the quality of the soil, was considered undesirable. Today these rancherías remain areas of refuge and are among the most important remaining sites of traditional Mayo culture.

Most of the rest of Mayo society was incorporated into the labor force of haciendas that were established and prospered in the area until the land reforms of the Mexican Revolution in the 1930s. Other Mayo communities dependent on small subsistence plots were considered important centers of labor supply and were allowed to retain small land areas adjacent to haciendas and the large tracts of mestizo farmers. Still other Mayo communities continued to survive within the borders of the old Mayo pueblos, which were taken over and expanded by mestizo settlers. These centers remain the principal areas of Mayo society settlement, altered in some cases only by the fact that some of the communities have become ejidos as a result of land reform programs.

It is important to note that Mayo resistance to external encroachment was initiated from the first instance of historical contact and continued through the various periods of increasing encapsulation. Indeed, the most recently recorded period of armed resistance took place a mere 60 years ago in the 1920s during the period of the Mexican Revolution. Clearly, enclavement of the sort endured by Mayo society is not a peaceful nor smooth process and involves much more than cultural dynamics. It includes a loss of control over economic resources, increasing dependency on outside society, and elaborate and desperate attempts to maintain some semblance of cultural integrity, as is the case with so many of the current Mayo religious ceremonies and the numerous recorded instances of cultural revitalistic movements in the 19th and 20th centuries and in recent years.

CONTEMPORARY SINALOAN MAYO SOCIETY: DIFFERING ECONOMIC AND CULTURAL ADAPTATION TO ENCLAVEMENT

Enclavement produced differing sociocultural and economic results in Sinaloan Mayo society. It has also perpetuated ethnic cleavages between Mayo and mestizo society and created a number of different types of Mayo communities and groups, not all of which are equally and openly identified with Mayo cultural traditions. The communities are different in their levels of economic well-being also. These differences represent the selective effects of historical and contemporary enclavement processes on specific Mayo populations throughout the Fuerte Valley.

Contemporary Mayo live dispersed throughout a number of Mayo and mixed Mayo-mestizo communities. The largest number of traditional as opposed to acculturated Mayo live in village enclaves along the banks of the Fuerte River. Others live in Mayo ejidos and mixed Mayo-mestizo pueblos. Despite this dispersion they share many common experiences as members of larger Mayo society and an identifiable minority. They are tied together or integrated as a society-at-large by language, religious beliefs, and cross-community ceremonies. These include regularly scheduled cross-community religious festivities during the Christmas and Lenten seasons. Although older civic-religious jurisdictions within the society have disintegrated, these religious ceremonies and the belief systems that underlie them continue to bind the society together.

Sinaloan Mayo society of today is distributed in several kinds of communities in the Fuerte Valley, including river bank rancherías located along the left and right banks of the Fuerte River. These river bank communities are the most geographically isolated and culturally traditional Mayo communities in the area. They are, in addition, among the poorest, if not the poorest, of all the Mayo and mestizo communities in the Fuerte Valley. All suffer from overparceling of their lands, or *minifundia,* that allows them, at best, to engage in subsistence agriculture. Because they are *comunidades indígenas* (Indian communities) and unattached rancherías rather than ejidos, they are not eligible for government technical assistance and farm loans. All adult males in these river bank communities work as day laborers on adjacent mestizo farms and ejidos for many months of the year in order to supplement their meager subsistence farming livelihood.

On the basis of my actual count and data from informants, I estimate that there are a total of 13 such river bank rancherías. They are the most socioeconomically and territorially marginalized Mayo communities in the area. They are distant from roads. They lack schools, and they have few, if any, of the community services such as electricity and potable water that are available to other Mayo and mestizo communities.

It is these communities that are most responsible for carrying on Mayo ceremonial and religious traditions. They have a larger number of Mayo speakers and celebrate more individually sponsored Mayo fiestas than other, more acculturated and mixed Mayo-mestizo communities. In a word, they are the most Mayo of all the communities and also the "purest" form of Mayo ethnic enclave in the area.

Other Mayo communities are ejidos or government land grant communities formed from lands taken from haciendas by Mayo tenant farmers and from hacienda work camp communities during the period of land reform in the late 1930s. These lands were taken as a result of Mayo grass roots political defense movements during the reform. Most of these lands were overparceled, because the numbers of Mayo tenant farmers and hacienda workers were greater than could be supported by the land area they were allocated by the competing land claims of adjacent mestizo land grant villages. There are eight such Mayo ejidos in total. They are among the most prosperous, though not equally so, of all the Mayo communities. None of these communities, however, rank in prosperity with the most successful mestizo ejidos. Consistently and systematically, Mayo ejidos receive less government assistance, farm credits, and benefits than do other ejidos. Moreover, some Mayo ejidos in the group receive no government assistance at all and must rely on renting their lands or borrowing from money lenders and growers who charge exorbitant interest rates. Those Mayo with the smallest parcels in these ejidos or those who cannot obtain loans or credits during a given crop cycle hire out as farm laborers for periods ranging from one or two months to six or more months, depending on employment opportunities.

Mayo ejidos may be defined as ejidos that were historically founded from two varieties of preexisting Mayo communities, dependent hacienda communities and comunidades indígenas. The Mayo in them tend to be bilingual, Mayo and Spanish-speaking. Many Mayo in these communities are highly acculturated as well and only minimally identified with Mayo society at large.

Another segment of Mayo society lives in mixed Mayo-mestizo ejidos. I counted seven such communities, with the Mayo representing a numerical minority. They live in their own residential enclaves or barrios in their villages. Because they live with mestizos, they share in some of the social services available to the mestizo population and hence are better-off than other Mayo. However well-off some Mayo may be in these communities, none tend to hold elected ejido offices and many others have most of the less desirable farm land in the ejido. Most of the Mayo population in these ejidos remains identifiable as Mayo, largely because of their family names, their origins, and the fact that mestizos label them as Mayo. Most do not speak the Mayo language. This group, then, is the most acculturated and least involved with Mayo cross-community religious and ceremonial activities.

The remaining segments of Mayo society live in old Mayo pueblos that have become, in the past 50 years, mixed Mayo-mestizo towns. These Mayo live in their own part of town in ethnically segregated enclaves. They have their own churches and public places for meeting. In addition there are places where, as Crumrine says about the Sonoran Mayo, "Mayos can meet mestizos" (Crumrine 1977). Two of these towns are major ceremonial centers, the pueblos of San Miguel and Mochicahui. The third center is a Mayo ejido known as La Florida. It is a suburb of the old Mayo pueblo of Ahome. These pueblos have some of the most acculturated as well as some of the most culturally and ethnically identifiable, loyal, and traditional Mayo. In each of these pueblos, the mestizo population keeps the Mayo at a social distance by insisting on not sharing church facilities and on having separate schools, bars, stores, and other segregated places of public meeting and entertainment.

ENCLAVEMENT, CULTURAL ASSIMILATION, AND CULTURAL IDENTITY AMONG CONTEMPORARY MAYO

Enclavement and marginalization processes have produced two cultural identity responses among the contemporary Mayo. Some Mayo, like many of their predecessors, have chosen to assimilate into the large mestizo society, while others, perhaps lacking the opportunity to do so and socialized by their families into traditional Mayo ways, have sought to perpetuate certain Mayo customs and rituals that publicly signal their loyalty and commitment to Mayo society. The latter situation is particularly true of the Mayo in nonethnically mixed and isolated communities. Hence enclavement processes and encroachment policies in Fuerte Valley society have led to the perpetuation of ethnic cleavages between Mayo and non-Mayo society and have encouraged both assimilation and separation.

Mayo who have not assimilated generally come from non-Mayo-mestizo mixed communities. As mentioned earlier, these Mayo rancherías tend to be the poorest of all Mayo and mestizo villages in the Valley. Mayo in these places bemoan the fallen ways of assimilated Mayo in other communities. Most of the inhabitants of these traditional Mayo rancherías as well as those of Mayo ejidos proudly display the Mayo Cross in the patio of their home as a public symbol of their identification with Mayo culture. Most Mayo rancherías and Mayo ejidos have a local place of Mayo worship, a ramada (arbor), or church. Most ranchería and many ejido inhabitants attend large cross-community religious ceremonies in nearby Mayo pueblos, where Mayo from distinct communities congregate during designated religious holidays. Traditional Mayo from both of these types of communities also tend to speak the Mayo language and prefer it, even when they know Spanish. Finally, most have married other traditional Mayo and have retained their Mayo last names rather than adopt Spanish last names as other Mayo have done.

It can be argued easily that the Mayo in traditional rancherías have retained most of their customs because of their isolation and the absence of direct daily contact with mestizo society. In line with this argument it can be said that the Mayo in these communities have been spared the need to assimilate and perhaps never had the chance to do so. The smaller number of traditional Mayo in Mayo ejidos perhaps can be traced to the greater contact that these communities have had with non-Mayo society since the land reforms of the 1930s and the government sponsored development programs of the late 1950s, the 1960s, and 1970s. The Mayo in these communities have found it necessary to deal with the mestizo world due to their economic involvement with outside society.

Traditional Mayo can be found in mixed mestizo-Mayo communities also, but they are smaller in number. There are even fewer in the large Mayo pueblos that are now mostly populated by mestizos and assimilated Mayo. The fact that traditional Mayo who reside in mixed mestizo communities, whether ejidos or pueblos, tend to be religious leaders is closely related to the organization of Mayo religious ceremonies. It is the combination of traditional Mayo from the various Mayo community enclaves in the Valley that keep Mayo traditions and ceremonies alive. But they are decreasing in number.

Most Mayo in contemporary Sinaloan Mayo society are highly acculturated individuals. Many others are fully assimilated and do not acknowledge their Mayo origins. Most of these individuals live in the large mixed-Mayo and mestizo pueblos with ethnically mixed ejidos. Their identification as Mayo stems from discrimination and exclusion on the part of mestizos. Many of these Mayo speak only Spanish and their children almost universally are Spanish-speakers. Some of the acculturated Mayo participate minimally in Mayo religious events, but they do not publicly proclaim their Mayo identity with the use of such symbols as displaying the Mayo Cross. Acculturated Mayo ridicule traditional Mayo for their "superstitious" and "curious ways," yet they are not themselves fully assimilated.

Indeed, the most successful cases of assimilation are found in the large urban centers and in Mayo-mestizo mixed pueblos. In sum, being Mayo and ethnically marginalized continues to exact a price from the members of Sinaloan Mayo society.

CONCLUSION

Enclavement is a multifaceted political, socioeconomic, and cultural process. Among the Sinaloan Mayo enclavement patterns are directly related to the policies of the Spanish and Mexican State. Through a series of territorial encroachments supported by State policies, the Mayo were systematically contained. They were also isolated in small numbers in the less prosperous of the over 130 rural communities and 10 towns and cities in the Fuerte Valley. As a result of this containment and sociocultural and economic marginalization, Mayo society has begun to distintegrate and to rely for most of its vitality on the poorest and least assimilated members of the group. In the midst of encroachments, Mayo society has been pushed and forced to retreat into sociocultural and residential niches within Fuerte Valley society that provide it with socioeconomically stagnant "areas of refuge" (Aguirre Beltrán 1967).

In those mixed Mayo-mestizo communities where Mayo also live, assimilation and acculturation are taking their toll by further reducing the cultural identities and ethnic pride of the Mayo. Enclavement is clearly not a neutral sociocultural process. It deserves further notice and analysis among those who have studied Mexican society and its independent Indian cultures. To do so we need to refine our conceptual notions about enclavement. Perhaps this chapter has made a contribution in that direction by positing a definition of the process that incorporates concepts in the work of several anthropologists who have examined Indian-mestizo relations.

Note. This chapter is based on field research I conducted in Mayo villages or rancherías, in mixed Mayo-mestizo villages and pueblos or towns, and in mestizo urban centers. Additionally, I have relied on the printed historical works of Edward Spicer (1969b), and Don Ernesto Gámez García (1955, 1985), a local Sinaloan historian. For comparative ethnographic data I have used the works of Charles Erasmus (1961) and Ralph Beals (1943), who are, to my knowledge, the only other anthropologists to have visited or worked among the Sinaloa Mayo. I wish to thank the Social Science Research Council (SSRC) for the support that made the research possible.

Aguirre Beltrán 1967
Beals 1943
Crumrine 1977
Erasmus, 1961
Gámez García 1955, 1985
Iwánska 1971
Spicer 1969b
Stavenhagen 1970
Warman 1976

CHAPTER FIVE

Production, Social Identity, and Agrarian Struggle Among the Tepecano Indians of Northern Jalisco

Robert D. Shadow (Universidad de las Américas, Cholula, Puebla, Mexico)

Early in the Colonial period the mountains and canyons of northern Jalisco and eastern Nayarit served as a refuge region for various Indian peoples fleeing Spanish expansion along the western and eastern flanks of the southern Sierra Madre Occidental. Initially this rugged area was of little value to the European invaders and it developed into the largest and most enduring refuge region in the province of Nueva Galicia (Weigand 1977). Much of it remained politically and militarily independent until the 1720s, and three major Indian cultures—Cora, Huichol, and Tepecano—evolved within the enclave and were reported on by the first ethnographers through the region in the late 19th and early 20th centuries: Lumholtz (1902a, 1902b), Hrdlička (1903), and Mason (1912a, 1912b, 1912c, 1913, 1948, 1952).

Since that time numerous anthropologists and others have visited the Cora and Huichol and have described their cultures in varying degrees of detail and completeness (see the references in Grimes and Hinton 1969; also Berrin 1978; Weigand 1972, 1976, 1978). In contrast, the Tepecano, who formed the easternmost component of the Colonial refuge region, have received comparatively little attention. After the pioneering and important observations provided by Lumholtz, Hrdlička, and Mason, no anthropologist is known to have visited the Tepecano until the 1960s. Two publications based on field data but limited in scope have appeared since then. J. A. Jones (1962) described Tepecano house types, and George Agogino, on the basis of a 1969 summer field trip, provided a short account of the town and residents of Azqueltán, the largest remaining Tepecano settlement (Mason and Agogino 1972).

A main reason for this lack of attention is that the contemporary Tepecano are a small, highly acculturated group that is less of an anthropological attraction than the more culturally distinctive Huichol and Cora. At one time, however, the Tepecano shared strong cultural affinities with their Huichol neighbors and occupied a large area of northern Jalisco east of the Sierra Madre (Pennington 1969: 16). With the gradual expansion and consolidation of Colonial society, however, and especially after Independence, large portions of the Tepecano's lands fell to non-Indian ranchers and farmers, and the Tepecano population was greatly reduced by disease and acculturation. At present there remain only about 300 Tepecano concentrated in a restricted area of the mid-Bolaños canyon of northern Jalisco (municipio of Villa Guerrero). In terms of material and ideological culture, they are almost indistinguishable from the larger regional population of impoverished, non-Indian campesinos. The native dress, language, ceremonies, and rituals have all but disappeared, remembered only by a handful of older individuals. Acculturation was well advanced even at the time of Mason's visit early in the century and, given the pervading culturalist orientation of succeeding anthropologists, it is not surprising that the Tepecano have failed to attract the interest accorded the more exotic Huichol and Cora.

Yet despite their advanced state of acculturation, the majority of Tepecano have not fully assimilated into the wider society and cannot be treated as simply another community within the larger, non-Indian (vecino) population. Fieldwork has shown that most Tepecano continue to identify themselves as Indians and to steadfastly support the corporate communal land structure they inherited from the Colony. Some years ago, however, a split developed and a small number of individuals disassociated themselves from the larger group. The members of this faction no longer actively espouse their Indian heritage or descent but seek closer identification with the surrounding vecino population. Because the process of acculturation has been uniform—there is little that outwardly distinguishes one group from the other—it cannot be argued that the retention or rejection of Indian identity is attributable to differential rates in the maintenance or erosion of culture traits.

In this chapter I examine this cleavage between the Tepecano factions and propose an explanation that focuses not on the cultural aspects of ethnicity but on its function as a component of political economy. Thus, rather than analyzing shifts in ethnic identity as the product of culture change, I adopt a structural perspective and consider ethnicity as but one of many tools manipulated by a minority group according to the benefits or liabilities that it conveys in the competition for resources or other desired goals within the wider social structure (Spicer 1971; Williams 1978). I argue that among the Tepecano both the preservation and abandonment of Indian identity are related to agrarian struggle and the competition between antagonistic modes of production. The maintenance of Tepecano identity is tied to the Indians' efforts to preserve their traditional, noncapitalist mode of production based on communal lands, while the abandonment of Indian identity by the splinter group is the result of the formation of an ejido movement. I analyze the contradictions inherent between ejido and communal systems of production and the manner in which conflict between these two systems has fragmented the once unified Tepecano and led to the differential utilization of social identity.

The two groups of concern in this analysis are the *comunidad indígena* and the *comunidad agraria* of San Lorenzo de Azqueltán. The comunidad indígena is composed of the 300 or so *comuneros* who support the continuation of the Colonial communal land system and who overtly embrace an Indian identity. The comunidad agraria, or *ejido*, on the other hand, is composed of some 50 family heads who were at one time members of the comunidad indígena but who split from the comunero group and accepted an ejido land grant from the State Government in 1969. As a result, the *ejidatarios* no longer view Indianness as a positive attribute and are in open conflict with their former comrades over the control of land.

THE SETTING

The remnant Tepecano are today clustered in and around the pueblo of San Lorenzo de Azqueltán, located deep in the Bolaños canyon in the municipio of Villa Guerrero, northern Jalisco. The Bolaños canyon is an impressive geologic feature sculptured out of Tertiary extrusives by the workings of the Bolaños River. Approximately 800 meters deep and 11 kilometers wide, the canyon runs in a general north-south direction for over 400 kilometers, bisecting the entire Región Norte of Jalisco before merging on the south with the canyon of the Río Grande de Santiago near Magdalena, Jalisco. From the western side of the canyon rise the mountain ranges that form the southern Sierra Madre Occidental, home of the Huichol and Cora. On the east the canyon is bordered by a large, rolling plateau where the town and cabecera of Villa Guerrero (population 2400) is now situated. The Indian population in this upland area has long since been removed and it is primarily inhabited by descendants of Colonial Creole immigrants. This upland comprises the municipio's core area; over 80 percent of the municipal population and the majority of its agricultural lands are situated here. In contrast to the relatively level uplands, canyon topography is generally rugged and lands amenable to plow agriculture are scarce.

From a modern farming perspective, the canyon is of little value. Except for those portions exploited by the agricultural comuneros and ejidatarios, the greater part of it is utilized as extensive, unimproved pasture by stockmen from Villa Guerrero. No motor roads enter the canyon in this region, travel is entirely by foot or horseback, and modern amenities such as electricity are totally absent.

The pueblo of Azqueltán was established alongside the Bolaños River during the Colonial period as part of the Spanish policy of *reducción* and *congregación*. The town possesses a Federal Primary school, one or two small retail stores operated on a part-time basis, and a large Colonial church. There is no resident priest and the church itself is in disrepair. Distributed loosely about this nucleus on both sides of the river are some 70 household compounds, usually defined by rock walls enclosing two and sometimes three domestic structures. Jacales of stacked stone and thatch roofs are the most common structures, although a large number of adobe houses are also present.

The population of the pueblo oscillates between 150 and 350 according to the season. With the arrival of the rains in June, many families move to agricultural ranchos, and only a small core of individuals with fields nearby remain in town. After the harvest and the onset of the dry season, families return to the pueblo, many in order to place their children in the primary school. The seasonal ebb and flow of population, then, involves rainy season dispersal and dry season concentration. Other settlements of importance in the canyon are the loosely aggregated communities of Izolta, La Gúasima, and San Isidro. Total population of these dispersed communities does not exceed 250 individuals. Like Azqueltán, Izolta is a riverine community and a major center for the comunero group. La Gúasima and San Isidro are located on mesas above the river bottoms and are ejidatario centers.

Both comuneros and ejidatarios practice rain-fed agriculture. Although there are a few small irrigated plots located on the alluvial *playas* alongside the river, their contribution to total subsistence is minimal; fishing also is of little importance. Average annual rainfall in the Azqueltán area is approximately 600 mm; yearly variations, however, can be extreme. The lowest recorded amount since 1939 was 182 mm, the highest 910 mm (CETENAL 1974). About 90 percent of the precipitation falls between May and October, dividing the year into the two periods of aguas and secas. In average years rainfall is sufficient to produce a crop, but drought is always a possibility. In addition, crop production, which consists of the familiar triad of maize, beans, and squash, can be seriously affected by the erratic distribution of precipitation during the growing season. Some craft production is engaged in by a small number of canyon residents, but it is primarily oriented toward satisfying household needs and is of limited commercial importance. Because of the precarious nature of their agricultural production and the absence of alternative sources of employment in the region, many men, some accompanied by their families, are forced to migrate temporarily in the dry season to work in the tobacco harvests on the coast of Nayarit.

THE COMUNIDAD INDIGENA

The Comunidad Indígena of San Lorenzo de Azqueltán was formally created in the year 1777. At that time the Indian pueblo received a charter from the Spanish authorities that defined the land area that was to remain the inalienable patrimony of the Indian community. According to some comuneros, the grant placed more than 94,500 hectares under exclusive Indian control; this would encompass most of the present-day municipio of Villa Guerrero. The available documentation, however, does not support this claim. For one, Spaniards had been granted *mercedes* to the level uplands east of the canyon as early as the third quarter of the 16th century. These private grants exceeded

12,000 hectares, and by the 1770s this upland area was thoroughly inhabited and controlled by settlers. It is unlikely that the Azqueltán grant would have usurped the existing status quo by including the uplands within its charter. Moreover, documents from the 18th century state that Azqueltán controlled only 12 to 14 sitios de ganado mayor (21,000 to 24,000 hectares) within the Bolaños canyon and did not include any large amount of land on the uplands (Velázquez Chávez 1961). Finally, the official petition filed by the comuneros themselves in 1951 to initiate proceedings for the restitution of communal lands (see below) claimed that only 4.75 sitios were contained within the original charter (Jalisco 1969).

Whatever may have been the precise amount of land originally granted to Azqueltán by the Crown, two things are clear: (1) the lands were located primarily, if not entirely, within the canyon; and (2) exclusive Indian control over even these lands was extremely short-lived. Beginning early in the 19th century, non-Indian cattlemen began to acquire the Indian lands at a rapid rate. The stimulus for this was the increasing vecino population (many of whom were drawn into the area by the silver mines at Bolaños, downriver from Azqueltán) and the suitability of the canyon for dry-season, winter pasture. Bills-of-sale contained in private archives in the cabecera of Villa Guerrero show that the principal participants in the vecino expansion into the canyon were large landowners resident on the upland plain. From about 1830 onward, and especially after the Leyes de Desamortización of 1856, these cattlemen began to put together relatively large holdings composed of both upland and canyon properties. The former were dedicated to the cultivation of maize and rainy-season pasture and the latter were utilized for dry-season grazing. By 1901 the transfer of Indian communal lands to vecino ranchers had progressed to such an extent that only 1,628 hectares were still under communal tenure. As might be expected, these lands were located in the most remote and unproductive sector of the original comunidad and were of little value for either pasture or crops (Archives of the Delegación de Hacienda, Villa Guerrero). Today, there are approximately 1,000 hectares still held communally by the Tepecano of Azqueltán. Most of these lands consist of the steeper slopes along the lower canyon wall, although there are a few areas of more level lands also under comunero control. However, many of these level lands are not held with firm, undisputed title by the comuneros and some have merely been taken over by them.

Under the communal system as presently practiced within the comunidad indígena, the ultimate control and ownership of the land is vested in the Indian pueblo as a corporate body, and the selling or alienation of land from the comunidad is prohibited. According to the communal charter, therefore, land is not a commodity to be freely bought and sold on the market, and access to and control over land is outside the sphere of the money economy. Rights to land flow from membership in the community; there are no private titles or deeds to land and individual community members obtain only the usufruct of land for agricultural and residential purposes. These agricultural use rights, for which no rents are charged, entitle the comuneros to cultivate lands and to retain the full fruits of their labor, but to no long-term control over individual fields. Lands that are not under crops are free goods and can be exploited by any member of the community for firewood, for the collection of wild foodstuffs, or for the grazing of the few head of cattle possessed by the comuneros.

The use rights to particular agricultural plots are flexible and unstable, and there is a great deal of mobility and shifting of comuneros from one agricultural rancho to another from year to year. When plots are abandoned due to declining fertility they revert to the community, which, through the direction of its locally elected Comité Ejecutivo, serves as the redistributive center, receiving and deciding on petitions for the extension of plots or the opening of new fields to cultivation. The flexibility inherent in this system is ideally suited to the type of shifting-field *(coamil)* agriculture practiced by the majority of comuneros.

In general, coamil agriculture conforms to the *swidden, roza,* or *tlacolol* agriculture described for other parts of Mesoamerica (Palerm 1967). Like all swidden systems, coamil agriculture depends on land rotation for the restoration of soil fertility and the control of weeds. It is technologically primitive and relies entirely on human labor power; no plows, draft animals, or fertilizers are employed and the basic tool kit consists of machete, pick, and hoe. Maize, beans, and squash form the crop complex and most fields are cultivated for three to four years and then left to regenerate. Hence, the system requires a rather large tract of land for its continuance even though the actual amount of land in crops at any given time is relatively small. Moreover, since coamil fields have little capital improvements, there is little interest in the maintenance of exclusive rights to particular plots after the cultivation period. Coamileros possess only a few head of cattle and the land in fallow or monte is consequently of little importance for grazing. Except for the small amounts of metal required for agricultural implements, coamil cultivation is largely a self-sufficient system. Little or none of the coamil production is sold outside the canyon and coamileros' participation in the agricultural commodities market is minimal. The entire system is land and capital extensive and, compared with plow agriculture, labor intensive (see also Lewis 1963).

Under present practices the communality of land does not entail communal forms of production, and each householder works his plot individually, retains all crops harvested, and pays no rent. The division of labor is extremely rudimentary and neither age nor sex necessarily excludes individuals from participation in agricultural activities. Women and the elderly of both sexes were observed working in coamiles, although the greater part of the agricultural labor is provided by males.

Because of communal land tenure all members of the community, ipso facto, receive rights to the basic means of subsistence. As a result there are no agricultural workers without land and sharecropping relationships are absent within the comunidad indígena. When viewed internally the land tenure system produces a classless system of production that neither engenders nor allows the existence of a landless proletariat or a landed bourgeoisie. None obtain their livelihood through the possession of property rights that enable them to extract an income of agricultural goods produced by the labor of another. Of course, due to variation in the sizes of domestic labor forces and differential productivity of particular plots, economic differences do emerge among comunero households. But the injunction against private property prevents the transformation of these differences into class distinctions.

Rodolfo Stavenhagen, in a summary article on the agrarian structure in Mexico, wrote that communal tenure in the country as a whole was plainly in a state of disintegration, and that "there are few internal forces within the communities themselves that attempt to maintain or revive it" (Stavenhagen 1970b: 236). This generalization does not account for the variety of comunidad response to capitalist expansion and it is certainly not valid as far as the communal systems of the Tepecano and neighboring Huichol are concerned (Weigand 1969). While these two communal systems (which differ significantly between themselves) ultimately may be transformed by the market economy, there have developed significant internal forces in the last quarter century for the revival and preservation of the comunidades. In fact, in 1950 the comuneros, faced with the continuing loss of lands to cattle ranches, initiated legal proceedings to regain their communal lands. It is inaccurate, therefore, to regard present comunidad organization in Azqueltán entirely as a fossil holdover from the Colonial period. Rather it must be seen as a resuscitation of a traditional form brought about not so much by isolation from the market economy as by a reaction to it, a reaction growing out of the desire of an increasingly marginalized group of Tepecano to stem and reverse the conversion of communal lands into private property. The comuneros recognize that the continued expansion of private tenure and the conversion of land into a commodity exchangeable for money has as its end result their transformation into a landless proletariat.

The Tepecano opposition to vecino cattlemen and private property has not been unique in the region but is part of a larger, though segmented Indian movement. In fact, the beginnings of the Tepecano legal actions seem to have been influenced by the neighboring Huichol Indians of the Sierra Madre. In the early 1950s the Huichol, under the leadership of Pedro de Haro, an Indianized mestizo, adopted a political and military strategy aimed at protecting their communal lands from the invasion of cattlemen, many of whom were from Villa Guerrero (Weigand 1969). The Huichol action undoubtedly had a "demonstration effect" on the Tepecano, stimulating them to renew and revive their comunidad system. However, whereas the Huichol number some 10,000, are culturally distinct from surrounding vecinos, and became a cause célèbre among Federal bureaucrats, the highly acculturated Tepecano numbered only a few hundred and lacked the official political support and military clout of the Huichol. Consequently, while the Huichol eventually obtained a Presidential Order confirming the validity and inalienability of their communal lands, and have for now slowed the process of land transfers to non-Indians, the Tepecano continue to struggle without much success in the attempt to regain firm communal title to even a portion of their original lands.

Nonetheless, the legal actions begun in the 1950s under various provisions of the Agrarian Code ushered in a new era in the agrarian struggle between comuneros and vecino cattlemen. The comuneros assumed the legal offensive, and the affirmation of Tepecano descent and identity became an important strategy of the comuneros' organization. Vecino cattlemen opposed to the Indians' efforts to obtain restitution of communal lands contend that many of the so-called "indios" are not really Tepecano at all but rather vecino opportunists who see the communal movement as a chance to receive free land. The landowners further argue that since the comuneros are no longer Indians in their dress, language, or ceremonies, what right do they have to land granted to the 18th-century Indian community.

In the face of this opposition it is clear why the Tepecano have made a concerted effort to systematically reaffirm and emphasize their Indian identity, especially in communications and dealings with agrarian officials, politicians, engineers, extension agents, and others involved in the litigation. Lacking economic and political power, especially at the local level, the comuneros' major resources in their struggle to maintain the viability of the communal system are the legal provisions of the Agrarian Code, their Colonial land title, and their Tepecano identity. However, any hope of success that the communal movement may have depends not only on how well the Tepecano are able to demonstrate the validity of their claims of illegal alienation of communal lands, but also on the interest and conviction of the Government in recognizing and enforcing the Indians' claims. In order to obtain a favorable assessment from agrarian officials and to rally maximum support within the agrarian bureaucracy, the Tepecano consciously manipulate the agrarian and Indian symbols of the Mexican Revolution by presenting themselves as an impoverished and exploited but proud and respectable Indian population.

While many comuneros express the hope that their strategy will be successful and that they will have restored to them the entire amount of land that some claim was contained in the original charter (approximately 94,500 hectares), this will never occur. Besides the practical and political barriers that preclude such an action—the town of Villa Guerrero itself would have to be handed over to the petitioners—there are the legal statutes that severely limit the amount of land the Indian community can claim as communal property. The Agrarian Law is explicit that only lands alienated between 1 December 1876 and 6 January 1915 are subject to restitution. Large parts of the canyon were "sold" to vecino cattlemen before 1876 and neither these lands nor the lands sold in accordance with the provisions of the Ley de Desamortización after 1856 are subject to restitution. The Agrarian Law specifically states that individual rights of private property to such lands are to be respected (see Articles

191 and 193, Ley Federal de Reforma Agraria 1971). Thus, in accordance with a strict interpretation and application of these statutes, the comunidad indígena is entitled only to those lands alienated in the 39 year period between 1876 and 1915. Moreover, to regain even these lands the burden of proof rests with the comuneros, who must demonstrate that such lands were alienated illegally from the pueblo, that is, that they were usurped by government or military authorities.

The communal movement, then, faces serious legal obstacles in achieving its goal of restitution. That is really not surprising, and indeed it is quite understandable, when it is realized that the Agrarian Reform has been primarily a political tool to restore to the countryside the stability and security necessary for the development of agriculture and the expansion of the capitalist economy (Gutelman 1971). The aim of the Agrarian Reform has been more the demobilization and defusing of a rebellious rural population than a far-reaching program oriented toward the economic improvement of the small-scale cultivator (Bartra 1974; Gutelman 1971). The Reform, despite the lip-service it pays to the poorer sectors of the rural population, was never intended to be a block to capitalist development nor to facilitate the expansion of noncapitalist forms of production, such as the comunidad indígena, at the expense of private property.

THE COMUNIDAD AGRARIA

Although certain details of the emergence of the ejido group from the comunidad indígena are yet to be determined, it is clear that the splintering occurred over the issue of the acceptability of the Governmental resolution. In its original form, this provisional decree restored to the Indian community a total of 9,086 hectares drawn from a number of properties located primarily in the canyon, but also including a section of the upland (Jalisco 1969). The largest single tract of land, 2,650 hectares, was expropriated from the Hacienda de La Gúasima, and was to be the future ejido. Another series of properties was located downriver from Azqueltán near Izolta, and others were on the western edge of the Villa Guerrero plain overlooking the canyon. In all, these dispersed properties totaled 5,662 hectares. It would seem, then, that the comuneros had achieved a degree of success in their petition. While they received nowhere near the amount of land that some claimed to be the property of the original comunidad, they did have restored to them a considerable amount of land, including the level mid-canyon mesas at La Gúasima. However, because of a series of injunctions obtained by landowners whose properties had been affected by the Resolution, the comuneros were not able to actually take possession of most of the 5,662 hectares located outside of La Gúasima. For example, the greater part of the lands of one large landowner-cattleman, some 2,100 hectares that included the lands on the upland plain, were later returned to the landowner. An additional 1,900 hectares belonging to three different vecino landowners also were removed from the Resolution, as were two other smaller properties.

After the landowners' judicial counteroffensive was completed, less than 1,660 hectares of the 5,662 remained for the comuneros, and most of these lands consisted of rocky canyon slopes. The lands at La Gúasima survived the landlord reaction and were retained as part of the Resolution to be restored to the community; a small group of comuneros moved onto these lands. While this group was prepared to accept the provisions of the Resolution, the majority of the comuneros, after seeing the largest part of the lands returned to the landlords, determined that the Government's Resolution was unacceptable and decided to continue the struggle for a more complete restitution of the original comunidad indígena. Those who had the good fortune and perspicacity to quickly take over the lands at La Gúasima were content with the Resolution and removed themselves from further agrarian activity. They abandoned the goal of achieving the restitution of the entire comunidad and established themselves as a comunidad agraria, independent of the comunidad indígena. In the 1970s, the ejido controlled approximately 2,600 hectares of mixed agricultural and grazing land, including level lands located on the first mesa above the Bolaños River. The total area of the ejido exceeded by twice the amount of land controlled by the comuneros and, more importantly, it encompassed some of the most valuable plow agricultural lands within the canyon. The 1970 census listed only 46 individuals as members of the ejido (Direccion General de Estadística 1972).

The general characteristics of ejido tenure are sufficiently well described that they require no detailed treatment here (Morenos Sanchez 1960; Silva Herzog 1959; Tannenbaum 1929). Suffice it to point out that the present day ejido, as a product of the Mexican Revolution, was developed as a mechanism for bringing political stability to the countryside through the break-up of excessively large, often unproductive properties and the distribution of the expropriated lands to petitioning communities that were land deficient. In contrast to comunidades indígenas that requested restitution of community lands, communities that sought ejido lands did not have to provide evidence of usurpation and alienation of lands but merely had to demonstrate their need for lands, and, very importantly, show there were privately-held lands nearby that exceeded the maximum size limits set out in the Agrarian Law. Under ejido tenure, the de jure ownership and control of the land rests with the community, and individuals obtain only the usufruct of individual parcels for agricultural and residential purposes. The buying, selling, renting, or alienation of land from the ejido is specifically prohibited by the Agrarian Laws, although in actuality these restrictions are often not enforced. With the exception of a small number of collective ejidos in northern Mexico (Wilkie 1971), production on most ejidos is in the hands of the individual ejidatario and his household.

The individualization of the ejido plots, however, together with the common practice of renting parcels, has allowed larger units of production to emerge, especially in the more fertile ejidos in which capitalist entrepreneurs consolidate a number of contiguous plots and exploit them as a single farm, often using the ejidatarios themselves as wage laborers (Barbosa and Maturana 1972).

On the surface, the formation of the ejido in Azqueltán and the resultant conflict between ejidatarios and comuneros simply represents a struggle between two groups over control of land. At a deeper level of analysis, however, the struggle represents a confrontation between competing modes of production. The ejido and the communal systems manifest radically divergent political economies. Contrary to some interpretations, ejido tenure cannot be treated as a variety of communal tenure, as is the modern, postrevolutionary equivalent of the Colonial comunidad indígena or pre-Hispanic calpulli. The differences between ejido and communal tenure are exhibited in a number of crucial characteristics. First, unlike communal tenure, ejidatarios receive firm rights to individual parcels and there is no periodic, community-wide redistribution and shifting of plots such as is found within the comunidad indígena. Most of the ejidatarios at La Gúasima are in possession of level lands and practice plow (yunta) agriculture, not coamil agriculture, and this has facilitated the development of individual rights and claims to particular fields. Second, rights to these individual parcels are inheritable, again unlike the communal system. Third, rights to land within an ejido are not extended to all residents and members of the community, as they are in the comunidad indígena, but only to those individuals named in the ejido grant and their heirs. Immigrants or children who fail to inherit a plot from their parents are left without lands, that is, they are proletarianized. In the ejido at La Gúasima this process has not had a chance to develop due to the youth of the ejido, but nevertheless it remains a possibility.

A fourth important difference is that ejido lands are commonly rented or sharecropped, despite the illegality of the practice, by individuals who were not named on the original ejido census. At La Gúasima a number of cases were recorded in which non-ejidatarios had obtained the use of plots either by entering into a sharecrop arrangement with an ejidatario or by paying a portion of their crop to the ejido executive committee. Ejido lands, therefore, can be used to earn rents while communal lands in Azqueltán cannot. Fifth, while it is not legal to sell ejido lands, it is common practice for ejidatarios who emigrate or for widows without heirs but with rights to parcels to sell, extralegally, the rights to the individual plots (see Barbosa and Maturana 1972 and Wilkie 1971 for extensive discussions of these practices). Again, in La Gúasima this practice was not common in the 1970s because the ejido was less than a decade old. But to judge from developments in ejidos in general and in the nearby ejido of Los Amoles located on the border between the municipios of Villa Guerrero and Mezquitic, such developments are likely to occur in time. Thus, despite its de jure façade of communality of land, the ejido easily creates a de facto landowning class as well as a landless class that often provides the bulk of the agricultural labor for the parcel-holding ejidatarios.

Finally, there are broad disparities in the degree of articulation and integration of the two systems within the larger socioeconomic framework. As noted, the comunidad indígena operates with a great deal of independence and is only weakly incorporated within either the external market or formal Governmental institutions. It neither pays taxes on its land to the state Tax Office nor, prior to the Echevarria administration, was it eligible for loans, grants, or other economic assistance aimed at improving the production capabilities or economic well-being of the comuneros. In a word, no surpluses are directly extracted from the comuneros' coamil production although, of course, significant exploitation occurs via their involvement in seasonal wage labor. The ejido, on the other hand, is not only subject to taxation of its lands but also has become eligible for participation in the Government's regional development programs. Through these development programs, the ejido serves as a workable mechanism for the penetration of capitalism into a group that formerly practiced a noncapitalist mode of production. (For other accounts of how ejidos have been used and modified to serve the needs of capital, see Wilkie 1971 and Barbosa and Maturana 1971.)

In addition, the ejidatarios, through their Comité Ejecutivo, are directly integrated within the municipal political structure as well as the State and Federal agrarian bureaucracies. Ejido representatives are included in official political gatherings held in the municipio and a past ejido president even served as municipal president, a position traditionally occupied by townsmen from Villa Guerrero selected by the stockmen and large landowners. The comuneros, however, receive no official recognition at the local level, are never included in the formal listings of municipal associations and organizations (such as the Cattlemen's Association or The Association of Small Property Owners), and possess only a semiofficial status in relation to the agrarian bureaus. In fact, a good deal of the comuneros' machinations to obtain restitution have been conducted through private agrarian channels and organizations rather than through official governmental organs.

The economic independence of the comunidad indígena is mirrored in the comuneros' conceptualization of the role of outside agents, especially those from the Government, with regard to their land. The comuneros view the Government's function in the land dispute to be one of confirmation and enforcement of land rights that have been theirs since time immemorial. Comuneros do not necessarily see the Government as the original creator and grantor of those land rights, but only as the protector and defender of rights that rest in the community and to which the comuneros have a prior moral claim independent of the Government.

Ejido lands, however, are a creation of the State, and lands granted as an ejido are usually independent of moral claims of prior ownership by the grantees. It is for this reason that the ejidatarios of La Gúasima have abandoned their claims of Indian ancestry; such claims have become superfluous now that they possess lands due to Government largesse rather than due to ancient community rights.

In the Azqueltán case, then, the ejido has served a variety of purposes. First, it has functioned as a political pacifier, not only by removing some individuals from engaging in a potentially disruptive agrarian struggle, but also by integrating them within formal political-administrative structures where their actions can be more readily controlled and directed. As well, the ejido serves as a vehicle to penetrate and transform semi-independent and archaic systems of production such as the comunidad indígena into forms more amenable to capitalist development. Finally, the ejido has diluted the traditional ethnic associations and allegiances rooted in the local community by forging stronger ideological commitments to and identification with the nation-state.

CONCLUSION

Through analyses of the differences between communal and ejido systems of production and of the historical relationship between the two in the community of Azqueltán, it is possible to identify the material conditions underlying the retention and rejection of Indian identity among the highly acculturated Tepecano. In addition to providing an examination of the crucial factors operative in the break-up and transformation of a traditional ethnic enclave, this study highlights the processes that internally differentiate a peasant population and impede coherent and unified class action. Despite the fact that both ejidatarios and comuneros are small-scale cultivators who occupy a similar disadvantaged position within the global social structure, there exists a good deal of conflict and antagonism between them stemming from their differential relations to landed property. The Azqueltán case, then, not only underscores the reality that the Mexican peasantry is exceedingly heterogeneous but also demonstrates the manner in which state intervention and the growth of the market economy produce internal differentiation within the peasantry. By creating conflicting loyalties and interests, such differentiation inhibits the formation of pan-regional peasant movements and contributes to the stability of the state.

Furthermore, I believe that it is reasonable to conclude that one, and possibly the most important, factor operating against the comuneros in their attempt to maintain the traditional comunidad indígena is that the communal system, unlike the ejido, provides no profits or surplus to the outside economy. The reproduction of the capitalist system is predicated on the continual creation of wealth and the production and accumulation of capital. Consequently, as the tentacles of capitalism expand, noncapitalist forms of production such as the comunidad indígena seem doomed to extinction; they neither reproduce the capitalist class structure nor produce an exploitable surplus.

In a provocative essay that has a bearing on this point, Diener (1978) suggested that the preservation of many Indian communities in Mesoamerica has been due to their elaborate civil-religious hierarchies and costly fiesta cycles. While investigators have long appreciated the importance of these hierarchies as boundary-maintaining mechanisms, what is novel in Diener's approach is that he analyzed their function in regional political economies. Diener pointed out that the Indians who accept the sponsorship of a cargo take on a heavy financial burden and are required to expend large sums of money on a variety of ceremonial and ritual goods. But the merchants who supply these commodities to the Indians are usually local ladinos. In this manner the civil-religious hierarchy serves as a device of appropriating Indian produced wealth by non-Indians. Diener contended that the income derived through this channel is substantial and that ladino stockmen-merchants, in order to decide whether to leave the Indians on their lands or to replace them with cattle, actually calculate the relative income obtainable from the sale of ritual paraphernalia versus that obtainable from grazing.

Unlike the Indians of southern Mexico, the Tepecano no longer possess an elaborate ceremonial cycle that provides significant income for local merchants. Their productive system also fails to produce surplus value for the larger system. The vacuum of profits in the comunidad indígena condemns it to either total transformation or disappearance.

Acknowledgments. Support for the various research periods was provided by The Research Foundation, State University of New York, Stony Brook through grants to Phil C. Weigand; by the Department of Anthropology and the Graduate School, Stony Brook; and by the National Science Foundation (grant number 75–19478). I am indebted to the peoples of Azqueltán, especially Sr. Desiderio Márquez Rojas and Sr. Reynaldo Pinedo Quiñones, agrarian leaders, for their forbearance and receptivity. To the people of Villa Guerrero I express my gratitude for their tolerance and permission in carrying out the research. My wife, Alexandra J. Lewis, greatly facilitated the collection of field data during the 1975–1976 season and I appreciate her professional and personal support. Phil Weigand provided valuable comments on early versions of this paper that improved its content.

Note. This paper is based on data collected during fieldwork over a period of 24 months between 1971 and 1976 in the municipio of Villa Guerrero. The summer months of 1971 and 1972 were spent in the pueblo of Azqueltán as part of an ethnographic research project directed by Phil C. Weigand. In 1974 fieldwork shifted to the municipal cabecera of Villa Guerrero. Between May 1975 and October 1976 I carried out an intensive land use–land tenure survey that enabled me to place the Tepecano situation within the wider context of the municipal agrarian economy. For a more detailed discussion, see Shadow 1978.

Barbosa and Maturana 1972
Bartra 1974
Berrin 1978
CETENAL (Comision de Estudios del Territorio Nacional) 1974
Diener 1978
Direccion General de Estadistica 1972
Grimes and Hinton 1969
Gutelman 1971
Hrdlička 1903
Jalisco 1969
Jones 1962
Lewis 1963
Ley Federal de Reforma Agraria 1971
Lumholtz 1902a, 1902b
Mason 1912a, 1912b, 1912c, 1913, 1948, 1952, 1981
Mason and Agogino 1972
Morenos Sanchez 1960
Palerm 1967
Pennington 1969
Shadow 1978
Silva Herzog 1959
Spicer 1971
Stavenhagen 1970b
Tannenbaum 1929
Velázquez Chávez 1961
Weigand 1969, 1972, 1976, 1977, 1978
Wilkie 1971
Williams 1978

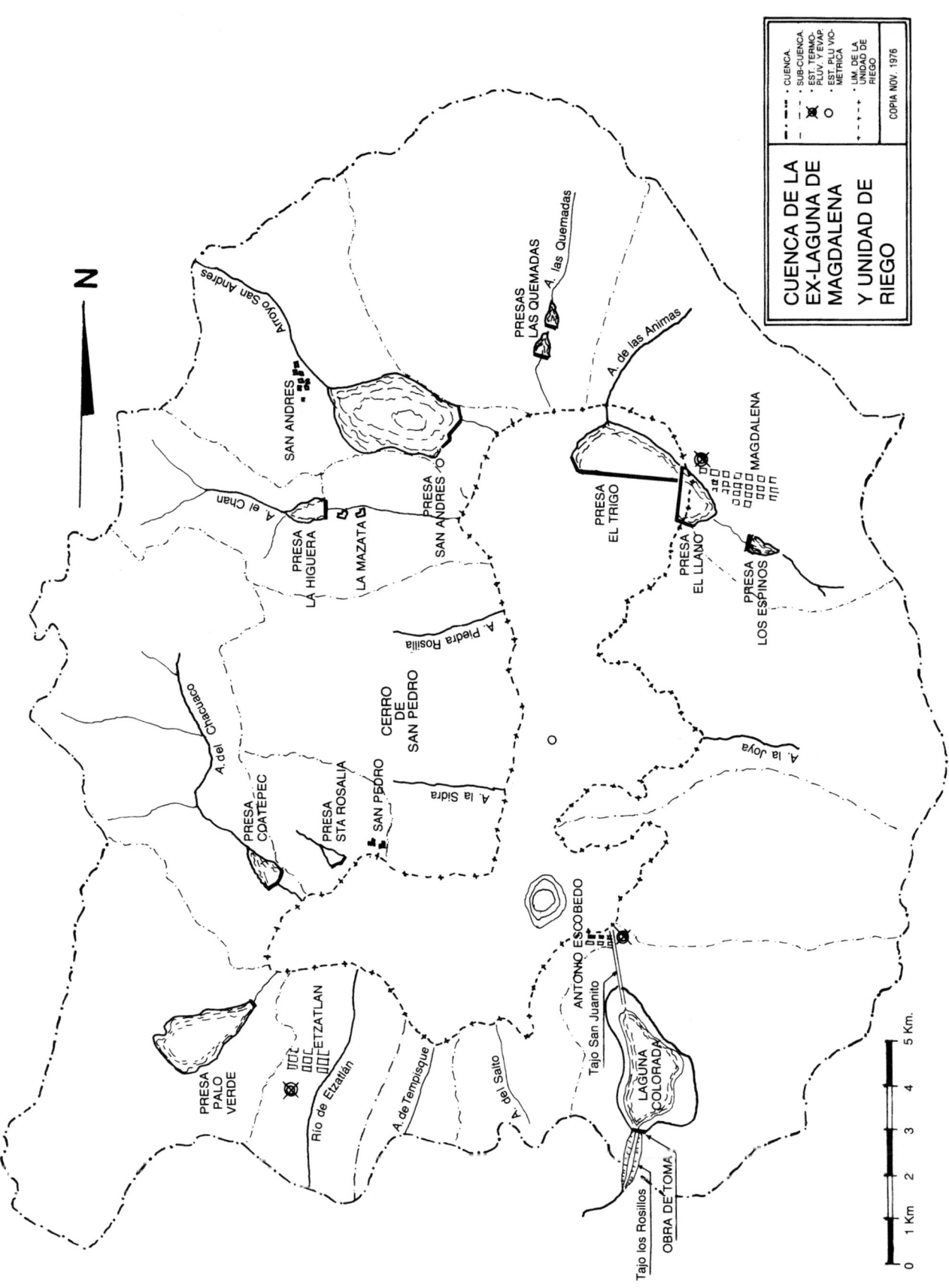

Figure 6.1. The Magdalena-Etzatlán Irrigation District, Jalisco. The outer dashed line is the catchment boundary. The inner dashed line is the shoreline of the lake before it was drained. The dashed lines between the outer and inner lines mark off the subdistrict catchments. The *Lagunas* and *presas* are reservoirs above the shoreline for irrigation purposes beneath the shoreline. (The map was drawn by Francisco Ron and is a composite based on information and drawings supplied to the Project by the Secretaría de Recursos Hidráulicas.)

CHAPTER SIX

The Marginalization of the Ejidos of the Magdalena-Etzatlán *Unidad de Riego,* Jalisco

Phil C. Weigand (State University of New York, Stony Brook)
Francisco Ron Siordia (Universidad de Guadalajara)

The literature is replete with examples of communities that are both marginalized and enclaved. Indeed, there is an undeniable historical and functional link between the processes of marginalization and the state of enclavement (compare Aguirre Beltrán 1967). While most enclaved communities are marginalized as a part of the process of their formation, it does not follow that most marginalized communities become enclaved. Obviously, the links between the processes of marginalization and its classic end result, enclavement, are strong, but many communities undergoing the course of marginalization escape becoming fully enclaved. It is our purpose to explore the processes of marginalization among the ejidos of the Magdalena-Etzatlán Basin, as well as assess the degree of enclavement represented in the communities that serve as bases for the ejidos. We hope that this study will help in the understanding of the relationships between marginalization and enclavement.

THE SETTING

The Magdalena-Etzatlán *Unidad de Riego* (irrigation and subirrigation district) is located in a closed basin that has a total catchment of 53,000 hectares (Fig. 6.1). At the northern end of the basin is the town of Magdalena, at the southern end is Etzatlán, and at the eastern edge is San Juanito (also called Antonio Escobedo). At the base of the catchment are 14,000 ha of relatively flat alluvial deposits, of which 6,986 ha are lake bottoms. The rest are alluvial fans or large playas (first terrace "beaches"). The dominant geographical features that surround the basin are the Sierra de Ameca to the south and the Volcán de Tequila to the east. The Sierra de Ameca is composed of a series of great, uplifted, sedimentary deposits that are rich in mineral content. The Volcán de Tequila is ringed by cinder cones, at least one of which sometimes emits gas and ash. The richness of the soils of the Unidad are due to the mixture of volcanic ash with the deep humus lacustrine alluvial deposits. These soils have no salinity and, when first exploited, were incredibly fertile. While the fertility has dropped, two crops a year are possible, and frosts represent no major danger during the winter dry season.

The Unidad is divided into two zones: 3,106 ha are classified as an irrigation zone, and 3,880 ha are classified as a subirrigation and drainage zone. During the spring-summer season, maize and sorghum are the major cultigens and drainage is the major technical problem. During the winter season, wheat and garbanzo are dominant, and the major problem is irrigation. Throughout the basin rainfall may vary from 500 to 1,600 mm per year, with about 85 percent falling during the wet, or spring-summer, season. That same range of rainfall may occur from year to year as well as interregionally, thus resulting in a year of drought followed by a year of flooding. Soil analysis has shown that the soils of the middle and southern parts of the Unidad are richer than those of the northern section. Rainfall also is higher in the southern section. About 70 percent of the total rainfall occurs in June, July, and early August. When the rainfall is exceptionally heavy, the drainage system is simply overwhelmed and the basin refills. This was well illustrated in 1977, when in July almost 5,000 ha were flooded. Over 2,000 ha were still under water in September, and a total harvest loss of 3,100 ha was experienced, though much of the lost harvest was plowed under for a badly needed green manure.

As mentioned, fertility is dramatically dropping throughout the Unidad. This drop is largely due to agricultural practices and poor management of the water table. Poor systems of crop rotation, especially on ejido land, and the persistent habit of burning stubble in order to clean fields are the two main problems. Overuse of chemical fertilizers, and overapplications of pesticides and herbicides are also in evidence. Burning on occasion has ignited the humus layers, and the land itself smolders for weeks at a time. Poor management is most evident during the dry season, when the basin's precious groundwater is "sold" to downstream sugarcane fields. The result has been a compacting of the soils that each year become more friable, harder to plow, and more prone to chemical damage. All this is complicated by the dumping of raw sewage into the major ditches of the Unidad. While much of the sewage is still largely organic, much of it is also chemical. Great mountains of soapsuds mark the flood gates—fish, reptiles, and birds have either died off or fled, and the ditches are now largely devoid of wildlife. Aside from *aguas negras,* several processing plants, such as that of Mezquital del Oro, dump unprocessed waste into the ditch system.

When the Spanish first arrived in Etzatlán in 1527, they noted a lake that fluctuated between about 5,000 to 8,000 ha in extent. The first organized program to drain the lake began in 1902, with a privately sponsored project that accomplished the drilling of a tunnel through the ridge that divides this basin from that of Ahualulco to the southeast. The next project was federally sponsored, and started in 1927. The heavy local fighting during the Cristero Revolt interrupted the work. The project was resumed in the 1930s, though work was sporadic until the 1950s. Then the great drainage ditch between the two basins was completed, and the lake could be managed. At this point, 7,000 ha could be more or less dependably utilized. The basin's proximity to Guadalajara was the reason for its development, and the planners hoped it would serve as another badly needed breadbasket for the expanding state capital. The basin was developed as an oasis to be used scientifically and mechanically (see Hewitt de Alcantara 1976).

There were two unanticipated side effects to the draining of the lake, one physical and one social. The physical effect was to lower the humidity level within the basin to such a degree that much of the mountain and hillside agricultural lands were forced out of production. The hectares gained by drainage do not offset the hectares lost because of changed microclimatic factors. In addition, forest cover changed and a remarkable series of plant replacements have taken place. Since the process started, mountain and hillside soil erosion has increased. The social effect was to provide a temporary labor vacuum in the area. Although the new oasis was to be mechanically operated as fully as possible, the machinery was not in place. Migrants (in order of their arrivals) came in from: Zacatecas, the Sayula Valley (Jalisco), the Altos de Jalisco, and most recently from La Piedad, Michoacán. Many of the older, traditional farmers of the basin did not make the transition easily, but the migrants were willing to leave subsistence farming behind and become rural proletarians in their new environment. The opening of the lake bottoms marked the end of subsistence farming on a large scale, and marked the beginning of full-scale commercial agriculture (Weigand and García de Weigand 1974).

LAND TENURE AND USE

The locally established ejidos were chartered during the 1920s and 1930s, a period of de facto formation of many of the ejidos. They were subsistence oriented and quite naturally sought, at times militantly, to expand into the lake bottoms as they were opened to agriculture. De jure entitlement often came much later, and was frequently accompanied by major changes in ejido structure, especially as the ejidos sought additional land from their original *dotaciones* (grants). The ejidos of Etzatlán and Nuevo Obelatos are the newest and were founded de facto and de jure after World War II.

Despite the resistance of planners and the private landholders, the ejidos gained control of 5,388 ha of the Unidad. Thus, the full development of a high technology oasis of the kind that Hewitt de Alcantara (1976) cites was compromised from the outset by difficulties in the overall tenure structure. The private landowners (*pequeña propiedad*), on whom the oasis developments most often depended, augmented by many from the migrant population, established control over only 1,598 ha of the Unidad, mainly in the most fertile southern sections of the basin. (See Table 6.1 for tenure according to type of legal possession in both irrigation and subirrigation drainage zones.)

Table 6.1. Land Tenure According to Type of Legal Possession

Legal Possession	Irrigation		
	Ha	Number of users	Average ha per user
Ejido	2006.00	645	3.11
Pequeña propiedad	1100.35	62	17.74
Total	3106.35	707	4.39
	Subirrigation and drainage		
	Ha	Number of users	Average ha per user
Ejido	3382.0	1277	2.65
Pequeña propiedad	497.8	24	20.74
Total	3879.8	1301	2.98
	Overall totals		
	Ha	Number of users	Average ha per user
Ejido	5388.00	1922	2.80
Pequeña propiedad	1598.15	86	18.58
Total	6986.15	2008	3.48

Actual Surface Irrigated from Total Potentially Irrigable Land

	Surface irrigated in ha		
Season	Ejido	Pequeña propiedad	Total
1967–1968	504	500	1004
1968–1969	585	620	1205
1969–1970*	337	35	372
1970–1971	No data		
1971–1972	600	310	910
1972–1973	446	216	662
1973–1974	514	370	884
1974–1975	475	389.5	864.5
1975–1976	420	538	958

* = dry year

It was the government's intent to promote the change from subsistence agriculture to commercial cash crops throughout the entire region, including, of course, the Unidad. Irrigation within the Unidad was to be the key for this transition, though even this goal was not achieved. The Unidad irrigation potential remains badly under used (see lower half of Table 6.1), especially among the ejidos. The cash crops promoted within the Unidad are sorghum and wheat, and the ratios of those two crops to maize and garbanzo (respectively) mark the ideal process and progress of the transition to commercial cash crops (Table 6.2). During the 1967–1968 season, the ejido farmers planted over 5,000 ha of maize and only 20 ha of sorghum. By the 1975–1976 season, they were planting around 1,700 ha of maize and nearly 2,500 ha of sorghum. During the same period, private landholders shifted crops in an even more dramatic fashion: 1,268 ha of maize and 330 ha of sorghum in the 1967–1968 season to 105 ha of maize and 1,267 ha of sorghum in 1975 to 1976. There have been irregularities in this transition, of course. The most prominent has been the rapid adaptation by the private landholders to the new system: by the late 1969–1970 season, they were already sowing 1,500 ha of sorghum.

Table 6.2. Area Cultivated by Season and Harvests

	Ejidal ha and (harvest ton per ha)							
	Maize		Sorghum		Wheat		Garbanzo	
Season	I[1]	RF[2]	I	RF	I	SI[3]	I	SI
1967–1968	64 (2.5)	5382 (3.0)		20 (3.0)	400 (3.0)	3300 (3.0)	40 (1.5)	1260 (1.5)
1968–1969		5000 (2.5)	40 (3)	200 (2.5)	535 (2.0)	3000 (2.0)	10 (1.0)	1390 (1.0)
1969–1970*	40 (2.0)	3940 (3.0)	40 (4)	1500 (4.0)	195 (3.0)		62 (1.0)	
1970–1971	No data							
1971–1972	92 (2.5)	1700 (3.5)		3800 (4.0)	297 (2.0)	800 (2.0)	211 (2.0)	2800 (2.0)
1972–1973	33 (3.5)	1450 (1.5)		3250 (3.5)	168 (2.5)	400 (2.0)	245 (1.5)	4800 (1.2)
1973–1974	82 (2.5)	1230 (2.5)		2850 (4.0)	230 (5.0)	400 (3.0)	147 (2.5)	4950 (2.0)
1974–1975	82 (1.5)	1686 (2.5)		3880 (4.0)	103 (2.0)	60 (1.5)	240 (1.5)	745 (0.8)
1975–1976		1695 (1.5)		2943 (3.5)	155 (1.5)	68 (1.5)	215 (2.5)	2694 (1.2)

	Pequeña Propiedad ha and (harvest ton per ha)							
	Maize		Sorghum		Wheat		Garbanzo	
Season	I	RF	I	RF	I	SI	I	SI
1967–1968		1268 (3.0)		330 (3.0)	500 (3.0)	1000 (3.0)		
1968–1969		700 (2.5)		800 (2.5)	620 (2.0)	245 (2.0)		500 (1.0)
1969–1970*		60 (3.0)		1500 (4.0)				
1970–1971	No data							
1971–1972		300 (3.5)		1200 (4.7)	17 (2.0)		239 (2.0)	1200 (2.0)
1972–1973		150 (1.5)		1450 (3.5)	26 (2.5)		170 (1.5)	
1973–1974		50 (3.0)		960 (5.0)	150 (5.0)	70 (3.0)	200 (2.5)	450 (2.0)
1974–1975		150 (3.0)		1100 (5.0)	47 (3.0)		275 (2.0)	320 (0.8)
1975–1976		105 (3.0)		1267 (4.5)	292 (5.0)	12 (1.5)	151 (2.5)	352 (1.2)

* = Dry year.
1. I = Irrigation.
2. RF = Rainfall.
3. SI = Subirrigation.

The ejidos have been far slower to experiment, for reasons that we cite below.

The transition of crops for the winter season was ideally completed at the time of the opening up of the lake bottoms. Wheat was the preferred crop of both the ejido and private farmers. By the 1967–1968 season, 3,700 ha were sown in wheat in the ejidos and 1,500 ha among the private holders, versus 1,300 ha and zero ha of garbanzo, respectively. Commercial cash cropping was almost an immediate benefit of the two-crop system made possible by the lake's drainage. Because of the drop in soil fertility and the lowering of the winter water table beyond the level of root penetration, wheat can no longer be profitably sown—a setback for the commercialization of agriculture of the Unidad, but in fact an act still in the service of cash crops. The water table is often lowered in order to supply the sugarcane fields of the Ahualulco Basin. In the overall planning, cane has become more important than wheat, and the Unidad is often left too dry for a major cash crop to be harvested. As mentioned, water is sold in such quantities as to have permanently damaged the subsoil structure of the lake bottoms. By the 1975–1976 season, ejido farmers planted around 225 ha of wheat, and the private holders about 305 ha

Table 6.3. Sorghum-Maize and Wheat-Garbanzo Contrasts in Ejido-Pequeña Propiedad
In Percentages of Area Cultivated

Season	Maize		Sorghum		Total % of area utilized
	Ejido	Pequeña propiedad	Ejido	Pequeña propiedad	
1967–1968	99.63	79.30	0.37	20.70	100.0
1968–1969	96.15	46.67	3.85	53.33	95.7
1969–1970*	72.43	3.84	27.57	96.16	100.0
1970–1971	No data				
1971–1972	30.90	20.00	69.10	80.00	100.0
1972–1973	30.85	9.37	69.15	90.63	90.0
1973–1974	30.14	4.95	69.86	95.05	70.7
1974–1975	30.29	12.00	69.71	88.00	97.6
1975–1976	36.54	7.65	63.45	92.35	85.8

Season	Wheat		Garbanzo		Total % of area utilized	
	Ejido	Pequeña propiedad	Ejido	Pequeña propiedad	Ejido	Pequeña propiedad
1967–1968	74.00	100.00	26.00	0.00	92.80	93.86
1968–1969	71.63	59.04	28.37	40.96	91.59	91.66
1969–1970*	75.87	0.00	24.13	0.00	4.79	0.00
1970–1971	No data					
1971–1972	26.70	1.16	73.30	98.84	76.24	91.10
1972–1973	10.12	8.67	89.88	91.33	100.00	12.26
1973–1974	11.00	25.28	89.00	74.72	100.00	54.43
1974–1975	14.19	7.32	85.81	92.68	21.30	40.17
1975–1976	7.12	37.67	92.88	62.33	58.12	50.50

* = dry year.

versus 2,900 ha and 500 ha of garbanzo, respectively. While garbanzo is largely a cash crop, it does not have the same high income factor that wheat has, especially among the ejido farmers to whom low yields and lower grain quality have meant a drop in overall farm income for the winter season. Wheat is now an unimportant crop for the Unidad. The lake bottoms are particularly underused during the winter season (Table 6.3). Large areas of the Unidad are used now as stubble pasturage during the winter, and hence still are used in some productive form, plus adding to soil fertility. The quality of cattle, however, is poor, and ejido-based cattle raising is not fully commercial. Among the cattle are high percentages of horses, donkeys, and mules.

The overall average size of plots held by the ejido farmers within the Unidad is extremely small: 2.8 ha per usuario (entitled ejido members), but even this figure, however small, does not represent the average minimum per individual with rights to ejido land. Many plots are still registered in the names of deceased or inactive individuals, and, through fractionization, working plots are often less than one hectare in size, with some as small as one-fourth of a hectare. All ejido members have plots outside the Unidad averaging around 7 to 9 ha of dry, rainfall fields, often coamil (dig-stick) hillside plots. Fractionization through the pattern of equal rights for all eligible inheritors has affected these holdings as well. Renting and the formation of family corporations within the ejidos serve to partly counterbalance the trend toward fractionization, but only approximately 15 percent of ejido land is so farmed. These holdings, while difficult to fully measure because of their temporary nature, seldom exceed 18 to 20 ha. These ejido-based family corporations have to contend with dispersed plots that are not managed as effectively as the concentrated holdings of the private owners. Despite this disadvantage, several corporations have been successful and are commercially productive. The operators, though, along with others of the ejido managerial hierarchy, are often accused of corruption, nepotism, and *priismo* (catering to the wishes of the P. R. I. politicians). Many of the ejidos are indeed corruptly managed.

Commercial agriculture among the ejido farmers still is not profitable on any scale. About another 15 percent of ejido land is rented to private farmers. This renting, contrary to intraejido renting, is against the law, and these plots often enter a hidden market of land rights subject to little or no control, either internally or externally. The freedom and extent of this type of renting only serves to further shrink the ejido land resource. The rents are small, and seldom if ever match the income that could be derived from the land if it were under ejido control. Actual alienation is happening as the renting to the private landholding sector gains momentum. Many ejido farmers are becoming a de facto landless peasantry. Stavenhagen (1966)

Table 6.4. Average Income in Pesos per Hectare

	Ejidal, pesos per hectare							
	Maize		Sorghum		Wheat		Garbanzo	
Season	I[1]	RF[2]	I	RF	I	SI[3]	I	SI
1967–1968	1564	2412		1834	2292	2467	990	902
1968–1969		1564	1834	1134	524	717	−198	−110
1969–1970*	714	2414	3224	3224	2292			
1970–1971	No data							
1971–1972	1564	3264		3224	524	717	2002	2090
1972–1973	3264	−136		2534	1417	717	900	330
1973–1974	1564	1564		3234	4634	2467	3102	2090
1974–1975	−136	1563		2534	542	−157	990	−550
1975–1976		−136		3234	−332	−157	3102	330
Average last 3 years	476	997		3000	1615	717	2398	623

	Pequeña propiedad, pesos per hectare							
	Maize		Sorghum		Wheat		Garbanzo	
Season	I	RF	I	RF	I	SI	I	SI
1967–1968		2414		1834		2292	2464	
1968–1969		1564		1134	542	717		−110
1969–1970*		2414		3224				
1970–1971	No data							
1971–1972		3264		4212	542		2002	2090
1972–1973		−136		2868	1417		902	
1973–1974		2414		4634	5792		3102	2090
1974–1975		2414		4634	2292	2464	902	−550
1975–1976		2414		3934	5792	−157	3102	330
Average last 3 years		2414		4400	4625	769	2369	623

* = Dry year.
1. I = Irrigation.
2. RF = Rainfall.
3. SI = Subirrigation.

notes that the distinction between ejido farmer and small, private landholder is often more formal than real. In this area, however, this distinction became a reality through fractionization within the ejidos as opposed to the pattern of primogeniture among the private holders.

PRODUCTION

Production (Table 6.2) and income (Table 6.4) from the Unidad show vast differences between the ejidos and the private holders. Obviously, the size of plots is a controlling factor, but so are the methods of production, credit arrangements, access to fertilizers, degree of mechanization, and access to markets. Despite the official rhetoric, credits are not available to the ejidos on the scale that they need for commercialization, nor are they on a par with the level of credits advanced to the private farmers. With the government-sponsored Unión de Ejidos, operated from a Reforma Agraria office in Magdalena, credits were supposed to be forthcoming on an appropriate scale. So far, the only result for the farmers has been the loss of ejido autonomy in many of their internal affairs. The improved credits to date have not even kept pace with inflation. Aside from the low level of credits, there are also problems with their timing, accountability, and management. In effect, the ejidos are trying to operate within a commercial system without the backup of investment—an impossibility, considering the tenure problems.

The ejidos are largely nonmechanical, reflecting not only the lack of credits but fractionization as well. A comparison of farm machinery, including trucks, between the ejidos and the private holders is presented in Table 6.5. No areas within the ejidos are fully mechanized, though some are partly so through the rental system or cooperative ventures. The machinery on the ejidos is most often vintage and undependable. Trucks are also in limited supply, which raises the costs of harvests on the ejidos and in effect serves as a limiting factor in marketing the produce. The government, through the CONASUPO program, serves as the major buyer for the produce from the ejidos. While the CONASUPO prices are pegged at the official rates, there are many "discounts" figured in the final amount. The

**Table 6.5. Mechanization
(Based on 1975–1976 census of machinery)**

Machinery	Land totally mechanized		Land partially mechanized	
	Ejido	Pequeña propiedad	Ejido	Pequeña propiedad
Tractors	0	27	22	15
Sowers	0	12	5	0
Harvesters	0	5	3	0
Combines	0	9	4	0
Trucks	0	32	30	0

ejido farmers do not have the mobility to look for other buyers. Within the ejidos, harvesting is almost always done by hand. This labor extends the harvest period, and may mean lower yields due to weather, rodents, and insects. Prolonged harvests and less access to the market seriously affect the productive potential of the ejidos, even under ideal circumstances.

Because of small plot size, lack of mechanization, lack of credits, and less use of fertilizers and insecticides (because of rising expenses and unequal distribution) production as figured in tons per hectare is considerably lower within the ejidos compared to that of the private holders and to national production figures as well. Complicating the circumstance of low production is the trend toward still lower production rates within the ejidos. Although there are fluctuations in harvests through the years, from the 1967–1968 season to the 1975–1976 season, Table 6.2 shows a drop in ton per hectare for maize, stability in sorghum production, a drop in wheat, and a slight drop in garbanzo for the ejidos. Over the same period, among the private holders, maize harvests were more or less stable, while sorghum harvests rose, wheat dropped, and garbanzo dropped slightly. Between 1972–1973 and 1975–1976, the production of maize within the ejidos on the irrigated land of the Unidad was at the same level as the coamil hillside plots.

Farm income, as expressed in pesos per hectare (Table 6.4), reflects not only the dramatic differences between the ejidos and the private farmers, but also the condition of economic collapse that has occurred when one thinks about the farming potential of the Unidad. Considering the amount of inflation, the point of equilibrium (which is expressed as the cost of production per hectare divided by the average rural price per ton, as figured in ton per hectare) has increased dramatically. It now costs far more to produce less. This especially affects the ejidos, within which the average in pesos per hectare over the last three years represented in this study was: $476 and $997 for maize (irrigation and dry, rainfall fields respectively), $3,000 for sorghum, $1,615 and $717 for wheat (irrigation and dry, rainfall fields respectively), and $2,398 and $623 for garbanzo (irrigation and dry, rainfall fields respectively). For the private holders, the figures are quite different: $2,414 for maize (dry, rainfall fields), $4,400 for sorghum (dry, rainfall fields), $4,625 and $769 for wheat (irrigation and dry, rainfall fields respectively), and $2,369 and $623 for garbanzo. For the 1974–1975 season, the points of equilibrium are shown in Table 6.6. From this perspective, farming within the Unidad is no longer a really viable and productive activity for the ejido farmers for a large percentage of their crops. While the ejidos hold 77 percent or 3.37 times the amount of land in the Unidad than the private holders, the latter group accounts for 35 to 40 percent of the total production value, and at times around half of the actual amount of grains marketed commercially. Harvests from ejidos may be considered about 50 percent subsistence oriented.

MARGINALIZATION

Commercialization of agriculture in the area, for the ejido farmers, has meant marginalization. The lack of mechanization, fragmentation of holdings, lack of credits, and low production rates have already been discussed. Compared to the level of development attained by the private sector in agriculture, the gulf in resources and goods between the ejido farmers and the private farmers is large and growing larger. In addition, marginalization can be measured to a degree by other criteria: living standards (as measured by the percentage of income devoted to staples) are dropping, illiteracy is increasing, and population is booming. Inflation is also rising in everything except the prices being paid for rural produce and wages. At the same time, the collection of rents, taxes, and fees has become more efficient. The response to date is migration, especially to Guadalajara, to the frontier zone of Baja California, and to the Los Angeles area of California. Almost every ejido family has someone in the United States. Whole families have picked up and left. Our estimates are that about 70 percent of the families remaining receive at least occasional remittances from the migrants, and about 40 percent depend on remittances for survival. The commercialization of agriculture has resulted in the differential formation of the rural proletariat class.

Although the private landholders are also affected by rising costs, inflation, and the lack of land for all of their offspring, their response has been different from that of the ejido farmers. Instead of fractionization, the private holders are using education in skills and services, including the professions, as the outlet for their expanding population. Migration to the United States from this sector certainly exists, and many families are so represented. The migration is not reflected in remittances, however, except when an individual wishes to invest in property or house lots, or to pay off debts, medical bills, and other such expenses. The migration from the private farming sector is far more individualistic and far less family-oriented when compared to that from the ejido setting.

Family corporations among the private holders also have formed in response to the pressure on the land and the need to have plots large enough to remain productive. Often these corporations hold more than the legal hectare limit permitted within an irrigated zone. Access to credits and plots of productive size have meant relative prosperity for the private holders.

Figure 6.2. View to the north of the Etzatlán Valley, with Etzatlán in the foreground and the Ejido of San Pedro in the background. The large irrigated parcels between the two settlements average approximately 20 hectares each and belong to private land holders. (Photograph by Phil Weigand.)

Their plots, even in the context of family corporations, are not overly large—there are no real *latifundistas* in the area, though some mountain holdings are extensive. This land is primarily pasture, although some of it is agricultural. The relative prosperity of this sector of the rural bourgeoisie is explained in part by the fact that, while working their own land, they were never actually *colonos*. For the most part, they were able to make the accommodation to commercial agriculture because their holdings were of a sufficient size to allow the adjustment to take place. The ejidos were never large enough to accommodate the shift.

Most colonos were *minifundistas* (very small, private landholders), and received their name from the fact that they were among the first to colonize the lake bottoms. They, along with *peones* (both from the hacienda setting and day-wage laborers), joined in the formation of the ejidos. The ejido de Etzatlán was formed almost entirely from ex-colonos and it remains above the ejido average in the number of ha per user (Fig. 6.2). San Juanito is one of the farthest below the average, and one of the most fragmented (Fig. 6.3). Prior to the opening of the lake bottoms, most of the colonos had been landless, and many were peones or sharecroppers.

Figure 6.3. The ejido lands of San Juanito, Santiago, and La Joya, showing the fragmentation of these plots; most of them are simple strips of less than one hectare.

Table 6.6. Points of Equilibrium: 1974–1975 Season

Crop	Cost per ha	Ave. rural price per ton	Quota of capital recovered	Total peso cost per ha	Point of equilibrium ton per ha
Maize	$2535.00	$1700	6%	$2687	1.58
Sorghum	2287.50	1400	6%	2424	1.73
Garbanzo I[1]	2253.50	2200	6%	2389	1.09
Garbanzo H[2]	2188.50	2200	6%	2319	1.05
Wheat I	2795.00	1750	6%	2963	1.69
Wheat H	2630.00	1750	6%	2788	1.59

1. I = Irrigation.
2. H = Humidity.

CONCLUSION

The ejidos have been economically marginalized during the transition from subsistence to commercial agriculture. As Stavenhagen (1969a, 1969b) notes, the persistence of great inequality in land distribution is the central cause of peasant marginality. This has been especially true since the end of the policies initiated by Cárdenas (Hewitt de Alcantara 1976). This enforced marginalization of the ejidos in the Magdalena-Etzatlán region has taken most of the Unidad de Riego out of full production. Indeed, we estimate that the Unidad is producing at about 50 percent of its potential, and even this production level appears to be still dropping. The ejidos are greatly overcrowded, and have apparently reached the point where agriculture without major income supplements, especially remittances, is no longer a feasible activity. Most ejido farmers do not consider the private landholding system to be their adversary, nor do they accept the argument that the latifundistas are the enemy. They blame the federal government for their condition.

Enclavement as such has not occurred, because the ejidos and their communities remain commercially oriented. To a large degree they have accepted the ethic of commercial agriculture and consumerism. Retailing activities are well developed and growing. Retailing is generalized in the communities, although, of course, some businesses are larger and wealthier than others. The government presence, especially CONASUPO, is also expanding. Because fertilizers, the little credit that does exist, and sales contracts all depend to a large degree on the government, a shift back to subsistence-based agriculture is simply not possible. In addition, the economic ties between these marginalized ejidos, their host communities, and the surrounding regional society have remained strong and prevailing. The ejidos and the rural proletariat in general are classes within a larger structure, which in its totality is varied and outwardly oriented. Cultural ties are also strong, and hence subregionalisms are de-emphasized. The communications networks, including highways, telephones, radios, and televisions, have precluded any isolation. Thus, while many of the conditions for enclavement are present within the economic sphere, they are not reinforced in the political and cultural spheres. Under these circumstances, marginalized communities cannot become enclaved. Even in the economic sphere, the migration to the cities and to California has retarded absolute marginalization. This migration has become the economic safety valve.

Acknowledgments. We wish to thank the personnel of the Secretaría de Recursos Hidráulicos, especially Ing. Jesús Lomelí; the Departamento de Asuntos Agrarias y Colonización; the Secretaría de Agricultura y Ganadería; and the Secretaría de Reforma Agraria, and the local municipios for allowing us access to their archives. The project, which was started in 1968, has been funded by grants from the MesoAmerican Cooperative Research Fund of Southern Illinois University Museum, under the direction of Dr. J. Charles Kelley, and from the State University of New York Research Foundation. Aid also has been forthcoming from local agencies and individuals.

Aguirre Beltrán 1967
Hewitt de Alcantara 1976
Stavenhagen 1966, 1969a, 1969b

Weigand and García de Weigand 1974

CHAPTER SEVEN

Families From Tarascan Villages

Mary Lee Nolan (Oregon State University)

Rapid socioeconomic change in 20th-century Mexico has unleashed forces that tend to modify or lead toward assimilation of members of ethnic enclavements long maintained in relatively isolated rural areas. Assimilation generally takes place along two fronts: (1) individual migration from rural areas to the cities, and (2) diffusion of modern culture traits and ideas from the urban centers to the countryside. Migration to the cities may result from economic difficulties such as expansion of rural populations beyond the carrying capacity of available land. In a more positive sense, migration may reflect an individual's perception of greater opportunities for self and family in the larger towns and cities. Many of those who leave their rural homes to seek new lives in the cities fail to enter the urban-industrial mainstream. They may be poorly adapted psychologically to urban life or may lack the necessary educational or technical skills for finding good positions in the urban work force. In either case, they may add to the growing numbers of the urban poor who have wrested their roots from the soil only to be frustrated in the search for fallow ground in the cities (Lewis 1961, 1966).

Some who migrate to the cities are successful. Either through the force of raw ambition or as a result of sufficient preparation, they, or their children, become part of the growing urban middle class. Because they usually maintain ties with their kinsmen in rural communities, these individuals play an important role in the diffusion of urban goods and ideas into the countryside (see Balan, Browning, and Jelin 1973; Whiteford 1964; Lewis 1952; Rollwagen 1974; Gilbert 1974). In some cases, they are also agents for idealization and reinterpretation of selected symbols of the ethnic group from which they spring.

Like the individuals who migrate to the cities, the rural communities vary in their collective responses to pressures for change. Some have resisted incorporation into the larger social order, while others have been much more receptive. Numerous rural villages have grown in size, adapted life-styles to such indicators of modernity as electricity, pure water systems, public health care, government schools, and new agricultural strategies, and expanded their economies from a predominantly agricultural base to light industry and commerce. Many of these changes have occurred rapidly, and communities differ substantially in their ability to maintain important local traditions and a sense of cultural continuity during the modernization process. As a result, a study of response to modernization in one community may present a positive picture of beneficial change, and the people of another may have paid the price for "improvements" in greatly increased levels of social stress and loss of the sense of community (Butterworth 1970; Kaplan 1965; Margolies 1969; van Zantwijk 1967; Foster 1948, 1967; Stanislawski 1950; West 1948; Miller 1973; Nolan 1973).

Striking examples of both individual and community variations in kind and degree of assimilation into a rapidly modernizing society are represented by the people of five villages in the Sierra Tarasca of Michoacán, which felt the direct impact of the Parícutin volcanic eruptions between 1943 and 1952. As a result of geophysical impacts ranging from destruction of two town sites by lava flows to severe ash fall damage of farmlands in three other communities, more than 6,000 people were jolted from a way of life deeply rooted in a Tarascan rural tradition. Within a short period of time, the region's people were forced to choose between traditional and modern adaptations to catastrophe. As a focus of government concern, they were given special opportunities for resettlement, for wage labor in the United States, and for advanced schooling for young people. Numerous other rural communities throughout Mexico have undergone major changes since 1940, but in the case of the villages affected by Parícutin, there was a special urgency imposed by ash fall and lava that had destroyed the traditional resource base. The communities and their individual citizens met the challenge of adaptation in a variety of ways. The five communities became seven when one town fragmented into three population concentrations composed of two refugee settlements and a remnant group that remained at the original townsite. The people of the two townsites buried by lava relocated in refugee settlements on opposite sides of Uruapan, while residents of the two remaining villages remained in place in the volcanic zone (Nolan 1973, 1979; Nolan and Nolan 1979). Some families left the area and never returned, while others left for various periods of time. Some young people obtained educations and entered the urban middle class, and others from the same communities and even the same kinship networks continued an agricultural existence in the face of growing population pressures on the available lands. The focus of this study is on the differential choices made by families and individuals within families.

The families considered in this analysis represent three generations starting with 26 ancestral couples native to the original five villages devastated by the Parícutin eruptions. Information on these family lines was obtained during the summer of 1971 through interviews with the few surviving ancestors and with second and third generation family members. An attempt was made to collect genealogies from persons representing the full range of socioeconomic variation present in the villages, and this was accomplished to some degree. However, the process of obtaining data on occupation, place of residence, and household composition on all consanguineal kinsmen over three to four generations is extremely time consuming and requires a high level of interest and cooperation from informants. It is possible, therefore, that the family lines here considered may overly represent the more outgoing, and possibly the more achievement-oriented, members of village society.

Regardless of social status, some individuals tend to keep better track of their kinsmen than do others. Several family histories collected during the field season could not be used in this analysis because they contained too little information on kinsmen other than immediate family members. I used only those genealogies containing information on the status of all members of a direct line of descent. Nineteen of the genealogies are complete in that they represent what has happened to all of the adult descendants of the ancestral couples. The other seven represent the status of all offspring of one of the ancestral couple's children. By restricting analysis to all descendants of either the ancestors or one of their children, bias toward information on only the more successful members of the kinship network is eliminated, as is emphasis on only those relatives living in the immediate area. Data are available on 292 descendants of the 26 ancestral couples, providing a fairly large body of information on Tarascan adaptations to geophysical and social change during the 20th century. It should be pointed out, however, that people from communities strongly affected by the Parícutin eruptions had different life experiences from those residing in other villages. These historical circumstances as well as the history of the region should be considered as a prelude to discussing the family lines.

PHYSICAL AND CULTURAL SETTING

The Sierra Tarasca is a highland in the Mexican state of Michoacán. It is a land of great beauty where cultivated fields fill valleys between numerous small volcanic cindercones. Forests of oak and pine cling to the sides of the older cones, cover ancient lava flows, and blanket the slopes of the massive Cerros de Tancitaro. Looming over the southern portion of the region, this 13,000 foot Pleistocene shield volcano is the highest peak in Michoacán.

The valleys lie at elevations of about 7,000 feet and thus are cool throughout the year. Winter nights are cold. Temperatures sometimes drop below freezing in the valleys and snow occasionally covers the top of the Cerros de Tancitaro. The possibility of late frosts limits the agricultural use of slopelands above 8,000 feet. The hottest season comes during the dry, dusty springs when farmers traditionally prepare their lands for maize and other crops. In the days before the deep wells and piped water, there were often serious water shortages when the springs and shallow wells dried up in late spring.

Toward the end of the dry season, the Sierra wilts under a hazy sun. Trees and shrubs take on a brownish tone from an accumulation of dust on leaves and needles. Then, in late May or early June, the clouds begin to gather in white billowing masses over the mountains. The first drops of rain freckle the brownish leaves with brighter patches of green. As the rains begin in earnest, vegetation is washed clean and the Sierra turns green. Corn pushes up through the earth of plowed fields and wildflowers decorate slopeland pastures. The haze clears and the pines on the mountains are etched against a brilliant blue sky for a few hours in early morning until the clouds gather and spread into a cold gray overcast bringing the life-giving rains. In fall, the bright greens of summer are replaced by golden tones and livestock graze on the remnants of the harvest. Corn is stored in granaries and choice ears are hung under the eaves of the region's traditional wooden houses. By October or November, the rainy season is over and the endless cycle repeats.

This highland of seasonal diversity forms the heart of the Tarascan culture region, usually defined as that area where substantial portions of the rural population still speak the Tarascan language. In addition to the sierra, the cultural region includes an area around Lake Pátzcuaro and outlying districts such as the villages on the shores of Lake Cuitzeo and the valley of the Once Pueblos between Morelia and Zamora.

The origins of the Tarascan linguistic enclave reach back to Precolumbian times. The Tarascans, or Purepeachas as they prefer to be called, came from the north and mixed with civilized peoples already inhabiting the region. By the early 16th century, the polyglot peoples of the Michoacán highlands were in the process of creating an organized state or "empire" that was administered from Tzintzuntzan on the shores of Lake Pátzcuaro. Use of the Tarascan language apparently was spreading throughout the region. After Tenochtitlán fell to Hernán Cortez in 1521, reasonably friendly contacts appear to have been established between Tarascan authorities and the Spanish conquerors.

In 1527, however, Cortez prepared to return to Spain and Nuño de Guzmán was selected as president of the first audiencia. Guzmán, unlike Cortez, appears to have been a particularly vicious person and a poor administrator. In 1529 he led a ruthless attack on the Tarascan region. When he was removed from power in Mexico City, he was cast into political oblivion by being made governor of Nueva Galicia, the region he had "reduced" the year before. Guzmán's men marauded the Tarascan region for six years, even as diseases introduced inadvertently from Europe decimated a population with little biological resistance. The survivors fled into the hills and almost all semblance of the Precolumbian social order broke down.

Guzmán was followed in Michoacán by a man of God, Vasco de Quiroga. A colonial administrator who took religious vows in middle age, Quiroga was a strong-minded man with utopian ideals. After his appointment as Bishop of Michoacán in 1538, he managed to eliminate through kindness most remnants of the Indian cultural tradition that had survived the Guzmán bloodbath. Working within the framework of a utopian socioeconomic model, Don Vasco and his missionaries imposed a new way of life on the people of Tarasco. The scattered remnants of the population were resettled, often near their original homes. Each new community was allocated a particular economic role. One was to make pottery, another was to work copper and another wood, and all were to prosper. Spanish crops, plow agriculture, large domesticated animals, and numerous other aspects of European technology were introduced, along with the Christian religion. Each community was given a patron saint and a proscribed set of ways for focusing social organization and the distribution of wealth in a pattern of honoring the saints. Although they kept their basic food crops of maize, beans, and chiles, and their language, by around the end of the 16th century the people of the Sierra Tarasca were molded into an idealized pattern of what a Spanish peasantry should be like. Craft specializations and the pattern of market exchange probably were not totally alien to the region. However, the emergent Tarascan enclave was highly Hispanicized. By the time anthropological focus was directed toward the region in the mid-20th century, the Tarascans represented something of a curiosity. Although linguistically Indian, in most respects they were more like a fairly isolated Hispanic peasantry than any other linguistic Indian group in Mexico.

There were a few highly conservative "closed" villages, but they were sufficiently rare as to be noted as unusual. For the most part, the Tarascan-speaking peoples had a fairly high level of identification with Mexico and the culture region had been steadily shrinking in size since at least the mid-18th century. Within the course of a generation, entire communities on the fringes of the enclavement had given up their identification with "Tarasco" and their use of the Precolumbian language. These communities stopped being Indian in self-identification, although the transition was not necessarily marked by any immediate changes in such physical manifestations of culture as dress or house-type (West 1948; this topic was discussed in two symposia on the Tarascans held at the 1974 and 1975 annual meetings of the American Anthropological Association).

It has been suggested that the Tarascans count as Indians only in terms of language (Beals 1946, 1953b; Foster 1948). Language may well provide the key to the initial enclavement. The 16th-century missionaries introduced the Latin alphabet and trained selected persons for literacy—but not in Spanish. Tarascan was the written language of the Sierra from the mid-16th century until the region was placed in the hands of the secular clergy in the 18th century. At the Augustinian monastery in Zirosto, long the religious center of the Sierra, the monks kept their records in Tarascan, and the literate elite of some villages recorded historical accounts in Tarascan well into the 19th century. In some places it was not unusual for Spanish-speaking families, who slowly filtered into the region borderlands and larger towns, to gain literacy in Tarascan so as to have access to the old documents. Thus, possibly in contrast to the situation elsewhere in Mexico, the Tarascan linguistic enclavement was firmly rooted in a written language. Until the 20th century, of course, most people of the region were illiterate and it is probable that by the late 19th century most of those who could read Tarascan were also competent in Spanish.

In the early 20th century, the Sierra Tarasca was a land of largely self-sufficient agriculturalists. The farmers lived in villages spaced a few miles apart in the valleys. Each village jealously protected its lands and even though most valley croplands were by then privately owned, custom decreed that they could not be sold to outsiders without consent of the council of village elders. Most villages also had forests and pastures that were in communal ownership. Tarascan was the predominant language of household and street, although in some communities an ever increasing number of people were using Spanish on a daily basis. Mule strings tied the Sierra with other places and some of the fringe villages were homes of *arrieros,* the mule-string owners and drivers. Others were key points in the mule-borne traffic of goods between highland and lowland. Bilingualism was prevalent in both the arriero and the trade-center towns. The ability to speak both Spanish and Tarascan provided an economic advantage in such places, a point not lost on entrepreneurs regardless of what language they grew up speaking around the family hearth. Indeed, the contemporary isolation of many of the old cultural borderland communities is relatively new, because it was created by the 20th century development of modern transportation routes. However, many communities of the Sierra were cultural microcosms in the late 19th century. Each village had its own distinct traditions and tended to be endogamous. Intervillage contact took place at market centers in the lower-elevation Hispanic towns and during the fiesta rounds when village after village celebrated the special day of its patron saint. Except for the most physically or culturally isolated villages, fiesta celebrations were intervillage affairs. The bands were from other communities, as were many of the celebrants. Marked by wild music, ceremonial dances (Fig. 7.1), religious enthusiasm, and often general intoxication, the round of fiestas highlighted the steady grind of the work year.

The traditional mayordomia system for sponsoring fiestas functioned as an economic leveling device. Those who worked hard and saved, or were lucky, were expected to share their good fortune with the entire community by paying fiesta costs. Thus stripped of their economic gains, they were rewarded with local power and a place in the council of elders who decided the use of communal resources. A young man worked his way up in the system by first providing his physical strength for the dances and some of his economic resources for the costumes. Later on he was honored by being allowed to pay for a band from another village or for a similar contribution. Ultimately, he hoped to be chosen as the mayordomo for the greatest fiesta of the year, and for that honor and the privileges it would bring in community decision-making, he gave his life-savings to meet the costs (Wolf 1959; Foster 1967). The mayordomia system instilled values of hard work and saving, and in villages of

Figure 7.1. San Juan fiesta dancers. (Photograph by Mary Lee Nolan.)

limited resources ensured that no single family would get ahead at the expense of others. It did not allow, however, for capital accumulation and for the kind of economic growth based on the input of local funds. By the mid-20th century, the socioeconomic balancing strategy that maintained steady-state exploitation of limited resources was considered a block to progress by the planners of the larger society. Thus, the mayordomia system introduced by Don Vasco de Quiroga gradually diminished. The fiestas, however, survived, paid for by a kind of "United Fund" campaign that still had overtones of the old system. Those who were better off were expected to make a greater contribution.

Villages of the Ancestors

The men and women who established the family lines considered in this study were born between about 1870 and 1900. One woman, born and raised in the relatively large town of Paracho, married a man from the conservative Tarascan village of Angahuan and moved to her husband's community in about 1900. The rest of the 52 ancestors were born in five small communities clustered in interlocking valleys near the northern foot of the Cerros de Tancitaro, about 25 kilometers from the provincial city of Uruapan. San Juan Parangaricutiro was the largest of the five communities, and the head town of the municipio, or administration district, of the same name. Included in San Juan's political jurisdiction were the communities of Parícutin, Angahuan, and Zirosto. Nearby Zacan was part of the administrative unit centered in the mestizo valley town of Los Reyes, but otherwise was linked to the socioeconomic network centered on San Juan.

In the days when the ancestors were young, the five villages were much alike in material culture and all were laid out on the grid pattern introduced by the Spanish missionaries of the 16th century. Social intercourse centered on the dusty plaza in front of the church. Homes surrounding the plaza tended to be of stone and adobe, but the house lots beyond contained two wooden structures. One, the *troje,* was a ceremonial structure that contained images of saints and other prized family possessions. It was passed on in the male line and because it consisted of huge notched planks, it could be removed from one site and reassembled on another like so many "Lincoln logs." The second wooden structure was the kitchen. Although not usually so well built, it was the heart of the home where the family cooked, ate, and slept around the warmth of the low stone hearth.

Most of the ancestors grew up speaking Tarascan as a household language, and even those who learned Spanish as children were able to speak the Indian language. Some of the bilinguals from San Juan and Zirosto were literate in both Spanish and Tarascan. All of the ancestral males either owned land or had rights to the use of communal lands, and 23 made their living as farmers on small plots. The other three ancestral males were the sons of a rich Zirosto mule-string owner who had invested in land during the 19th century. Each of these men had holdings of more than 1,000 acres that were worked by tenants while they engaged in mercantile activities. They were, of course, much wealthier than the other ancestors.

Eight of the ancestral couples were from San Juan, and they produced 114 of the 292 descendants (Table 7.1). San Juan was the largest and most important of the five villages. In addition to being a local political center, it was an important regional pilgrimage destination. Spanish-speaking mestizos had been incorporated into the community during the 18th century, and by the 1940s it was described as a community that contained two, rather sharply defined ethnic groups: a Spanish-speaking majority and a large Tarascan-speaking minority. The Tarascan-speakers apparently held near equal access to the resource base, possibly because they were more inclined to rise in the mayordomia system of sponsoring fiestas, thus gaining decision-making power over use of communal lands. The mestizos had the counter advantage of closer ties to the larger society through outmarrying kinship networks and other contacts. Old mestizo families are more or less equally represented with Tarascan-oriented kinship networks in the San Juan genealogies.

The other predominantly mestizo town was Zirosto. The community was a monastic center from the mid-16th century until 1775. Its people, therefore, were in close contact with the Augustinian friars who provided religious administration for the region during much of the colonial period. Even after the region came under the jurisdiction of the secular clergy, the old monastery complex served as a retreat for young men studying for the priesthood at Zamora, a valley town that had become the seat of the bishop.

Although Tarascan remained the predominant community language until the second decade of the 20th century, Zirosto's socioeconomic structure by then was far more like that of the mestizo valley towns than like that of the highland Indian villages. By the early 19th century, Zirosto had become a center of commerce and finance due to the growth of mule-driving and mule-string ownership as local occupations. The wealth from trade tended to accumulate in the hands of a few families who acquired control of large portions of the surrounding lands and most of the local business establishments. For a time, these wealthy families sponsored fiestas in keeping with tradition, but by the 1930s the mayordomia system was abandoned and more modest fiestas were paid for largely from the resources of the entire community. By the early 1940s, Zirosto was in economic decline as a growing network of railroads and paved highways undercut profits from mule-driving. Some descendants of the wealthy families relocated in cities during the early 20th century. Others remained in the community where

Table 7.1. Ancestral Couples and Descendants by Town of Origin

Town of Origin	Number of Ancestral Couples	Number of Adult Descendants	Percentage of Sample
Angahuan	3	24	8
Parícutin-Calzontzin	4	25	9
San Juan	8	114	39
Zacan	1	42	14
Zirosto	10	87	30
	26	292	100

they engaged in trade and managed their extensive landholdings. As the generations passed, the amount of land available to each descendant decreased and the differences between the rich and the poor may have been narrowing before the volcano erupted. Three of the Zirosto ancestors were direct male descendants of one of the town's wealthy 19th-century mule-string owners. Two came from very poor families with Tarascan surnames, and the other five occupied middle positions in the Zirosto socioeconomic structure.

Four ancestral couples originated in Parícutin. This village was small and isolated from outside contact other than with neighboring communities, the closest of which was the politically dominant San Juan. Although almost entirely Tarascan in language and custom, Parícutin people had indicated an interest in new opportunities by the 1930s when the first school teachers arrived. Village men became involved in an agrarian movement sponsored by the Mexican government to encourage peasants to win back land from large private holdings in haciendas. However, there were no haciendas within the grasp of Parícutin's farmers, so the agrarian movement tended to pit them against other villagers. The result was a series of land wars with San Juan.

Zacan, like Parícutin, was small and physically isolated. Its people, however, had a tradition of going elsewhere to work for a time, then returning to the village. Men from Zacan were employed in the Guanajanto mines as early as the 18th century, and during the early 20th century several worked in the United States. By the late 1930s, Spanish was replacing Tarascan as the local language, and, because of the influence of the locally born head of the elementary school and a visiting priest, the villagers decided to give up the mayordomia system in 1941. It was agreed that the money could be better spent in providing education for the children (Figs. 7.2, 7.3). The one large kinship network I recorded in Zacan was founded by a Tarascan-speaking couple in the early 1900s. It displayed a range of residential and occupational variation that seemed reasonably representative for this educationally oriented community.

Information on three family lines was collected in Angahuan, located a few miles from Zacan in the volcanic zone. It was noted by anthropologists as a closed, highly conservative, Tarascan community before the Parícutin eruptions, and the village had maintained the same kind of reputation through

Figure 7.2. Elementary school graduation in Zacan, 1971. (Photograph by Mary Lee Nolan.)

Figure 7.3. Secondary school graduation in Zacan, 1971. (Photograph by Mary Lee Nolan.)

1971 in spite of a tourist influx that began in about 1944. In contrast with the other communities, it was not easy to obtain extensive genealogical information in Angahuan because it was difficult to gain sufficient access to people on a personal basis except through the mediation of the numerous tourist guides, whose function was as much to protect the local people from outsiders as to gain income from tourism. As a consequence, two of the three genealogies collected in this highly endogamous community derived from interviews with women who had married into the community more than fifty years earlier. One was known as "the old lady from San Juan" and the other was the "old lady from Paracho." Although both had produced a share of the town's current inhabitants, they were atypical of Angahuan women of their generation in that they were not born locally and the woman from Paracho was fluent in Spanish. Therefore, the family lines from Angahuan may reflect community norms to a lesser degree than those from the other villages affected by the Parícutin eruptions.

Volcanic Eruption in the Mid-20th Century

The 26 ancestral couples had a total of 91 children who lived to adulthood. Most of this next generation was born between 1900 and 1934, although differences in the ages of the ancestral couples and long child-bearing spans make this a rough estimate. Nearly all of the ancestors and their children were living in the five villages in 1943, when a new volcano suddenly appeared in the cornfield of a Parícutin farmer.

The economic basis of village life was severely disrupted as a result of the nine-year eruption. Subsistence farming was not possible on most of the lands of Angahuan, Zirosto, and Zacan until at least seven years after the eruptions began. Some ash-covered lands remain infertile. Lava covered the San Juan and Parícutin townsites and most of the best agricultural lands. In 1943, the people of Parícutin village were resettled at Caltzontzin, a former hacienda near Uruapan. Men of San Juan chose a new townsite about 14 kilometers east of Uruapan and the community relocated there in 1944 when lava covered the old town. Zirosto fragmented into three communities. Some people refused to leave the original townsite despite extremely heavy ash fall. Other Zirosto families migrated to the refugee settlement of Miguel Silva nearly 100 kilometers away at a lower elevation. A few stayed there, but the majority returned to the highland community. Later on, more than half of those remaining in Zirosto resettled at Rancho Baranca Seca near the old town. Today the original town is known as Old Zirosto while Rancho Baranca Seca is called New Zirosto. The Miguel Silva community contains the remaining fragment of the original Zirosto community.

The people of Angahuan stayed in place. Few left the community even on a temporary basis. During the eruption period they survived by salvaging community forests and guiding tourists and scientists to the volcano. Zacan also survived in place, but many families lived elsewhere in Mexico during the worst years of the eruptions.

In addition to government aid in resettlement, all able-bodied men from all of these towns were given preference as contract laborers in the United States under the terms of the World War II bracero program. Special attention was drawn to the educational needs of these villagers whose lives had been so suddenly disrupted, and a more than usual number of scholarships were provided for young people during and immediately after the eruption period. Thus, the volcanic eruptions precipitated greatly increased contacts between the people and the world beyond the village.

Villages of the Grandchildren

Most of the ancestors' grandchildren were born after 1935, and 190 of them had reached adulthood by 1971. The remainder were still children and teenagers living with their parents. Only 11 great-grandchildren were among the adult descendants, and of these, 8 were students not yet fully established as self-supporting. Many of the children and grandchildren did not live in the ancestors' home communities, but the bonds of kinship generally kept them in contact with the villagers.

Meanwhile, life in the original villages and relocation settlements had changed substantially from what it was when the ancestors were young. All communities except Old Zirosto had electricity, pure water systems, six or more grades of local schooling, post offices, and direct access to bus transportation. Although the majority of local men still made a living as farmers, there was more occupational diversity than had existed in the past in all communities but the fragments of Zirosto. Only New San Juan had preserved the mayordomia system and then only for one fiesta. In this large town, modest wealth or political influence provided other routes to local status. Use of the Tarascan language was declining in all towns other than the highly conservative Angahuan community, and even there most male inhabitants were bilinguals. The idea that advanced education for the young was an important means for adjusting to modern conditions had taken strong root in two communities. In Caltzontzin-Parícutin, the thrust toward education remained a predominantly family matter implemented by proximity to Uruapan schools. In Zacan, located in the volcanic zone outside of commuting distance for schooling beyond the local sixth grade, education of children became a status symbol at the community level much as sponsoring fiestas had been a route to local status in the past. This small, isolated community had produced 88 offspring with professional degrees between 1930 and 1971 for the record achievement of all the towns studied in terms of both population percentages and absolute numbers.

Only Angahuan could be considered part of a Sierra Tarascan ethnic enclavement in 1971, although the social and economic ties of this linguistic Tarascan community were more pervasive with linguistically Hispanic communities than with most other conservative Tarascan communities. Tourism, which first bloomed in Angahuan during the eruption period, was flowering in the 1970s, a period during which Angahuan's cultural ethnicity was beginning to prove as great an attraction for visitors as the chance to inspect the aftermath of eruption. People of Angahuan constantly referred to themselves as the last of the "pure" Tarascans, but it seemed likely that most such statements were made at least as much to promote tourism as to express ethnic identity and avoid disenclavement.

ANALYSIS OF FAMILY LINES

There was considerable variation among the ancestral couples in terms of wealth, access to resources, and cultural-linguistic orientations. None, however, were atypical for the region in the early 20th century. All men in the ancestral generation either owned land or had rights to village lands. Twenty-three were farmers and resin-gatherers before the volcanic disruption, and although some worked at other jobs during the eruption period, they remained agriculturalists throughout their lives. The other three, all from Zirosto, owned extensive amounts of land and were merchants and landlords before the eruptions.

All male ancestors were descended from families that had lived in the same community for generations. Of the 26 wives, 22 were from their husbands' communities; the other 4 women were born in nearby towns and villages and had settled in their husbands' villages upon marriage. All of the ancestral couples could speak Tarascan, although only 12 used the language for household communication throughout their lives.

The linguistic orientations of the descendants were not fully ascertained, but many of the children and an even larger proportion of the grandchildren had little command of the Indian language. Many of the descendants could not speak or understand Tarascan, and it is doubtful that any of the ancestors' grandchildren were literate in Tarascan, with the possible exception of some urbanites who liked to compose songs and poems in the traditional language. The descendants were widely scattered geographically and made their livings in a variety of occupations.

Location of the Descendants

Sixty-two percent of the descendants lived in the home town or in a refugee settlement founded by members of the ancestral community (Table 7.2). A few lived in other Michoacán villages and ranchos, and six percent lived in Michoacán towns with populations ranging from 5,000 to 50,000. Many of the town dwellers lived in Paracho and were descended from the early 19th century marriage between an Angahuan farmer and a Paracho woman.

Of the descendants, 28 percent were urban dwellers living in Mexican and United States cities of more than 50,000 people; 35 of the urbanites were in the Michoacán cities of Uruapan and Morelia, and 29 were in other Mexican cities including Mexico City, Tijuana, Puebla, Guadalajara, Leon, Jalapa, and Ciudad Victoria. The 17 descendants who lived in California were all in the San Diego and Los Angeles areas.

When residential patterns are considered by generation, the trend toward exodus from the villages becomes more apparent (Table 7.3). In spite of the disruption of their lives created by the Parícutin eruption, all but one of the ancestors was living, or had died, in the community of birth or marriage. A vast majority of the numerous great-grandchildren were still living with their parents and were not counted as adult descendants. Of those who were married, self-supporting, or in school beyond the primary level, fewer than 10 percent were in the home communities. It was possible that some of the students would return home but the majority would go elsewhere due to lack of opportunities for the well-educated in most of the villages. A trend toward urban residence is also apparent; 18 percent of the children lived in cities compared with nearly 30 percent of the grandchildren.

Table 7.2. Residence of Descendants

Town of Ancestral Origin	Percentage of Descendants				
	Remaining in Ancestral Town	Residing in Mexico, by Town Population			Residing in the United States
		Below 5,000	5,000–50,000	Over 50,000	
San Juan (N = 114)	75[a]	4	2	16	4
Parícutin (N = 25)	48[b]	12	4	36	0
Angahuan (N = 24)	71	0	25[c]	4	0
Zirosto[d] (N = 87)	60	2	7	17	14
Zacan (N = 42)	36	10	2	50	2
All Towns	62	4	6	22	6

a. In new location, San Juan Nuevo Parangaricutiro.
b. In new location, Caltzontzin.
c. Descendants of Paracho woman who married an Angahuan man. All in Paracho.
d. Includes those in Old Zirosto, nearby New Zirosto (Rancho Baranca Seca), and in the refugee settlement, Miguel Silva.

Table 7.3. Location by Generation

Location	Percentage of			
	Ancestors (N = 26)	Children of Ancestors (N = 91)	Adult Grand-children (N = 188)	Adult Great-Grand-children (N = 11)
Home Town	96	79	57	9
Mexico, town less than 5,000	0	1	6	9
Mexico, town 5,000–50,000	0	2	7	0
Mexico, city over 50,000	0	9	25	82
United States	4	9	5	0

Table 7.4. Occupations of Adult Descendants

Occupation	Number	Percentage*
Housewife	89	0.30
Farming and resin collecting	71	0.24
Small-scale commerce or industry without land	18	0.06
Secondary, preparatory, or normal school student	18	0.06
Unskilled labor (mostly in the local area)	15	0.05
Skilled blue-collar work	12	0.04
Traditional crafts and market vending	11	0.04
Primary school teaching	10	0.03
University or normal superior student	9	0.03
White-collar work	9	0.03
Small-scale commerce or industry with land	8	0.03
Professionals other than teachers with college or university degrees	7	0.02
Priest or female religious worker	7	0.02
Secondary, preparatory, or normal school teaching	6	0.02
Unskilled labor, mostly migrant labor in the United States	3	0.01

*Percentages do not total 1.00 due to rounding.

Table 7.5. Occupation Groups of Adult Descendants*

Occupation Group	Number	Percent of Total
Farmers	123	42
Unskilled Laborers	35	12
Merchants	38	13
Skilled Workers	34	12
Professionals	33	11
Students	27	9

*Housewives and other female descendants primarily dependent on husbands' income are categorized by husbands' occupations. In this and subsequent tables related to occupation, the number of offspring totals 290 rather than 292 because of lack of data concerning husbands' occupations in the cases of two female descendants.

Descendant Occupations

The range of occupations found among the descendants of these farmers and village merchants was extremely varied (Table 7.4) and has been consolidated into occupational categories in Table 7.5. Eighty-nine females were classified as full-time housewives and categorized by their husbands' occupations, as were most of the other women who worked part-time in crafts and market vending but who were primarily dependent on their husbands for financial support. Some of the men followed in the ancestral footsteps as farmers, resin-gatherers, and merchants. Others made a living primarily from traditional crafts and market vending, and a few were owner-operators of backyard industries such as woodworking shops and brickyards. A fairly small group of unskilled laborers without access to land had emerged, many of whom either migrated periodically to other parts of Mexico and the United States or went for long periods without work. Among the skilled blue-collar workers were bricklayers, auto mechanics, electricians, and factory workers. These people were as well off financially as many of the white-collar workers who included secretaries, bank clerks, shop clerks, a beautician, and a radio announcer. A fairly substantial number of the descendants were either schoolteachers or married to schoolteachers at the primary, secondary, and normal school levels. Two taught at the college level in Normal Superior schools that prepare Mexican teachers for jobs above the primary level. One was a superintendent of schools in a middle-sized Mexican town. Seven descendants were either priests or female religious workers. The priests had long years of training behind them and although the female religious workers were not so well educated, they worked primarily as parochial schoolteachers or nurses. There were in addition seven university-educated professionals in a variety of fields, including a Mexico City banker with a University of Mexico degree in economics, a captain in the Mexican forestry service, a land-use planner trained as a geographer, a veterinarian, two engineers, and a lawyer. It was difficult to classify the professional musician whose face graces numerous Mexican record albums, but because he had relatively little formal education he was included in the category with blue- and white-collar workers. Married female schoolteachers and other descendant women who were gainfully employed outside the home were classified according to their own occupations.

Finally, there were the students. It was necessary to leave five of the seven villages in order to attend school beyond the primary level, so all descendants at the secondary school level and beyond were considered students. Many of the students at lower levels hoped to attend universities. (Occupational totals in the following tables number 290 rather than 292 because no information was available on the occupations of the husbands of two California housewives.)

Occupation and Place of Residence

As should be expected, there was a relationship between location and occupation (Table 7.6). The vast majority of farmers lived in the communities of ancestral origin. Their land base included both inherited lands and rights to use of land controlled by village councils or granted to refugee settlers in ejido. Families supported from farming in other communities represent female descendants who married farmers from neighboring villages. There were no cases of descendants acquiring farm lands elsewhere except through marriage, unless the Tijuana upholsterer who sold tomatoes from his acre house lot is taken as an exception to the rule.

Nearly 70 percent of the merchants, small-scale industrialists, and unskilled laborers also lived in the ancestral communities. In the first generation removed from the ancestors, more

Table 7.6. Occupation of Descendants by Residence

Descendant's Occupation	Percentage Living				
	In Home Town	Elsewhere in Mexico, by Town Population			In the United States
		Below 5,000	5,000–50,000	Over 50,000	
Farmers (N = 123)	96	2	2	0	0
Unskilled laborers (N = 35)	69	0	0	17	14
Merchants (N = 38)	68	3	3	24	3
Skilled workers (N = 34)	18	3	3	50	26
Professionals (N = 33)	9	24	21	46	0
Students (N = 27)	22	0	15	63	0

than half of the merchants also owned or had rights to farm land. In the grandchild generation, however, only two of the merchants supplemented their incomes with farming.

The unskilled laborers were largely a pathetic group of often unemployed men whose families were among the poorest of the poor. A few of the younger workers who left their families at home while they sought work elsewhere in Mexico or the United States apparently took responsibility for their wives and children and were attempting to save money to buy land or shops. This fits the eruption period and postvolcanic village patterns of gaining capital to get started through migrant labor. However, most of the unskilled laborers either stayed home and were unemployed most of the time or went elsewhere and "forgot" to send money home to wives and children who were being marginally maintained by the kinship networks. The majority of unskilled laborers came from one San Juan family, but 11 other kinship networks, including some of those that produced the highest percentages of professionals, had to cope with the son who never amounted to anything or the daughter who married a man who could not or would not support her and the children. Possibly many of these families were in the home villages because they could not survive without the aid of kinsmen.

In contrast to farmers, merchants, and unskilled laborers, only 18 percent of the blue- and white-collar workers lived in the communities of ancestral origin. Many of those who did either commuted to jobs in Uruapan or spent most of their time away from home. There simply were not many jobs of this kind in the villages, and some men decided it was better to have their wives and children stay home rather than uproot them in a move to the cities. Half of the family lines included people in this occupational category.

Fewer than 10 percent of the professionals were residing in the home communities, and all of these were local school teachers. None of the university-educated professionals lived in the ancestral villages, although most made frequent visits. Of the 26 family lines, 13 had produced professionals, and 6 included both professionals and blue- and white-collar workers. Out of 26 family lines, 20 included kinsmen with essentially middle class occupations, most of whom lived in cities or large towns.

All of the students were from family lines that also included blue- and white-collar workers, professionals, or both. In the cases of two extremely conservative families, one from Angahuan and the other from Zirosto, all descendants made a living from the land. The other four families with no obvious ties to an urban middle class included merchants and backyard industrialists, and only one of these four also included an unskilled laborer. There were no examples of family lines composed only of farmers and unskilled laborers, although such kinship networks surely exist in the Sierra Tarasca.

Change in Occupations Through Time

Change in occupation through the generations was even more dramatic than change in place of residence (Table 7.7). All of the ancestors either owned or had access to land; 88 percent made their primary living as farmers and the rest were land-owning Zirosto merchants. Of their children, 65 percent were farmers or married to farmers, but only 34 percent of the grandchildren lived from the land. Even as the percentage of farmers decreased, the actual number of families living off the land increased.

In the ancestral generation, 23 couples were primarily dependent on land for subsistence. In the generation of the children, 59 offspring and their spouses lived off the land, a number that rose to 64 adult offspring and spouses (if married) in the grandchild generation. Many of the grandchildren who had not yet reached adulthood had no apparent career plans other than farming. It was impossible to calculate the number of great-grandchildren who intended to be farmers. The adult grandchildren and their spouses had already produced an estimated 500 to 600 offspring and more were being born every year.

The amount of land available to farmers from these communities was probably not much greater than in the early 20th century. Many of the original holdings damaged by volcanic ash in the mid-20th century were back in production, but a sizable acreage buried under lava and deep ash may remain agriculturally useless for centuries. Some of this loss was offset by ejido grants to the founding members of the refugee communities and by purchases of land from profits made through migrant labor in the United States and elsewhere. By the 1970s, however, there were virtually no opportunities to acquire more land in the areas around the villages except through purchase from other farmers. Access to land varied from family to family. Some of the families that were land poor before the volcano received more in ejido grants than they lost to the eruptions. Others, especially from Zirosto, bought damaged lands at low prices from richer families who left the region, and they were reaping rewards as fertility slowly returned. Still other families, especially from the New San Juan that was not originally awarded an ejido, lost more than they gained and several of the

Table 7.7. Occupation by Generation

Occupation	Ancestral Couples (N = 26) %	(No.)	Children of Ancestors (N = 91) %	(No.)	Adult Grandchildren (N = 188) %	(No.)	Adult Great-Grandchildren (N = 11) %	(No.)
Farmers	88	(23)	65	(59)	34	(64)		(0)
Unskilled laborers		(0)	11	(10)	13	(25)		(0)
Merchants	12	(3)	17	(15)	12	(23)		(0)
Skilled workers		(0)	6	(5)	15	(29)		(0)
Professionals		(0)	2	(2)	15	(28)	27	(3)
Students		(0)		(0)	6	(19)	73	(8)

rich Zirosto families sold their lands at a low price to get established elsewhere.

Descendants of the same ancestors made different choices in the face of volcanic crisis, and thus affected the opportunities that would be available to their children. For example, one descendant of a land-rich Zirosto ancestor dramatically burned the deeds of title of his land and moved to California. His sister and her husband also left for California, but prudently kept the deeds to their Zirosto holdings. The latter couple worked as grape pickers, but paid their taxes and within a few years were renting out their Mexican acreage as pasture. From grape picking, this family turned to contracting Mexican labor for California vineyards, using the profits to buy cheap, not yet fully productive, lands in the Zirosto area. In about 1960, they began planting their extensive holdings in cold-tolerate avocado trees developed to withstand the California climate, but equally suitable for the relatively high elevation lands in the Sierra Tarasca. Avocados thrived in lands still marginal for corn because of the droughty nature of the top surface of ash and the wind-whipped sand damage of the dry spring months. By 1971, this couple was building a summer vacation home near New Zirosto and contemplating a comfortable retirement. It was said that the brother who burned his deeds sometimes got very depressed.

Most family lines, of course, had never controlled anything comparable to the land base of the three richest Zirosto ancestors. A late 1960s agricultural census in New San Juan provides a better overall view of land distribution in these villages than the rich Zirosto examples. In San Juan, only 55 percent of the household heads owned or controlled any farm land in addition to their house lots (if they had house lots). Of the local landowners, more than half held 2 ha or less. The land baron of this community, which had reached a population of nearly 5,000 in 1970, owned 80 ha of cropland and 17 head of livestock. The largest San Juan landowner from whom a genealogy was collected held fewer than 20 ha.

A finite amount of land cannot be infinitely subdivided and still provide even a marginal living, whether at the level of the village or the family. Even the most extensive ancestral holdings did not allow all descendants to become farmers except at the price of a precipitous decline into peasantry. The consequences of land-base fragmentation were especially apparent in the situation of a descendant family with 13 children ranging from 1 to 20 years of age. The father of this Zirosto family owned 80 ha inherited from his father. He had married a landless woman, so there were no resources from her side of the family. None of the 10 sons or 3 daughters were being educated beyond elementary levels and those who had left school had no apparent plans other than farming their father's lands or, in the case of daughters, marrying men of the vicinity. Yet, when the father's lands are eventually subdivided, each child may expect to receive little more than 6 ha. Some of this land is at high elevations and not suited for much but forest and pasture. If the father's estate should be equally divided between the 13 children, and if each marries a landless spouse and has 13 children, the next generation will be reduced to roughly an acre apiece. One more such subdivision would provide each descendant with about enough dirt for a flowerpot. Family history and old cadastral maps on file in Morelia indicate that the father of the man who sired this family owned 560 ha. This holding was equally subdivided among 7 descendants. The ancestor's father is said to have owned 5 square leagues of land, an indefinite figure when transmitted orally, but probably more than was made available to any of the refugee communities in ejido. In this case, the transition from land wealth to land poverty has required only three generations. Continued subdivision of a limited resource base, no matter how extensive to begin with, is not, in the case of this family, a hypothetical abstraction.

Considering the rate of population growth that has marked most of these communities over the past few decades, it has been inevitable that the percentage of farm-supported families would decline with the generations. A critical question is what happens to the descendants of farmers when the number of offspring outstrip the carrying capacity of the agricultural resource base? If the communities are growing economically in an expanding society, there is room for more merchants, craftsmen, and small-scale industrialists at home. Only in New San Juan, however, was that kind of growth of important magnitude. None of the three fragments of the Zirosto community could support the variety of goods and services that had been present in the mother community before the volcanic eruption. Caltzontzin and Angahuan were expanding slightly in terms of local mercantile opportunities, but Zacan was more or less stationary. The percentage of families supported from small-scale commerce and backyard industry showed relatively little fluctuation through the generations. The major difference was that all of the merchant ancestors owned land as did the majority of the merchant and small-scale industrialist children. Most of the grandchildren in that occupational category had nothing other than their shops or backyard industries for support.

The numbers of unskilled laborers with no access to land increased through the generations, but not so much as might have been anticipated. Only 11 percent of the children and 13 percent of the grandchildren were landless laborers. In contrast, 8 percent of the children and 30 percent of the grandchildren had found an alternative to traditional village livelihood by becoming white-collar workers, skilled blue-collar workers, teachers, and university-educated professionals. An additional 6 percent of the grandchildren were students and most of these would launch middle class urban careers. All of the great-grandchildren counted as adults were either professionals or students, although it was certain that as this generation came of age it would include people supported by a great variety of occupations.

The trend of generational change in these families may be simplified in two ways. One breakdown segregates descendants into middle class versus popular class occupations as suggested by Miller (1973) on the basis of González Cosio's (1961) classification scheme (Table 7.8). The other group places farmers and merchants into a "traditional" occupational category as compared with a "modern" occupational niche (Table 7.9). Rich farmers may be considered "middle class" in the village context, as are most merchants. Therefore, the latter scheme may be a more reasonable means of ordering the data. The generational trend toward modern occupations with middle class status is evident. As previously pointed out, people with relatively rewarding modern occupations tend to be in the cities, and the small component of unskilled laborers is based primarily in the villages. Obviously for these families, migration to the cities has not resulted in a hand-to-mouth existence as part of an urban "culture of poverty." There is no reason to suspect that the achievements of urban cousins, nephews, or even grandchildren were overemphasized. All genealogies were collected from villagers, and there was a certain propensity to argue that urban kinsmen were not really doing all *that* well comparatively, and that city life had made some kinsmen "go wrong."

ANCESTRAL ETHNICITY AND DESCENDANT OCCUPATIONS

When opportunity or necessity for adjustments to a modernizing larger society affects previously isolated villagers of various ethnic orientations, is one ethnic group likely to benefit more than another? This study cannot provide a general answer to such a critical question, but it does suggest that ethnic Tarascanness as of the early 20th century was not highly limiting. Some aspects of the traditional Tarascan orientation may even have conferred a special advantage when self-sacrifice on the part of parents was required to ensure educational opportunities for children.

Table 7.8. Generational Change in Terms of Cosio's Socioeconomic Categories

Occupational Classification	Percentage of		
	Ancestors (N = 26)	Children of Ancestors (N = 91)	Adult Grandchildren (N = 188)
Popular Class	88	76	45
Middle Class	12	24	53

Reference: González Cosio 1961.

Table 7.9. Traditional and Modern Occupations by Generation

Occupational Classification	Percentage of		
	Ancestors (N = 26)	Children of Ancestors (N = 91)	Adult Grandchildren (N = 188)
Traditional (Farmers and merchants)	100	81	47
Modern: Popular (Unskilled laborers)	0	11	13
Modern: Middle Class (Skilled workers, professionals, and students)	0	8	40

Twelve ancestral couples spoke Tarascan as their primary language on a lifelong basis, although most of the men and some of the women could speak Spanish. Language may not be the most adequate measure of ethnic orientation, but it is presumed that these couples were oriented toward tradition to a greater extent than the others. They produced 55 percent of the descendants. Eight couples used Spanish as a household language while their children were growing up and apparently identified more with rural mestizo culture than with a Tarascan ethos. These bilingual mestizos produced 30 percent of the descendants.

The other six couples were classified as transitionals. Three of these couples adopted Spanish as a household language during the period when they were raising their children. In at least one such case, the motive was to rear families with a good command of Spanish. The other three couples represented ethnically mixed marriages. In one case a Zirosto man from one of the rich Spanish-speaking families married a local girl who spoke only Tarascan at the time of marriage. Although she eventually learned some Spanish, it was recalled that she preferred to speak Tarascan in her old age. In another case a Tarascan speaker from Parícutin married a girl from San Juan who was literate in Spanish. In the third case, a man from conservative Angahuan brought a Spanish-speaking girl from Paracho into his community. The linguistic orientations of this couple's descendants were particularly interesting. One of the two daughters married an Angahuan man and her children were raised as linguistic Tarascans. The other married a man from her mother's home town, and her children and grandchildren, raised in Paracho, never learned the Indian language. Several either became schoolteachers or married schoolteachers and displayed strong middle class orientations. Nevertheless, they frequently visited their grandmother, aunt, and cousins in Angahuan. Fifteen percent of the descendants came from six transitional couples.

The ethnic Tarascans out-reproduced the mestizos and transitionals. The average number of children and adult grandchildren descended from these couples was 13.4 persons. The mestizo couples were next with an average of 10.8 adult descendants each. The transitionals had an average of 7.2 descendants each or only slightly more than half as many descendants as the Tarascans. Yet although, or perhaps because, they produced fewer descendants, their children and grandchildren on the average had done remarkably well in socioeconomic terms.

The highest percentages of merchants, teachers, other professionals, and students came from the six transitional family lines, as did the lowest percentage of farm-supported families (Table 7.10). Far fewer of the descendants of these ancestors were living in the community of male ancestral origin than was the case with descendants of the Tarascans and mestizos. This was partially a result of descendant location in a female ancestor's home community, but also reflected occupational choices. It is tempting to speculate that the transitional couples were more flexible in their abilities to cope with physical, environmental, and social change than in general were ancestors in either of the other categories. Had they not been adaptive people to begin with, they probably would not have made the early 20th-century decisions that led to mixed marriages or adoption of Spanish as a household language in young adulthood.

Descendants of the mestizo ancestors had not faired as well as might have been expected considering that two were extremely rich for the region before the volcanic eruption, and that all had the advantage of fluency in Spanish. These couples had produced the largest number of merchants and the highest percentage of blue- and white-collar workers. However, less emphasis was placed on advanced education for offspring than was the case with the other two groups. Interestingly, the only one of the three rich Zirosto ancestors whose progeny included professionals was the one whose wife came from a Tarascan-speaking family.

Nearly as high a proportion of descendants of the mestizo couples was in full-time farming as was found among descendants of the ethnic Tarascans, partially due to the fact that the mestizo ancestors, in general, tended to own more land initially. Therefore, in spite of volcanic devastation and reduction of holdings through the generations, the mestizos of the early 20th century controlled a resource base large enough to allow many of their sons to become farmers or to tempt other farmers to marry their daughters.

The ethnic Tarascans had produced about the same proportion of farm families as the mestizos and the highest number and percentage of landless, unskilled, laborers. They also, however, had produced higher percentages of teachers, other professionals, and students than the mestizos. In terms of actual numbers, the more numerous and biologically fruitful Tarascans accounted for the most descendants in all occupational

Table 7.10. Ancestor Ethnicity and Descendant Occupations

Descendants' Occupations	Descendants of					
	Tarascan-speaking Ancestors (N = 161)		Transitional Ancestors (N = 43)		Mestizo-oriented Ancestors, Spanish-speaking (N = 86)	
	%	(No.)	%	(No.)	%	(No.)
Farmers	45	(72)	30	(13)	44	(38)
Unskilled laborers	16	(26)	7	(3)	7	(6)
Merchants	7	(11)	26	(11)	19	(16)
Skilled workers	10	(16)	7	(3)	17	(15)
Professionals	12	(20)	16	(7)	7	(6)
Students	10	(16)	14	(6)	6	(5)

Table 7.11. Socioeconomic Status of Parents and Offspring

Occupation Class of Offspring	Occupation Class of Parents			
	Popular Class[a] (N = 212 Offspring)		Middle Class[b] (N = 78 Offspring)	
	%	(No.)	%	(No.)
Popular Class	64	(136)	28	(22)
Middle Class	36	(76)	72	(56)

a. Popular class includes farmers and unskilled laborers.
b. Middle class includes merchants, skilled workers, professionals, and students.

categories other than merchants. It can be concluded that ancestral ethnic Tarascanness as indicated by language was not a major stumbling block in the course of upward socioeconomic mobility for the subsequent generations.

It should be pointed out, however, that there was a large amount of variation within and between family lines regardless of ancestral ethnicity. For example, the two largest kinship networks were founded by Tarascan couples. One, a San Juan family, had produced 43 percent of all the unskilled laborers, but only 3 percent of the professionals and 7 percent of the students. In contrast, the Zacan kinship network accounted for only 6 percent of the unskilled laborers, but 30 percent of the professionals and 33 percent of the students.

Parents and Children

Although ancestral ethnicity was not a determinate of the status of descendants, there was some indication that parental occupational choices were beginning to play a role in the opportunities available to the offspring. Most of the farm-supported families were descended from full-time farmers and nearly all the rest were descended from land-owning merchants, whereas children of unskilled laborers as well as professionals tended to follow in their parents' occupational footsteps. The children of parents with middle class occupations were more likely to achieve middle class status on reaching adulthood than the offspring of either farmers or unskilled laborers (Table 7.11). However, the doors toward upward socioeconomic mobility were not closed to children of parents with popular class occupations. These parents had produced a larger number of middle class offspring, even though the percentage was much lower.

Family orientation rather than actual support occupation was the key. For example, two of the three skilled workers raised by a parent engaged in unskilled labor were the son and daughter of a woman whose husband went to California as a migrant laborer and disappeared. She took the two young children to Uruapan where she worked at whatever jobs she could find while she got them through school. One is now a bank teller in Uruapan and the other a radio announcer in Leon.

A NEW KIND OF TARASCANNESS

At the time fieldwork was conducted, only Angahuan had insisted on retention of overt ethnic characteristics to the point of a self-enclavement supported by tourism. Otherwise, the people of the communities affected by the Parícutin eruptions had largely reinterpreted their ethnic identity. For the most part, they took pride in a Tarascan background that in no way interfered with their being totally Mexican. As is usual in Mexico, the higher status urbanites tended to proclaim the values of an Indian heritage to a greater extent than did their kinsmen in the villages. Because the middle class city-dwellers frequently visited their home communities, they were important agents for diffusion of urban ideals about the kinds of customs that should be maintained in a modern world.

There was no indication that the urbanites from these villages had formed ethnic enclavements in the cities. There were associations to raise financial help for modernization of the home communities such as the Uruapan association of the "Professionals from Zacan," and Mexico City meetings of Sierra Tarasca people interested in the maintenance of song-writing and scholarship in the native tongue. In both cases, these were leisure activities of the middle class.

Maintenance of ethnic traits in the villages was a curious mix. In outward appearance, Zacan was nearly as traditional as Angahuan, but for different reasons. In Zacan, a modern house built by a family that had not provided the highest possible level of education for the children would probably have led to social ostracism. Educated children from Zacan helped improve kinsmen's living quarters, but usually by extending water systems or by purchasing furniture and electrical appliances rather than by making major changes in residential architectural style.

San Juan had modernized to a considerable degree in architecture, but remained conservative in dress for elderly women and in retention of socioreligious responsibilities. Certain symbols of Tarascan ethnicity were regarded as community icons and the fiesta dancers of San Juan won prizes in national competitions. The fragments of Zirosto had retained little in terms of any kind of community symbolism, but it was interesting that the people of the Miguel Silva refugee settlement, located far from the Sierra Tarasca, had the strongest interest in maintaining the Indian language and the traditional dances.

This Zirosto-derived community also had produced the highest proportion of professionals for a Zirosto fragment and in many ways was the most dynamic, although the poorest in physical resources.

In the Parícutin resettlement village of Caltzontzin, which as a suburb of an expanding Uruapan is now essentially an urban-fringe community, the poorest people encountered knew only a few words of Tarascan, if any, and had no apparent sense of ethnic identity. In contrast, the Tarascan language was used as a family ritual when a college professor son and his brothers, who were finishing degrees in engineering at the University of Mexico, gathered for holidays in a modern-style brick house on a corner of the plaza. This was not an isolated example. In Caltzontzin, as in San Juan and Zacan, pride in Tarascan heritage was something that the successful could afford without any threat to status locally or in the larger society.

Only in Angahuan had being Tarascan become a commercial advantage; there the ethnic difference was marketable but only at what appeared to be a major psychological cost. The Angahuanese did not object strongly to North American tourists. They disliked the Mexican tourists, however, who included the children and grandchildren of the Tarascan speakers from villages down the road and who drove up in their automobiles to look at the people living as their ancestors had lived (Fig. 7.4). The Angahuanese said, and probably believed, that they had never had a choice because they were just poor Indians. The historical record indicates that they had just as much chance as the people of any of the other communities affected by the Parícutin volcano, including an offer of a resettlement location and bracero work in the United States. Thus, Angahuan was self-enclaved in its image of a past Tarascanness that explained their problems, yet offered little hope for the future of the children who would have to leave the community as land resources were subdivided past the subsistence level. There were other ways of coping without giving up all traditional values, but the people of Angahuan had not yet accepted these adaptations. In 1971, most children who left the community were forced into the ranks of the alien Mexicans and thus could not play quite the same role of integration at the family and community level as did urbanites from other communities.

CONCLUSION

This analysis of 26 family lines, deriving from specific ancestral couples, conforms with the well-documented trend of migration from village to city in Mexico. It illustrates, at the family level, the pressure on the land of an exploding population of still largely subsistence rural communities. More and more people depend on land controlled and passed on through inheritance of ownership or ejido rights, *even* when the majority of the increasingly numerous offspring leave the land. For those families in which a majority of descendants cling to the land, the patrimony has been diminished with each generation to the point where the children and grandchildren of once reasonably

Figure 7.4. Angahuan child *(right)* and girls from urban Mexico. (Photograph by Mary Lee Nolan.)

prosperous farmers have been reduced to a marginal existence. Ejido grants judged sufficient to support a farm family a generation ago often cannot provide even the barest living for the ejiditaro along with his grown children and their numerous offspring.

In an age when capital investment per unit acre of land and mechanized farming that requires reasonably large holdings or cooperative effort are becoming increasingly important, the problem in many Mexican rural communities is of serious dimensions. As a Caltzontzin merchant-farmer put it, "There are few fields for growing corn. Now one must go to school and learn some way to make a living other than farming because there are more farmers than there is land to farm."

The positive implication of this study is that the majority of those descendants with little or no land did go to school and learn other ways to make a living. Only a few of the offspring of these ancestral couples are found among the many hand-to-mouth unskilled laborers of Michoacán. Substantial numbers of people from these villages have worked in cities at one time or another, and nearly one-third of the descendants are urban residents. Only a few have become locked into a marginal existence by wit and occasional day labor in city slums. The majority of city-dwellers have carved out places for themselves at various levels of the Mexican middle class spectrum.

The fact that both unskilled workers and educated professionals were found in many family lines indicates the variability in life-choice and chance open to these people. It helps explain why many who have reached a status in life that they find acceptable believe that they made the best of the opportunities available, and why many think that some of their children will do even better given good fortune and hard work. The success of the children and grandchildren of Tarascan-speaking farmers provides explanation for the new kind of Tarascanness expressed in ideals of achievement thought to reflect rural virtues. In what may be one of the most positive forms of disenclavement, many people from these families viewed their Tarascan heritage as a special aspect of being Mexican. It gives them roots in their rural traditions plus a sense of being able to make a unique contribution to the cultural heritage of the nation with which they identify. It also, however, leads toward an idealized version of the Tarascan heritage that may have little meaning in some villages, and almost inescapably a feeling among the more successful that those less well-adapted have only themselves to blame.

Acknowledgments. The fieldwork on which this paper is based was partially supported by a grant from the Environmental Quality Program, Texas A & M University, College Station, Texas. Quantitative analysis of genealogical materials was made possible through a grant for support of computing services from the Oregon State University Computer Center. Assistance with fieldwork was provided by Sidney Nolan.

Balan, Browning, and Jelin 1973
Beals 1946, 1953b
Butterworth 1970
Foster 1948, 1967
Gilbert 1974
González Cosio 1961
Kaplan 1965
Lewis 1952, 1961, 1966
Margolies 1969
Miller 1973
Nolan 1973, 1979
Nolan and Nolan 1979
Rollwagen 1974
Stanislawski 1950
West 1948
Whiteford 1964
Wolf 1959
Zantwijk 1967

CHAPTER EIGHT

Insistence and Persistence in Cultural Enclavement: Villages That Progress Chose?

George Castile (Whitman College, Washington)

Ralph Beals worked in the Michoacán community of Cherán in 1939 and declared it "one of the most isolated of the mountain Tarascan towns" (Beals 1946: 1). He considered it as "almost wholly Indian," while at the same time noted "the essentially European origin of most of the culture and the relatively small number of traits of native provenience" (Beals 1946: 1, 210). This report of Beals's was essentially descriptive, but in his brief analytical section he wondered about the persistence of some qualities that constituted the "uniqueness of Cherán culture" and that seemed to involve "fierce attachment to costumbres," an attachment that "persists despite the fact that Cherán culture not only changes visibly but that such change is accepted. . . ." (Beals 1946: 211). Julian Steward, in his introduction to Beals's report, asked the question, "Why is Cherán considered Indian?"

In my restudy of the Sierra Tarascan community of Cherán in 1969 and 1970 (Castile 1974), I was not concerned with the question of ethnic identity and its persistence, but concentrated instead on some consideration of the goodness of fit of Eric Wolf's model of the closed corporate community to the analysis of Cherán (Wolf 1967). Later, however, I asked much the same question of myself as did Steward, but in terms of the "Tarascanness of the Tarascans" (Castile 1981). In this chapter I combine some of these concerns and address some broader problems in the understanding of social enclavement or what Spicer once labeled "Persistent Cultural Systems" (Spicer 1971). My title is obviously in part a purposeful twist of Redfield's (1950) title of his classic work, "A Village that Chose Progress . . . ," and in its selection I direct attention to the continued emphasis in the literature on choice and choosing as the mechanisms of cultural change and persistence. I suggest that communities like Cherán do not "choose" to become isolated defensive enclaves and, furthermore, they do not exercise choice as to whether they will remain in that condition or become integrated into the larger society. We have long since abandoned the "great man" theory in our acceptance of determinism in human affairs, but we cannot seem to give up our romantic notions of the "little man" who, Horatio Alger fashion, chooses progress (usually under the guidance of a community development project).

THE CULTURE OF THE CONQUERED

Because the archaeology of the Sierra Tarasca is not well developed, we can do little more than speculate as to how long Cherán existed as an integral part of the Tarascan "empire." With the descent on the region of Nuño de Guzmán and his ravages, we can be certain that Cherán was disarticulated from such larger aboriginal social and political contexts sometime between 1529 and 1533 (the duration of Guzmán's campaigns and administration). Don Vasco de Quiroga was appointed Bishop of Michoacán in 1537, and with him and others of the religious order working in the vicinity it is likely that Cherán came quite early under the utopian influence of the Church. Indications are given in the survey of the area by Aguirre Beltrán (1952: 82–83) that Cherán was being visited by Franciscans in the 16th century and that it had become a sujeto of the town of Sevina, which was held as an encomienda. Cherán, like all other Tarascan communities, had become subject to the pressures of Spanish tribute and labor demands at some level. Presumably it was disrupted socially and demographically by disease and Guzmán's ravages and, in this time of crisis, was probably in contact with the reorganizational opportunities offered by the Church.

The indefatigable traveler and chronicler Lumholtz wandered through Cherán in 1897, and though he appears to have disliked the town and its people, he gives us our first glimpse of its adaptations. He tells us enough, in fact, to clearly suggest the firm establishment of a civil-religious hierarchy that appears typical of the Latin American versions of the defensive enclaves Wolf has labeled closed corporate communities. The evidence is in his outrage with the town's conservatism and in his reports of the complaints of the Priests against the existence of folk Catholic ceremonials and their unsuccessful attempts to suppress them (Lumholtz 1902a: 398). The next glimpse is the clearest and comes from the work of Beals (1946) himself. By that time he was able to present a thorough description of a clear cut "typical" Mexican peasant community in which life was centered around a civil-religious hierarchy, with all of the accompanying elements such as a firmly established compadrazo system. Cherán had not become identical to other archetypical communities such as Tepotzlan or Zinacantan, inasmuch as its "costumbres" differed and its ecological situation was not precisely the same, but no one may argue against the remarkable similarities found all over New Spain among these "Indian" peasant adaptations.

What is the role of "choice" in this initial process of enclavement that led to the establishment of Cherán as a defensive isolate? Cherán did not choose to be shorn of its connections with the Tarascan state. It did not bring Spanish overlords to exact tribute and labor nor the diseases that created severe population decline. It did not invite the Franciscans to offer new alternatives for community organization. No person in Cherán, be he conservative or progressive, made any of these events come to pass. The only choice open to members of that community, and most others in Mexico, was to somehow adapt to these new circumstances, and virtually everywhere the same inward-turning closed community seems to have developed as the "right" choice.

It is a maxim of adaptive logic, of course, that one is ultimately free only to make the right choice, the one that is possible and workable. The people of Cherán, under the guidance of some charismatic leader, might have chosen to rebel militarily. This "choice," if full blown, would have presumably led to the destruction and dispersal of the community and to further disruption at all levels. The abortive Mixton War in this area suggests the possibility of the choice and its likely outcome. Similarly, messianic or other movements of revitalization, designed or "chosen" to restore some integrity to the Tarascan communities, of necessity would have been broken up, as happened elsewhere with others such as the Mayan cult of the Talking Cross in the Caste War of Yucatan. A dominant society cannot allow the continued existence of any such threatening forms of adaptation and of choices that challenge its dominance and reduce its control.

In fact, only two broad categories of "choices" existed and they were embraced in various ways in Mexico—enclavement or assimilation. The defensive isolates such as Cherán arose and endured only in those areas that Aguirre Beltrán (1967) has properly called "Regiones de Refugio." In most of Mexico, within a relatively short time, new, entirely Spanish defined and controlled, institutions centered on the cities and mines, and the large supporting agricultural complexes acted as instruments to atomize and absorb as individuals the bulk of the "Indian" population. This process of "mestizaje" was most complete and earliest in such areas as the Bajio and often has been described in terms of the workings of the hacienda system (Wolf 1955). In most cases, this process of assimilation did not transform existing communities, *as communities,* but bled the membership of the surviving Indian enclaves into new contexts. In time these new structures, particularly the "open" peasant communities, underwent further change and adaptation. After the revolution, the products of this process, the mestizos, came eventually to be the dominant cultural element and force in Mexico, but by this time they had ceased to be "Indian" in any sense appropriate to this discussion.

The enclaves like Cherán, however, adapted *as units* and retained their identity and some degree of boundary-maintaining structural integrity. The people of Cherán, today as much as in the 16th century, regard themselves as Tarascans and are so regarded by their neighbors. The key in the first days was the relative degree of isolation of Cherán and other similar communities. Disruptive pressures were brought to bear but at a low intensity, because the area had no large Spanish population and was lacking attractive exploitable resources of minerals or even land. There are few places in the Sierra Tarasca where the land is not broken by topography into small parcels, making the large-scale market farming of the haciendas impractical. I have commented elsewhere in regard to U.S. reservations: "Land held by the Indian was by definition economically undesirable, else the Indians would not have been given it or allowed to retain it" (Castile 1979: 205). The same is true in Mexico for the surviving enclaves.

Disrupted and under pressure (but limited pressure), the people of Cherán were given a breathing space by virtue of their isolation, in effect an opportunity to adapt. As everywhere else, the model offered them as an alternative was organization around the structure of the Church. The necessity for adaptation obviously existed because pre-Columbian structures were no longer permitted or viable, while the civil structure of secular Spanish society relegated the native peoples only to subordination, tribute production, and other distasteful conditions. Given necessity and opportunity, another essential ingredient was also present—tolerance. The adaptations of a subordinate sector of a society must be "tolerated" by the larger dominant sector. The Spanish were content to treat communities like Cherán as units, interfering minimally and leaving them to the Church for supervision of their internal affairs, so long as tribute and labor demands were met. For a variety of reasons of its own, the Crown was not only tolerant but even worked to purposefully separate the Indians from the secular Spaniards, and leave the Indians to the sole guidance of the Church. While this was only successful where there were relatively limited numbers of Spaniards, as in the regions of refuge, it still provided a framework permitting the formation of the enclave in the isolated zones. It is obvious, of course, that no one in the Spanish sector chose or intended to produce anything like the closed corporate communities. The formation of the enclaves is ultimately the choice of neither of the parties to the change transaction and is as much an Indian adaptation as the desired end of a Spanish program of planned change.

IMAGES OF LIMITED GOOD

So long as my analysis remains in the distant historical realm, few would attempt to argue the influence of conservative or progressive individuals or the importance of "Indian" versus non-Indian mental sets. However, if we proceed further and ask how these communities have endured into the present or examine the prospects for their "development" or "integration," a shoal of mentalistic views of the nature of the peasant mind begins to fuddle the issue. At a fundamental level we stray into theoretical debates over emic and etic explanations and their relative utility and validity. In its simplest form, the mentalistic approach leads to statements that peasant communities are conservative because peasants are conservative. Somewhat more useful are the arguments raging around Foster's (1967) presentation of the "image of the limited good" or the discourse by Erasmus (1968) on the "encogido syndrome," both of which have served as models for the nature of the peasant mind and as "explanations" of their resistance to change.

Marvin Harris (1974: 243) gave forth the admonition that "etic outputs require etic inputs" and that "a single cognitive model can generate a variety of etic outputs depending on the etic inputs." Put in the terms of this discussion, it is a simple and seemingly obvious fact that no matter what is going on in the peasant's mind (encogido, limited good), the primary determining element in the fate of the community and the individuals is the effectiveness of their adaptations in coping with "the others." This does not deny the fact that some attention must be paid to whether peasants do indeed have characteristic mental sets and how they come to have them. It seems fairly clear that they do have such sets, but that these are the product of the general defensive "cultural lifeboat" quality of their adaptation and not its cause. As the adaptations of the peasant communities alter, the mental sets alter along with everything else, although perhaps not quickly enough for those who seek developmental change. The encogido becomes *mas entron* and the image of the limitations of the good becomes less limited.

Erasmus and Foster themselves, despite many acccusers to the opposite, clearly never meant to suggest encogido and limited good as inherent qualities of the peasant mind. In an article flaying them both for such belief, Huizer (1970: 303) suggested that such characteristics were the consequence of a "culture of repression" and "seem to disappear to a large extent as soon as the power relations in rural areas are drastically changed. . . ." In their replies, both Erasmus and Foster point out that they had long since made similar observations and that the only new element in Huizer's discussion was his emphasis on the concept of "culture of repression," which Foster appeared to accept and Erasmus found wanting (Foster 1970; Erasmus 1970).

Foster (1970: 314) makes the observation that, "That is what is most peasant about peasants—throughout history they have been oppressed and repressed." It seems clear that some general agreement could be reached that peasants and "Indians" have some of the self-defending characteristics normally described by terms such as conservative, encogido, and the like, precisely because they have a need to defend themselves and that few other mechanisms are available to them. I think Foster (1970: 314) is quite wrong, however, when he says, "When repression is removed, whatever the means, people don't stay peasant for long." Erasmus (1968) is more nearly correct in his observations about the self-sustaining qualities of some peasant communities where mechanisms such as "invidious sanction" tend to retard change under circumstances where it "ought" to occur if repression is the only factor.

To some extent I suspect that the appearance of peasant conservatism in situations where rational analysis suggests that change is clearly possible and desirable is an artifact of a microtemporal view. Peasants only appear unreasonably conservative because there is a lag time in their adjustment to a changing environment. Geared to holding their limited own against a repressive external order, time is needed to reorder attitudes and expectations when that order changes. Over macrotime the peasant comes to accept the reality of change through some process like "frequency analysis" (Erasmus 1961), which is simply to say he believes it when he sees it—repeatedly. In a general way much is explained by this simple concept, but it leads to a second possibility as suggested in Spicer's (1971) writings on the concept of persistent "peoples" or "persistent identity systems." In his definitive book, *The Yaquis: A Culture History,* Spicer (1980) clearly suggests that the Yaqui go on being Yaqui not only through repeated shifts in the actualities of their articulation within a single society, but even through relocation to entirely different societies. It would appear that the enclavement process can act in some cases as the instrument for the creation of a "people," and that this "people" persists independently of the circumstances that called it forth.

Before pursuing this problem of persistence, further observations may be made about the concept of a "culture of repression." As Erasmus (1970) notes, labels like "culture of poverty" and this "culture of repression" usually lead to fruitless attempts to cram the data into conceptual straitjackets prescribed by ideology. I suggest a more severe problem, that such terms as "oppression," "repression," and "exploitation," while reasonably descriptive, tend to lead us into the theoretical trap of personalization and blame fixing. We cease to look for process and begin to point the finger at the villain. It is certainly true that the peasant condition is one of subordination and exploitation by a dominant sector of a plural society. That is close, as Foster notes, to being the definition of peasantry. But recall my observation at the beginning that we have abandoned the "great man" theory but clung to the "little man" as mover and shaker. In the search for the oppressors we find ourselves with something of a demon theory or "rotten man" explanation for social affairs. Carlos, in this volume, has some tendency to fixate on the conscious and purposeful exploitation of the peasantry in this fashion only to obscure an otherwise insightful analysis.

If we are prepared to abandon the view that peasants are peasants because they want to be, then it is equally necessary to jettison the view that they are peasants because the patrón wishes them to remain so. The patrón has no more control over the eventual disruption of the subordination of the peasantry than do the peasants, although in microtemporal perspective it may appear otherwise. The superior power at the disposal of the elite does indeed serve to maintain subordination for the purposes of exploitation, but surely any examination of peasant rebellions and ultimate revolutions shows the illusory quality of this power in macrotime. In Mexico the collapse of Don Porfirio is surely a classic reminder that power is ephemeral in the face of large scale change in the nature of a society. Both Don Porfirio and Zapata are products, not causes, and more symbol than substance.

I once wrote of an "Unethical Ethic" in an attempt to deal with some of the dilemmas in "action anthropology," or what another called the "Applied Man's Burden" (Castile 1975; Jansen 1973). It still seems to me that there are vast dangers for anthropology as a science in "activist" approaches to understanding such as is advocated by Stavenhagen (1971) and others. To focus our studies in support of some political stance or constituency can only lead to confusions such as are inherent in the "culture of repression." A "rightist" view would lead us to presume that subordination is a natural condition of peasants and is good for them in view of their limitations, racial or otherwise. But does the "leftist" orientation, which leads us to search for the grinder of the faces of the poor (portrayed by the Mexican muralists in the guise of *hacendado*), lead us much further? There was something terribly frightening and somewhat sad about a recent statement coming from Chinese "ethnologists" saying:

> We no longer have what you call anthropology and sociology because to us they have no usefulness. We already have a comprehensive theory of social formations: the theory of historical development that has been explained successively by Marx, Engels, Lenin and Mao Zedong. We had anthropology and sociology in the past but after liberation they quickly withered away (Braybrooke 1980: 264).

I doubt that peasant or ethnic studies will be much advanced by our moving toward any such social Lysenkoism, whatever our degree of sympathy with the plight of these peoples.

FROM INSISTENCE TO PERSISTENCE

Returning to the Tarascans as an example of enclavement and its persistence, it is clear that Cherán was initially "chosen" to become an enclave by the circumstances described relating to its isolation and relative lack of interest to the Spanish conquerors. Its status as an "Indian" community at this stage can be seen as a function of "insistence" by the invaders, because they defined the range of possible variation that they would allow to exist and the role that communities of this kind would be allowed to play. The place of the Indian was well defined throughout most of the colonial period and the definition was one of subordination and exploitation. Indians were Indians because the Crown said they were—insistence. With Independence and then the 1910 Revolution, the quality of insistence altered markedly.

I want to use the Tarascan situation, and particularly Cherán, to comment on the phenomena previously mentioned of the persistence of ethnic identity when insistence is much reduced.

If all that keeps peasants peasants is repression, as Foster suggests, what keeps some communities or peoples apparently "Indian" when few such restraints that could be called repression operate? Pursuing this thought, of course, could lead to the unfruitful fields of speculation as to "who is an Indian?" It is more helpful to use Spicer's thought on "persistent identity systems" to reach some understanding of the continuation of the supposed Indian communities.

The Sierra Tarasca remained an isolated "region of refuge" until a main road penetrated the area at the time of Beals's study (Fig. 8.1). In some sense it still remains a region of refuge because the pressures from outside forces are by no means overwhelming. The area has no significant industry or resource base to exploit beyond maize cultivation and some small-scale crafts. There are no large and expanding population centers to draw the Sierra into their orbit. The levels of contact, however, have increased steadily. The people of Cherán, for example, travel freely and frequently on the excellent bus service to the towns of Zamora and Uruapan and less often to Morelia, Guadalajara, and Mexico City. Many workers engage in seasonal farm labor in the tierra caliente and in the far north, and many of them even spend time in the United States, as some had already done in Beals's time.

In their increasing contact with the larger world, the people of Cherán and the Sierra remain a subordinated enclave, and traditional mechanisms still function to protect against exploitation by the dominant elements. On a national level, the cult of Indigenismo has created a political stance favorable toward the "Indian" past and, as a side effect, a favorable policy toward the enclaves that represent the surviving "Indians." The presence of the I.N.I. Regional Coordinating Center on the outskirts of Cherán (Fig. 8.2) vividly illustrates to its people the reality of the government's programs aimed at their development. At a local level, however, the "Indian" identity is still a low status, and economic affairs are largely controlled by the local non-Indian elites.

The I.N.I. personnel at the Cherán center at the time of my study illustrated this ambivalence, showing considerable indications of disdain for the Tarascans and their perverse peasant conservatism and failure to cooperate in programs designed for their own good. More realistically, Grindle (1977) has given an excellent analysis of the workings of a Mexican bureaucracy that shows the accuracy of the peasant judgments about the risks in cooperation. Programs are designed *for* peasants not *by* them, and "higher" purposes than peasant needs and wants generally prevail. The condition of subordination remains, but the terms have altered favorably for the people even if they must continue to accept the domination of the "others."

In his discussion of the Mayo in Sonora, Erasmus (1967) reveals some important elements that stand in useful contrast to the Tarascan circumstance. The Mayo and Yaqui rivers have been the sites of massive irrigation projects that have altered their status as regions of refuge and have attracted an invasion of outsiders through various schemes of colonization of the desirable resource of newly fertile lands. In many cases, the

Figure 8.1. Modern transportation to Cherán. The road completed during Beals's study is probably the greatest single factor in the "choice" of Cherán. "La Flecha," the bus serves Cherán every half hour, but once it was the "most isolated of Tarascan communities." (Photograph by George Castile, 1969.)

Mayo have been placed in direct social and physical association with non-Indians when they are mixed together in the membership of ejidos. Erasmus (1967: 112) observes the result, saying, "The Mayo River Mayos, living as they do in almost daily contact with Yoris and forced as they have been by the irrigation and land developments to interact with them more, have drifted noticeably further from the 'encogido' end of the character continuum." While some communities and individuals in the area continue to maintain a strong adherence to traditional "Indian" values (Fig. 8.3), it would appear that in many cases such mechanisms are not able to survive in the face of truly massive assault, and many Mayo cease to be Mayo. However, the seeming importance of isolation may be overstressed, because the Yaqui who serve as Spicer's principal example of a "persistent indentity system" are in this same region and obviously have been subjected to similar intrusions and pressures (Spicer 1976, 1980; Erasmus 1967). The presence or absence of exploitable resources explains much but not all.

The question of the viability of an ethnic identity in the face of pressures against its continuance leads us to Spicer's paradoxical notion of the "oppositional process" as the principal mechanism for the persistence of enclaves (Spicer 1971). It is a paradox because on the one hand, as in the Mayo case, it appears that enclaves cannot survive if the pressures put on them are too great, but on the other hand Spicer seems to suggest that *some* degree of "opposition" is necessary for the initial formation and continuation of the enclaves. Here we may fall into the usual pit of circular adaptive logic and say that there must be "enough" pressure but not too much. Some "Tarascan" communities such as Tzintzuntzan have ceased to

Figure 8.2. The coordinating center of I.N.I. Located on the edge of Cherán, this center is a major influence toward "nationalization." (Photograph by George Castile, 1969.)

identify themselves as Tarascan (although outsiders continue to make the identification). Cherán and Ihuatzio still make claim to the Tarascan identity and outsiders ratify it. Where are the critical differences to be found?

In his discussions of persistent identity systems, for which he also uses the term "enduring people," Spicer cites numerous examples but suggests in "all of these instances a continued conflict between the peoples and the controllers of the surrounding state apparatus. The conflict has occurred over issues of incorporation and assimilation into the larger whole" (Spicer 1971: 797). At a point in this oppositional process the enclave is formed structurally around some set of "identity" symbols that mark off the members from outsiders. In another place Spicer (1966: 264) says, "A cultural enclave is a part of a political society which maintains distinctive traits from the members of the larger whole and which places positive value on the maintenance of these differences." Here, then, is a key to the peculiar property of persistence, not only under oppressive insistence but beyond it. The members of the enclave *must* at some point be forced into the defensive posture that produces the symbolic identity system, but once produced it becomes like any other "culture," a self-sustaining end in itself that will persist so long as it can meet the "functional prerequisites of a society," including the all important retention of the loyalty of the membership (Aberle and others 1950). Peasants think well of their "culture" even when they recognize its subordinate status and need "reasons" to abandon it.

Cherán, like all other "Indian" communities, underwent the requisite oppositional process during the colonial era and later years and did develop into a defensive enclave, as we have already suggested. It would seem that the critical difference that has left Cherán still more or less intact is probably more the degree of actual physical and economic isolation than any special form of continuing "opposition." It differs little from

Figure 8.3. The procession of the *panaleros*. This traditional ceremony indicates an adherence to "Indian" values. (Photograph by George Castile, 1969.)

other villages that progress did, in fact, choose except with regard to this isolation, and other villages that are also supposedly "Indian" such as Ihuatzio appear to share the quality of isolation. Cherán does not have a special history of persecution and resistance such as apparently forms the core of the Yaqui identity system, or at least no more so than any other Tarascan community.

There are some indications of a "special" status for Cherán that might promote persistence. Aguirre Beltrán (1952: 92) quotes an 18th-century source who commented on Cherán's resistance to ladinization. "No son ladinos, pero si inquietos, inclinados a la bebida y pegados a sus antiguas viciosas costumbres, declarados enemigos de los de rason, mentirosos, amigos de pleitos, lo mengua sus facultades. . . ." Lumholtz (1902a) similarly frothed at the mouth about the character of the people of Cherán. Beals (1946: 156) notes in his study,

"For many miles around, Cherán has the reputation of being the outstanding center for witchcraft among the Tarascans." Traces of this reputation existed at the time of my study among local peoples that I encountered, and once I was even offered "place of the witches" as a translation of the word Cherán. Cherán, it would appear, has long had a bad press.

In all of this, however, there seems little reflection of the fact that Cherán has changed drastically and embraced many aspects of "modern" Mexican culture (Fig. 8.4). In my attempts to compare it with Janet Moone's scaling of Tarascan communities in terms of national integration, I found it ranked very near the top in spite of the self-identification as Tarascan and the insistence on its conservatism by outsiders (Moone 1969). The factor of "insistence" seems still important since Cherán continues, at least in part, to persist because its neighbors continue to believe in its Tarascanness.

Figure 8.4. One example of "modernization." This notice of a dance at the main school seems particularly ironic confronting the student of the "closed corporate community." (Photograph by George Castile, Cherán, 1969.)

CHERAN IS CHOSEN?

Up until the time of the study by Beals, and to a lesser extent up until the time of my own research, the factors of isolation and disinterest on the part of the larger political society seem to have operated to allow the enclave of Cherán to persist and, as I have suggested, may have insisted on it to a considerable extent. Is the symbolic identity system of Cherán (or other "Tarascans") strong enough to carry it into the condition of one of Spicer's (1976) "enduring peoples," who persist in a cohesive and separate identity no matter what is going on around them in the larger society? Has Cherán survived until now *only* because the pressures for its assimilation have not been very strong? There are a number of problems in giving any definite answer to such speculations.

In the first place, there is no clear agreement by anyone as to what is meant by "Tarascan." Foster, for example, insists that Tzintzuntzan is not Tarascan and he appears more often than not to be fixated on language as a criterion, saying in one place, "By about 1850 I estimate the non-Tarascan population *(defined as monolingual Spanish speakers)* equalled or exceeded the Tarascan population" (Foster 1967: 26, emphasis mine). Obviously this is not his only criterion but it is his most frequent. Spicer (1976: 4), however, points out that it is perfectly possible to assert Yaqui identity and have it recognized without being a speaker of that language.

Spanish is increasingly the language of daily life in Cherán, but its people still regard themselves (and are regarded) as Tarascan. No one presumably takes seriously any claim to genetic purity of any particular community as a criterion of Indianness, although it is interesting that the claim is made. This leaves us with adherence to Tarascan "culture" or "way of life," what the people of Cherán identified as "costumbre," as the most common means of defining who is Tarascan. This is a problem of a different order because, as Spicer (1976: 1) says of his enduring people, such systems are best thought of as "the entity that maintains continuity at the same time that it undergoes change." As I have discussed elsewhere, there seems to be very little Tarascan about the Tarascans and their costumbre if one means by that some pattern of unaltered pre-Columbian survivals (Castile 1981). Beals (1946), as we have noted, made the same observation at the time of his study.

Obviously we are back to the problem of defining the nature of the symbols and the structure that maintains them, and this problem is complicated by the obvious fact that whatever these symbols may be, they clearly have changed over time. Whatever Cherán was, or thought it was in 1520, it is not that now and has not been for a long time—but it remains somehow Tarascan. Spicer (1976: 7) comments that "Identification of the symbols by which the meanings of a people's existence become known from generation to generation is the means for describing their identity system." Unfortunately, so far as I am aware, no coherent study like Spicer's (1980) Yaqui work has attempted to make such a description for the Tarascans.

Kay Warren, in her book *The Symbolism of Subordination*, has made an attempt at an analysis of a related nature for a community of Cakchiquel Indians in Guatemala, but the only work for the Tarascans that approaches this is van Zantwijk's study of Ihuatzio (Warren 1978; van Zantwijk 1967). Until more study of this kind is done, speculation about the precise nature of a Tarascan symbolic identity system is largely fruitless. For the moment, we can deal only in terms of the existence of simple self-identification with the awareness that it has a base in such a system.

But what of the viability of such an identity system, whatever its precise nature? It would appear that virtually everywhere in the Tarascan area where villages have been "chosen," by the intrusion of outsiders or by involvement in external economic enterprises, many formerly autonomous communities have rapidly become integrated and lost their separate "Indian" identity. Cherán and other villages are only just now at the point of being tested in this way, because many new pressures are coming to bear at ever higher levels.

Most of all, Cherán faces the same demographic crisis that challenges Mexico as a whole and that demands change of some sort. The population has more or less doubled since the study by Beals, while the amount of land remains exactly the same. Many cannot now choose to follow traditional pursuits based on subsistence cultivation because they are completely landless, and the minifundio holdings of others will not allow them to choose this closed self-sufficient life. Like it or not, the people of Cherán have had to turn to new enterprises to feed themselves, and these endeavors require greater and greater involvement with the doings of the outside world. Even this demographic crisis is scarcely a matter of choice, because the health and environmental conditions that have led to a decline in infant mortality and other death rates are artifacts of national level campaigns, and the limits on land holdings that have long existed are equally due to externally determined boundaries.

At the time of my study, the people of Cherán, unlike many other peasant villages, had managed so far to make this adaptation to new pressures without extensive permanent outmigration. Certainly there is an increasing number who migrate elsewhere, whether it be for a season or a few years, but virtually all eventually return to the community bringing new goods and still more new wants to fuel the process of change.

In my study I pointed out in some detail the wide range of new occupations developing as individuals respond to these pressures, and Cherán's increasing importance as a commercial center is a community-wide result. In the midst of this directly economically prompted change, much else has occurred, including a considerable "opening" of the closed community to the values and expectations of the larger Mexico. I referred to it as the "Global Village," because with radio, television, movies, newspapers, tourists, I.N.I., the schools, and anthropologists, the people of Cherán are today surely not isolated. They hear every day the messages of Mexican nationalism (Fig. 8.5), along with the blandishments of world capitalism, and see on every hand the material possibilities in the larger world.

In understanding the pattern of change overtaking the Sierra and other Tarascans, too much weight is sometimes given to the effects of "community development" efforts like that of I.N.I. Such agencies of planned change in all nations certainly tend to award themselves credit for any beneficial events occurring in areas in which they work, regardless of their actual source. Erasmus has rightly warned against the idealistic and myopic focus of such efforts, which frequently seem to be encouraging cooperation for its own sake and the promotion of "household economics," of which he says, "Any government promoting the household economy works against itself. . . . Natural developments . . . generally involve increasing political and economic participation in modern national culture. . . ." (Erasmus 1968: 66, 69). To the extent that I.N.I. has acted to promote such participation, it has served to accelerate change in Cherán, but it is change that was already taking place and that has proceeded only seldom in the ways and directions envisioned by the planned programs.

The belief by the people that they are Tarascan remains in Cherán, but much of the traditional structure of the closed corporate community that supposedly is necessary to support such an identity system is in ruins. The carguero system already had started to disintegrate during the study by Beals, and my own observations suggested that the burden of serving the saints largely had been diffused evenly over the community through a system of commissioners responsible for raising necessary ceremonial funds. The rich are expected to pay more than most but not at a level sufficient to beggar them and provide them with the poverty essential to the rewards of shared poverty. There *are* men today who have far more than others and Cherán is not a society of equals in any real economic sense, but the ideological lag we suggested leads many to continue to insist that all are still equal and to resort to "treasure tales" to explain the obvious appearance of inequality. Similarly, the once vital mutual support web of kinship and fictive kinship is still highly valued, but wealthy storekeepers complain quite accurately that the compadre relation brings them little and costs them much.

Figure 8.5. The town council and the local schoolteachers taking part in the "Day of the Flag." Teachers, as well as the I.N.I. staff, function as important "priests of nationalism." (Photograph by George Castile, Cherán, 1969.)

Their economic ties in large part are dependent on those outside the community, and hence they are relatively independent of the sanctions of the traditional world and increasingly inclined to ignore them.

Overall it would seem that there is mounting pressure for involvement in the affairs of the larger society, and fewer and fewer effective restraints to such involvement. Cherán is no longer a closed corporate community and, with the shift away from subsistence farming, it is far less "peasant." The question remains as to whether or not, in the face of these shifts, it will continue to be "Indian" in any realistic sense, including the persistence of identity. The only element that would seem to promote in a positive way such continued Indian identity is to be found in the encouragement of the national government, principally through I.N.I., but also through less formal recognition of a special place for "Indians" in the complex maze of "sectors" that make up the power structure of the ruling party, P.R.I. Today's spontaneous delegations of "Tarascan" representatives to Morelia and Mexico City, seeking collectively to influence political affairs in Michoacán, would seem to have some potential to coalesce into a pan-Tarascan federation, and in such a collectivity may lie a structure whose benefits could reinforce and sustain ethnic identity.

If the principal purpose of adherence to ethnic identity and membership in an enclave is defensive isolation, then neither the isolation nor the necessity for it appear to be intact. As Barth and others have pointed out, accepting subordinate ethnic status may not be as illogical as it sounds because the ethnic player, in effect, confines himself to a closed game in which he can win—Foster's "rewards of shared poverty"—and avoids the humiliations of foredoomed competition in the larger game (Barth 1969; Foster 1967). Today, however, the people of Cherán are increasingly forced into playing in the larger game, and some of them seem to be winning more than others. Poverty is no longer universally shared and, therefore, presumably less rewarding, and the limited goods visibly appear to be less limited. Under these circumstances, which will surely intensify as Mexico continues to grow in population and modernize economically, there seems little to justify an expectation that Cherán will not be drawn down the path of Tzintzuntzan and other formerly Tarascan communities into Mexican society and Mexican national identity.

Aberle and others 1950
Aguirre Beltrán 1952, 1967
Barth 1969
Beals 1946
Braybrooke 1980
Castile 1974, 1975, 1979, 1981
Erasmus 1961, 1967, 1968, 1970
Foster 1967, 1970
Grindle 1977
Harris 1974
Huizer 1970
Jansen 1973
Lumholtz 1902a
Moone 1969
Redfield 1950
Spicer 1966, 1971, 1976, 1980
Stavenhagen 1971
Warren 1978
Wolf 1955, 1967
Zantwijk 1967

CHAPTER NINE

Old World Diseases and the Dynamics of Indian and Jesuit Relations in Northwestern New Spain, 1520–1660

Daniel T. Reff (University of Oklahoma)

In the summer of 1591, Fathers Martín Pérez and Gonzalo de Tapia began the first permanent Jesuit mission in northern New Spain. The mission was founded along the banks of the Sinaloa River at San Felipe, which was at the time the northernmost Spanish settlement along the western slopes of the Sierra Madre Occidental. About the same time that Tapia and Pérez began working in Sinaloa, several Jesuits established a residence in Durango, several hundred miles southeast of San Felipe, along the eastern slopes of the Great Divide. From these humble beginnings, the Jesuits in a short span of about 80 years established missions throughout northwestern Mexico. In the process, over 500,000 natives were baptized, the majority of whom accepted the protection and supervision of the priests. Not to be denied further converts, the Jesuits advanced into Baja California and southern Arizona during the closing decade of the 17th century. Missionary efforts continued in both areas as well as in northwestern Mexico until 1767, when a bankrupt Charles III expelled the Jesuits from his overseas empire (Bannon 1955; Bolton 1936; Dunne 1940, 1944, 1948; Pérez de Ribas 1896, 1944; Polzer 1976; Shiels 1934; Spicer 1962).

Although the Jesuits clearly enjoyed remarkable success in northern New Spain, the reasons for this success are not altogether apparent. For many years it has been assumed that, aboriginally, most native groups in the Greater Southwest lived in small rancherías that lacked sophisticated economic and sociopolitical systems (Spicer 1962: 8–15). Against this backdrop the Jesuits have been cast in a role analogous to modern day extension agents. Through the introduction of new crops, tools, cattle, and other innovations, the priests are said to have made possible for the first time in many areas native settlement in towns, permanent houses, intensive agriculture, craft production, and other advances in native economic and sociopolitical organization. Many researchers have suggested further that native recognition of Spanish technological and economic superiority played a dynamic role in acculturative processes (Bannon 1955; Bolton 1917; Dunne 1940, 1944; Fontana 1976; Hu-DeHart 1981; Spicer 1962: 58, 285–298, 1980: 19).

The traditional view of aboriginal culture and the dynamics of Jesuit and Indian relations have never been adequately scrutinized, particularly in light of historical evidence of Old World diseases and their impact on native populations during the 16th and 17th centuries. This chapter reviews extant evidence of disease and how epidemics of smallpox and other maladies affected mission and Indian relations. It is argued that Old World diseases undermined the structure and functioning of native societies prior to sustained contact with the Jesuits, and that native interest in and acceptance of missionization had little to do with the introduction of wheat, chickens, cattle, plows, or Jesuit knowledge of irrigation agriculture. Rather it is argued that native acceptance of missionization was largely influenced by the fact that the Jesuits pursued a policy of reconstituting native productive and organizational strategies that faltered or collapsed following exposure to introduced-diseases. From the point of view of the indigenous population of northern New Spain, acceptance of missionization was an opportunistic endeavor; the presumption that this opportunism was a function of native recognition of the inherent superiority of western civilization is not supported by empirical data.

EPIDEMICS IN THE GREATER SOUTHWEST 1519–1660

The idea that Old World diseases had a profound impact on native peoples during the historic period is not novel. For many years historians and anthropologists have recognized the probable importance of disease. However, with the exception of Sauer (1935), few researchers have acknowledged the relative abundance of historical data regarding disease episodes and their consequences in northern New Spain. The historical record indicates that Old World diseases first may have been introduced during Nuño de Guzmán's conquest of Nueva Galicia (1530–1531). Guzmán's expedition largely destroyed the fabric of Indian life in western Mexico (Sauer and Brand 1932). It was not primarily Guzmán's slave raiding and military exploits, however, that undermined the once populous and advanced cultures of northern Nayarit and southern Sinaloa. The numerous accounts of Guzmán's entrada suggest that the invaders also brought with them one or more devastating diseases. Indeed, we know from Guzmán's own *Memoria* that he was harboring *Plasmodium Malariae* (Carrera Stampa 1955: 40), and on at least one occasion during the Conquest, suffered an apparent relapse of quartan malaria (Bancroft 1886: 364). Guzmán, in fact, may have been the source of an infection that swept through his army in September of 1530, while it was encamped for the winter at Aztatlán, along the Río Acaponeta. The epidemic reportedly killed 8,000 of Guzmán's Indian allies, and left the province of Aztatlán largely depopulated (Carrera Stampa 1955: 154, 185). The symptoms mentioned by various eyewitnesses such as intense fever, chills, and bloody stools (Carrera Stampa 1955: 108–109, 138–139, 154) are all highly suggestive of dysentery (*Shigella* spp.), typhoid, and malaria (Ashburn 1947: 92; Cloudsley-Thompson 1976: 137; Kitchens 1949: 1017). Significantly, shortly after the epidemic subsided, Guzmán's army pushed into Sinaloa, where several participants in Guzmán's entrada (Carrera Stampa 1955: 125, 175) as well as many later observers (for example, Arregui 1946: 46; Cuidad Real 1976: II, 122; Mota y Escobar 1940: 85–86; Tello 1891: 611) commented on the large numbers of mosquitoes. In modern times, and most likely at the time of Guzmán's conquest, coastal Nayarit and Sinaloa were home to Anopheline *Albimanus*, a most efficient malaria vector (Faust 1949: 756).

The introduction of malaria, dysentery, and typhoid undoubtedly played a major role in the dramatic decline in the native population of northern Nayarit and southern Sinaloa during the decades immediately following Guzmán's conquest (Borah and Cook 1963; Sauer and Brand 1932). Acute infectious diseases also exacted a heavy toll. About 1534 to 1535, measles, which had raged for several years in southern and central Mexico (Ashburn 1947; Dobyns 1963; McNeill 1976), ravaged northern Nayarit and southern Sinaloa. According to Tello (1891: 251–255), measles and "bloody stools"—probably dysentery and typhoid that were introduced during Guzmán's entrada—killed 130,000 natives of the province of Culiacán, apparently along the Río San Lorenzo, Tamazula, Humaya, and Culiacán. Again from 1545 to 1548, an epidemic of what appears to have been typhus claimed hundreds of thousands of lives in southern Mexico and Nueva Galicia (Bancroft 1886: 529–530; Grijalva 1924: 213–214; Mendieta 1945: 174; Zinsser 1934: 194–195). After the epidemic subsided, from roughly 1548 to 1574, southern Mexico enjoyed a period of relative calm, excluding the interval from 1559 to 1564 when New Spain suffered from a major epidemic of what was probably, in part, influenza (Cook and Simpson 1948: 14; Grijalva 1924: 216; Ocaranza 1934: 84–85). Except for an epidemic characterized by sore throat ("hinchazones en la garganta") in 1551 (Tello 1891: 549), Nueva Galicia also seems to have been spared the ravages of disease. The chronicles of Baltasar Obregón (Hammond and Rey 1928) and Antonio Ruíz (AGN n.d.; Sauer 1932), specifically their comments about the size and complexity of native populations encountered during Ibarra's expedition (1564–1565), also suggest that northern Sinaloa and Sonora were not affected by Old World diseases.

While the third quarter of the 16th century may have been a time of relative calm, epidemiologically speaking, there were a number of developments during this period that contributed to the introduction and rapid spread of disease in northern New Spain. The most significant development was the discovery of vast silver deposits in and around Zacatecas in 1546. Shortly thereafter, muleteams and wagon trains began frequent journeys northward along what became the *Camino Real de la tierra adentro*, bringing men and supplies to Zacatecas (Bakewell 1971; Powell 1952). This movement of goods and people predictably provided numerous opportunities for the northward spread of disease–opportunities that multiplied between 1550 and 1580 as new mines were opened to the north and east of Zacatecas at Fresnillo, Sombrete, Topia, Indehe, and Santa Barbara. The rapid expansion of the mining frontier led not only to commerce and communication between Nueva Vizcaya and southern Mexico, but to extensive trade and communication with Nueva Galicia. After 1565, muleteers began hauling large quantities of salt, fish, fruit, and other commodities from Chametla, Culiacán, and San Felipe to the burgeoning mining frontier on the eastern slopes of the Sierras. This commerce was conducted via the "Topia road," a mule trail that stretched for about 140 miles from the Villa of San Miguel to the Real of Topia, and then down the eastern slopes of the Sierras to Tepehuanes (West and Parsons 1941). Alternatively, fish and other commodities from Nayarit and Sinaloa were taken by muleteers southward along the camino real of the coast to Guadalajara. Here a thriving commercial center developed after 1560 that funneled west coast exports over the Sierras to Zacatecas or southward to Michoacán and Mexico City. Muleteams owned by residents of Mexico City, in turn, brought items like rope and cloth from the Capital to Guadalajara as well as to Compostela, Chametla, and San Miguel (Arregui 1946: 103–104; Cuidad Real 1976: II, 122; Mota y Escobar 1940; Navarro García 1967: 29–37; West 1949: 77, 79, 90; West and Parsons 1941).

The rapid expansion of the mining frontier led to an extensive trade and communication system that became "the routes of contagion" during the closing decades of the 16th and throughout the 17th and 18th centuries. Although it is difficult to determine precisely when disease agents first made their way northward along the camino reals of the coast and the interior, both roads apparently were functioning as conduits for the spread of disease from 1575 to 1581. At this time, typhus raged in southern Mexico, killing millions of Amerindians (Alegre 1956: 184–185; Bancroft 1886: 657–658; Florencio 1955: 257–270; Mendieta 1945: 174; Tello 1891: 623; Zinsser 1934: 256). Significantly, not long after typhus reached epidemic proportions in the south, it appeared in Zacatecas. In 1576 and 1577, "the Great Matlazahuatl" killed more than 2,000 native mine workers in Zacatecas (Bakewell 1971: 126–127). There is also indirect evidence that typhus subsequently spread farther northward to Spanish mining centers and Indian villages along the eastern slopes of the Sierras. Some disaster must have befallen Durango and southern Chihuahua between 1575 and 1579, because in 1579 Royal officials in Durango petitioned the King for the right to import 1000 Tlascaltec and other civilized Indians to increase the supply of Indian miner workers in Nueva Vizcaya (Mecham 1927: 231). Often requests of this nature or for new encomiendas were correlated with disease episodes (Friede 1967: 339; Griffen 1979: 100).

There are several additional lines of evidence that indicate that typhus and other Old World diseases affected native populations along the eastern slopes of the Sierras as well as in the mountains around Topia during the closing decades of the 1500s. Of particular interest are a wide range of behaviors, beliefs, and fears regarding disease that were present among the Zacateco, Irritila, Tepehuan, and Acaxee at the time of Jesuit contact (Alegre 1958: 74–94; DHM 1596: 30; DHM 1598: 51, 57; DHM 1601: 65; Pérez de Ribas 1944: III, 13–22). Indeed, shortly after the mission of Parras was founded among the Irritila and Zacateco, the Jesuits reported discovering a mass burial that logically may be attributed to an epidemic that occurred before the Jesuits began working in the Laguna region (Pérez de Ribas 1944: III, 263–264). Actually, a letter written by Father Juan Augustín de Espinosa that recounts the first Jesuit entrada into the Laguna region clearly indicates that Old World diseases, specifically smallpox, had affected the Zacateco and Irritila prior to 1590. In his letter, Espinosa recounts how he and a fellow Jesuit set out from Zacatecas for Cuencame in the summer of 1594. While Espinosa's companion, Father Gerónimo Ramírez, preached to the Zacateco at Cuencame, Espinosa went farther north to a pueblo at the base of the Cerro Gordo. Here the priest was visited by numerous caciques from the Laguna region and three from the Río Nazas, who asked Espinosa to visit their pueblos because their children were dying of smallpox. Espinosa acceded to their request and in one pueblo baptized 17 or 18 children who were sick and in danger of dying (Alegre 1956: 423–424; Pérez de Ribas 1944: III, 251–253). Significantly, Espinosa makes no mention in his letter of adults being ill. From what is known about smallpox (Dixon 1962), it is reasonably safe to assume that the Irritila and Zacateco of the Laguna region had been exposed to smallpox on a previous occasion, leaving those who survived—namely the adults encountered by Espinosa—with an active immunity to variola.

During the closing decades of the 16th century, northern Nayarit and southern Sinaloa apparently also suffered from typhus and other maladies (Tello 1891: 623, 692–694). Several early historians believed that by 1590 Old World diseases had contributed to a 90 percent reduction in the aboriginal population of Nueva Galicia (Bancroft 1886: 552–553). Unfortunately, we know little about what impact diseases such as smallpox had on native populations in northern Sinaloa and other areas farther to the north. Shortly after their arrival in Sinaloa in 1591, Fathers Tapia and Pérez wrote several letters describing native life that seem to indicate that Old World diseases did not have a profound or lasting impact on northern Sinaloa (AGN 1593; Shiels 1934: 109–113, 132–135). This situation changed dramatically, however, in 1593. An epidemic of smallpox and measles occurred at this time that claimed at least 1,000 of the Jesuits' new converts along the Río Sinaloa, Ocoroni, and Mocorito (AGN 1593, 1594; Pérez de Ribas 1944: I, 172–173). Significantly, many accounts seem to indicate that all age groups suffered equally during the epidemic, suggesting a lack of prior exposure to smallpox and measles. Moreover, one priest, Juan Bautista de Velasco, noted that many Indians complained to the Jesuits that it was only after the Jesuits came to Sinaloa that the natives suffered from disease (AGN 1593: 41; Dunne 1940: 32; Alegre 1956: 392–393). On balance then, it would appear that northern Sinaloa had not suffered from Old World diseases prior to 1591.

The outbreaks of smallpox that occurred along both the eastern and western slopes of the Sierras in 1593 and 1594 were the first of many disease episodes during the Jesuits' tenure in northern New Spain. In the decades that followed, epidemics occurred at regular 5 to 7 year intervals. The annual reports and occasional correspondence of the Jesuits as well as the works of Pérez de Ribas indicate there were epidemics from 1601 to 1602, 1606 to 1607, 1612 to 1613, 1616 to 1617, and 1623 to 1625. This pattern reflects, in part, the appearance of a new generation of susceptibles, specifically children that lacked an active or passive immunity to disease. Another of Father Velasco's letters, from the year 1601, provides some support for this thesis. That year Sinaloa again suffered from what apparently, in part, was fulminating smallpox. According to Velasco (AGN 1601: 109), the *cocoliztli* had its greatest impact on children who had not yet reached juvenile age—presumably those who had been born since the epidemic of 1593. In the *anua* of 1602 we learn that the epidemic involved not only smallpox, but measles, typhus, sore throat ("garrotillo"), and several other unspecified diseases. Reportedly, almost everyone suffered from one or more illnesses, and large numbers of natives died along the Ocoroni, Sinaloa, Mocorito, and Río Culiacán (AGN 1602).

Like many disease episodes, the epidemic of 1601 to 1602 was preceded by several years of hunger, caused by drought and poor harvest. Poor harvests were reported again from 1604 to 1605, following heavy rains that destroyed mission and nonmission crops (AGN 1604). The ensuing hunger and malnutrition undoubtedly lowered native resistance to disease and set the stage for the third major epidemic to affect Sinaloa, as well as Durango and Chihuahua. The epidemic of 1606 to 1607 was truly widespread and, like many epidemics, it apparently originated in southern Mexico where several diseases raged from 1604 to 1607 (Alegre 1958: 144–146; Gibson 1964: 448). During the winter of 1606 to 1607, smallpox and several other maladies became widespread in Sinaloa and thousands of natives died, particularly along the Río Fuerte (Alegre 1958: 120; Pérez de Ribas 1944: I, 342–346). During the spring of 1607 at least several thousand additional converts and countless gentiles died in the Sierras among the Chicoratos, Cahuemetos (Pérez de Ribas 1944: I, 247; 1896: I, 218), Acaxee (Alegre 1958: 158–162; Pérez de Ribas 1944: III, 29, 49, 54–55, 79–84), and Tepehuan (Alegre 1958: 154). That same year, 1607, the Irritila and Zacateco of the Laguna region also were devastated by smallpox and other diseases (Alegre 1958: 151–153; DHM 1607: 86–87; DHM 1608; Dunne 1944: 109–117; Pérez de Ribas 1944: III, 269–285).

The epidemic of 1606 to 1607 was the first of many epidemics that are known to have affected mission communities on both the eastern and western slopes of the Sierra Madre and the valleys and barrancas of the Topia region. Significantly, like many disease episodes, the epidemic predictably spread beyond the mission frontier, as is apparent from a letter written by Father Juan Fonte, describing the first Jesuit entrada among the southern Tarahumara. At the time of his visit, Fonte was working among the northern Tepehuan of Ocotlan, where he had been visited by several Tarahumara caciques who requested baptism and priests. Wishing to know more about the Tarahumara, Fonte traveled some 18 leagues beyond the Valley of San Pablo in November or December of 1607, visiting several Tarahumara rancherías in which he found a number of children who were sick and in danger of dying, including one child who was quite ill with smallpox (Pérez de Ribas 1944: III, 159–161). The fact that Fonte did not report that the child's parents or other adults and children had contracted the disease suggests that the southern Tarahumara had been exposed to smallpox on a previous occasion.

Fonte's experience among the Tarahumara was not unique. In 1612 to 1613 many natives in Sinaloa as well as among the Acaxee, Xixime, Tepehuan, and Laguneros (Irritila and Zacateco) suffered from typhus, smallpox, *cocoliztli,* influenza, and bloody stools, probably dysentery or typhoid (AGN 1612; AGN 1613; Alegre 1958: 234–235, 237–238, 244–245; Decorme 1941: II, 33–34; Pérez de Ribas 1944: I, 350; III, 66–67, 106–108). One or more of these diseases also must have spread beyond the mission frontier. Some acute or chronic infectious disease apparently was afflicting the Mayo when Father Pedro Méndez began working among them early in 1614. In a letter to his Superior, Méndez noted that during his first 15 days among the Mayo he baptized over 500 children and adults who died (Alegre 1958: 255; Pérez de Ribas 1944: II, 12–13). Later that same year, in December, Méndez again wrote to his Superior, noting that there had been numerous occasions when he made the rounds of his nine or so new missions, finding those people that had been baptized because they were sick or dying (AGN 1614: 22; Pérez de Ribas 1944: II, 21–23).

It is perhaps indicative of the extent to which maladies like typhus were spreading at this time that 350 Pima Bajo, an entire village, left their home in the Sierras in January of 1615 and traveled to San Felipe to ask for baptism (AGN 1615a; AGN 1615b; Pérez de Ribas 1944: I, 253–256). During the spring of the following year (1616) another group of 174 "Nebomes" came south, as did a third group late in 1616 (AGN 1615; AGN 1616). Although the Jesuits attributed this mass exodus to Nebome impatience for baptism, the Nebome, like other native peoples, apparently had suffered from Old World diseases and hoped that baptism might provide a measure of protection from and a cure for disease. Accordingly, three of the adults who came south in January of 1615 died en route and another reached San Felipe in a "death trance, . . . so leprous that there was not a part of his body, from his head to his feet, that was free of that plague" (Pérez de Ribas 1944: I, 255–256).

Not surprisingly, the Yaqui also suffered from diseases that outdistanced the northward moving mission frontier. In a letter describing his and Father Tomás Basilio's first entrada to the Yaqui, undertaken in the spring of 1617, Pérez de Ribas (HHB 1617) wrote that the two priests began their entrada at a time when the Yaqui were suffering from an epidemic of *cocoliztli* that had raged from a year among the Indians of Sinaloa. Pérez de Ribas went on to note that the two Jesuits baptized 1,600 infants, and 100 adults who were sick. Significantly, while many infants died, only some ("algunos") adults reportedly died, and still others regained their health. The apparent high case frequency and mortality rate for children as opposed to adults indicates that the Yaqui had suffered from the dreaded *cocoliztli* years before the first entrada by Pérez de Ribas and Basilio.

The epidemic that afflicted the Yaqui in 1617 was widespread and affected groups as distant as the Guasave and the Varohio. In his letter discussed above, Pérez de Ribas mentions that he and Basilio were visited by delegations of Varohios (Yhios), Baciroas, Tetaribes, Tehatas, Conicaris, Tepagues, and other groups who brought their sick children to the Río Yaqui to be baptized. According to Pérez de Ribas, the natives also visited and petitioned Father Diego de la Cruz on the Río Mayo to come to their lands to baptize. He did as the natives requested, and apparently found many who were ill, as Ribas noted that de la Cruz in one day baptized over 100 individuals (HHB 1617).

It is apparent from Pérez de Ribas's letter that fulminating smallpox or *cocoliztli* spread well up into the foothills of northern Sinaloa and southern Sonora in 1616 to 1617. This same area again suffered during the epidemic of 1623 to 1625. Like earlier disease episodes, the epidemic followed several years of great hunger caused by drought and poor harvests (AGN 1622; AGN 1623; Alegre 1958: 353). Coincident with this hunger were scattered outbreaks of disease that took on epidemic proportions in Sinaloa in October of 1623 (AGN 1625). The epidemic reportedly was the worst ever seen, and involved a variety of diseases, including smallpox, pneumonia ("dolor de costado"), typhus, and sore throat, possibly influenza or streptococcus (AGN 1623). Over the course of two years these maladies spread throughout Sinaloa and southern Sonora, up into the foothills and Sierras among the Acaxee and Xixime, over the Sierras among the Tepehuan, and from Zacatecas at least as far north as the mission of Parras (AGN 1623, 1624, 1625, 1626; Tello 1891: 779–780). According to Father Juan Lorencio, by the time the epidemic had run its course, over 8,600 natives died in Sinaloa alone (AGN 1625). This number, Lorencio noted, included only those who were baptized; there reportedly were many others who died during the epidemic whom the priests were unable to baptize. Included among these gentiles were many Chinipa, Pima Bajo, Eudeve, and Opata, including, apparently, the Opata cacique "Gran Sisibotari" from the Río Sahuaripa (AGN 1628: 345).

The devastation wrought by the epidemic of 1623 to 1625 contributed to a temporary slowing of mission expansion on both the eastern and western slopes of the Sierra Madre. It was not until the second half of the 1630s that the mission frontier again made significant advances, principally among the Opata and the Tarahumara. Predictably, the incorporation into the mission system of thousands of new converts ushered in a new and almost relentless wave of epidemics that were particularly destructive of the Opata and the Tarahumara, the first coming in 1636 to 1639. During these years, smallpox and *cocoliztli* raged among the Tepehuan and Tarahumara near Parral (AGN 1638) and destroyed nearly 20,000 Indians in New Mexico (Hackett 1937: 108). Some unidentified disease also claimed many lives among the Opata of the Sonora Valley (AGN 1639). Between 1645 and 1649 (AGN 1647, 1647a, 1647b, 1649; AHH 1666; Polzer 1972: 270; DHM 1645; Pérez de Ribas 1896: I, 304) and on numerous occasions during the 1650s (AGN 1653, 1653a, 1656; DHM 1652, 1653, 1658; Pérez de Ribas 1896: II, 498, 556) and 1660s (Alegre 1959: 266, 285; Decorme 1941: II, 33; DHM 1662, 1669), northern New Spain was beset with outbreaks of smallpox, "malicious" fevers (malaria or yellow fever?), bloody stools (dysentery or typhoid), sore throats, and other diseases. This situation did not change for at least another century. However, by 1678 the damage had already been done, and the native population of northern New Spain largely had been destroyed.

DEMOGRAPHIC CONSEQUENCES OF SPANISH-INTRODUCED DISEASE

Although the Jesuit materials clearly indicate that Old World diseases were a prominent feature of life in northern New Spain, the Jesuits seldom commented on case frequency and mortality rates during epidemics. The demographic consequences of Spanish-introduced disease are reflected, however, in a comparison of baptismal and census figures compiled by the Jesuits and other Spanish colonial officials. Not surprisingly, what the figures show is a dramatic decline in native population during the Jesuits' tenure in northern New Spain.

Among the Tepehuan, Zacateco, Irritila, and Acaxee, the decline was particularly rapid and pronounced. During the 1590s, when the Jesuits founded the mission of Parras, the Irritila and Zacateco of the Laguna region reportedly numbered 16,000 to 20,000 (Pérez de Ribas 1944: III, 293). As a consequence of disease, particularly the epidemics of 1607 and 1623 to 1625, only 1,569 Irritila and Zacateco survived in 1625 (Hackett 1926: 152–159). Similarly, between about 1593 to 1624 the Acaxee were reduced in number from approximately 14,000 (Pérez de Ribas 1944: III, 17) to less than 2,000 (Hackett 1926: 152–159). Census figures from 1625 also suggest that the Tepehuan lost 90 percent or more of their population by this date (Hackett 1926: 152–159). In 1638, Pérez de Ribas noted that there were more converts in one pueblo in Sinaloa than in all of the Tepehuan pueblos combined (Hackett 1937: 101–102), and that less than 10,000 of the 100,000 Laguneros, Tepehuan, Acaxee, and Xixime that had been baptized were still alive in 1638 (AHH 1638; Hackett 1937: 100).

The mission population along the west coast also underwent a significant reduction in size during the closing decade of the 16th and throughout the 17th century. Baptismal figures show that by 1624, about 106,000 natives had been baptized in Sinaloa and southern Sonora (Dunne 1940: 218). Census figures for the same year show that the mission population numbered only around 67,000 (AGN 1624a); some 40,000 native converts, in effect, died between 1591 and 1624. In 1638, 18 years later, the Jesuits reported the total number of baptisms on the west coast reached 200,000 (AHH 1638; Hackett 1937: 100). Despite almost a 100 percent increase in baptisms since 1624, the mission population increased by only around 47 percent, to about 90,000 (AHH 1638; Hackett 1937: 97, 100).

Between 1591 and 1638, then, roughly two-thirds of the mission population of northwestern Mexico died; some 200,000 native converts in all. After the years 1636 to 1639, when a new wave of epidemics began in northern New Spain, an even larger percentage of native converts perished. This decline is reflected in a census conducted in 1678 by Father Juan Ortiz Zapata (AGN 1678). At the time of Zapata's census, the Jesuits had completed the reduction and missionization of all but a few native groups in northwestern Mexico. The total number of Indians that had been baptized since 1591 numbered over 500,000, as Pérez de Ribas (1896: II, 562) reported that the number of baptisms reached 400,000 as early as about 1654. Despite a significant increase in baptisms, the total mission population for all of northwestern Mexico declined from its previous high of 100,000 in 1638, to some 63,000 in 1678 (AGN 1678).

Census figures for individual groups and missions further testify to the destruction of the native population of northern New Spain during the 17th century. The Mayo and Yaqui, for instance, were each reported to have numbered around 30,000 at the time of missionization (Pérez de Ribas 1944: II, 24, 64). By 1678 the Mayo and Yaqui numbered 7,807 and 7,549, respectively (AGN 1678); a reduction in population of 75 percent. A comparison of baptismal and census figures for other Cáhita groups and the Pima Bajo also reveals a decline in population of 75 percent or more by 1678. Predictably, because many Opata and Tarahumara communities were exposed to Old World diseases at a later date, they retained a larger percentage of their population in 1678. However, as a consequence of epidemics in 1638 to 1639, 1645 to 1647, 1649, and 1652, already by 1653 the Opata numbered only about 25,000 (AGN 1653). By 1678 this number was further reduced by half, to approximately 13,500 (AGN 1678). The population of the Opatería continued to decline until approximately 1730. At this time the Opata numbered about 7,000 and the author of the anonymous *Estado de la Provincia de Sonora* commented that there were in all of Sonora only 12,132 adults—a mere fraction of the more than 70,000 souls recorded in "the ancient catalogs" (DHM 1730: 627).

The decline in native population documented above for the Opata and other groups pertains to mission converts. How many natives died from Old World diseases that spread in advance of the mission frontier we do not know. Groups such as the Irritila, Mayo, and Yaqui, however, suffered from smallpox and other maladies prior to sustained contact with the Jesuits. Probably many native groups lost between 25 to 40 percent of their populations prior to missionization. A decline in population of this magnitude is suggested, in part, by studies of virgin populations exposed to diseases such as smallpox (Ashburn 1947; Dixon 1962; Shurkin 1979). A premission reduction in population of 25 to 40 percent is also suggested by demographic observations made by Spanish explorers. In his chronicle of the Ibarra expedition (1564 to 1565), for instance, Obregón estimated that 15,000 men could be found along the lower Yaqui (Yaquimi; Hammond and Rey 1928: 257–258). If it is assumed that Obregón was referring to all able bodied men between the ages of 15 and 40—those who might be apportioned through *repartimientos* or assembled for military purposes—then it may be inferred on the basis of the 1930 Mexican census (see Cook and Simpson 1948: 25–26) that this cohort constituted approximately 30 percent of the Yaqui's total population, which would have been about 50,000 in 1564. This figure is 40 percent larger than the 30,000 Yaqui who were reported at the time of Jesuit contact.

CULTURAL CONSEQUENCES OF SPANISH-INTRODUCED DISEASE

The great loss of life and the suffering that many communities experienced during the 16th and 17th centuries predictably had a profound impact on the structure and functioning of native societies. The general character of the changes wrought by Spanish-introduced diseases is reflected in the incongruous descriptions of native life that were compiled by Spanish explorers, and later by the Jesuits. In the explorers' accounts, dating from 1530 to 1565 (Nuñez Cabeza de Vaca 1944; Di Peso 1974: IV; Hammond and Rey 1928, 1940; Hedrick and Riley 1974, 1976; Reff 1981; Riley 1976, 1982; Sauer 1932; Sauer and Brand 1932; Undreiner 1947), the Greater Southwest frequently is described in terms of large populations living in rancherías as well as in villages and towns. Through the use of a variety of agricultural techniques, including floodwater farming and canal irrigation, many settlements enjoyed crop surpluses and were said to be involved in extensive trade of salt, turquoise, shell, macaws, slaves, obsidian, copper, bison hides, coral, and a host of other basic commodities and luxury goods (Riley 1976). The explorers also mentioned or alluded to native elites, and noted that native settlements in a number of areas were integrated into sophisticated sociopolitical systems, or what the Spaniards termed "Kingdoms" (for example, Senora, Marata, Tototenac, Cibola). By comparison, the later Jesuits described the Greater Southwest in different terms. The priests made little or no mention of "Kingdoms," and frequently described native life in terms of small, economically and politically autonomous communities that lacked intensive agriculture, regular surpluses, extensive trade, and elites (Spicer 1962). The priests also reported, particularly the Jesuits, that many native groups were quite willing to accept mission tutelage—a response that differed markedly from the hostility directed toward the explorers.

Although it is true that we have been unable to identify or correlate many settlements and groups described by the explorers with those later discussed by the missionaries (Di Peso 1974: IV; Hedrick 1978; Reff 1981; Riley 1976; Sauer 1932; Undreiner 1947), this lack of continuity is precisely what would be expected, given the introduction of Old World diseases during the interlude separating the time of the explorers and the Jesuits. Infectious diseases would have had their greatest impact on large, nucleated settlements, prompting the abandonment of villages and towns and a proliferation of dispersed rancherías, an inference borne out by recent archaeological data from the Sonora Valley (Reff 1981). Disease-induced reductions in population and shifts in residence also would have had an impact on productive and organizational strategies. A community that lost 25 to 40 percent of its population in a short time would have great difficulty clearing, sowing, and harvesting agricultural fields; constructing and maintaining irrigation systems; organizing communal hunts; or preparing food for peak periods of consumption and scarcity. Without regular surpluses of food and other basic commodities, craft specialization would decline and local and long distance exchange would languish. The collapse of productive and organizational strategies likewise would undermine the status of elites empowered through differential access to or control of crop surpluses and trade. The status of religious specialists also would suffer because of the lack of experience in dealing with unprecedented suffering and loss of life. In point of fact, all aspects of native life would suffer from outbreaks of smallpox and other maladies. Given the uncertainty of life, native peoples also would be expected to show an interest in alternative behaviors and beliefs like those offered by the Jesuits.

Was it really "new" or "different" behaviors and beliefs, however, that prompted and sustained native acceptance of programs for reduction and missionization? In the past, many researchers have concluded that native interest in and acceptance of mission ways of life were prompted by a recognition of the benefits that accrued to missionization. Although this idea can be traced back in time at least to the works of a number of 18th century mission historians (for example, Alegre 1956–1960; Nentvig 1980; Treutlein 1949), it was Bolton who popularized the notion. In many of Bolton's works as well as those of his students (Bannon 1945, 1955; Dunne 1940, 1944), the missionaries are credited with the introduction of a variety of "innovations" that transformed the "barbarians" of northern New Spain into civilized Christians. This theme was clearly spelled out in one of Bolton's earliest works on the mission frontier, wherein he likened the mission to a "great industrial school," where besides learning good manners, agriculture, and self-government, "the women were taught to cook, sew, spin, and weave; the men to fell the forest, build, run the forge, tan leather, make ditches, tend cattle, and shear sheep" (Bolton 1917: 57). According to Bolton, once the missionaries taught the "erstwhile barbarians" the rudiments of civilization, they turned the wilderness of New Spain into a veritable bastion of progress, with imposing structures, fertile farms, and great stock ranches (Bolton 1917: 58).

The conclusions reached by Bolton in this early work were amplified in many of his later publications (1932, 1936), and have been generally accepted by modern anthropologists and historians. No less a scholar than Spicer has described the missionaries as "agricultural extension workers," and the mission as "a center for the diffusion of agricultural improvements" (Spicer 1962: 58). Purportedly native recognition of the technological and economic superiority of Spanish tools, crops, cattle, and other "innovations" prompted many communities to petition for baptism and missionization, and subsequently revolutionized aboriginal culture (Spicer 1963: 58, 292, 295–297; 1980: 32, 86).

The traditional model of culture change and contact is based on a number of assumptions of questionable validity. Implicitly, at least, it has been assumed that, aboriginally, most groups in the Greater Southwest lived in small rancherías, without permanent houses, sophisticated agricultural practices, regular surpluses, extensive trade, and some form of political organization that involved more than war captains or charismatic leaders. This characterization of aboriginal culture had been based largely on observations that postdate the founding of Jesuit missions in northern New Spain and on modern ethnographic fieldwork. As noted, it is contradicted by the exploration chronicles. Also, native populations that were not affected by Old World diseases prior to missionization frequently were described by the early missionaries as being far more numerous and complex than later historians and anthropologists have recognized. This is true, for instance, of the Cáhita and Guasave, who were described by Fathers Tapia and Pérez in 1593 in terms very different from those used by later Jesuits and modern researchers (AGN 1593; HHB 1633; Shiels 1934: 108–116).

The idea that Spanish or mission innovations were an important inducement for missionization, and that these innovations revolutionized native life, also lacks empirical support. Although the Jesuits seldom discussed the economic side of mission life (Bannon 1945: 194), there were several occasions when their interests were threatened by civil and ecclesiastical encroachment that prompted reports on the wealth and functioning of the missions. In 1638, Pérez de Ribas, who was at the time the Father Provincial, compiled one such report that was sent to Spain along with testimony taken from a number of civilians in Nueva Vizcaya (AHH 1638; Hackett 1937: 95–127). Some 20 years later, in 1657, Father Francisco Xavier de Faría prepared a much more detailed report on the status of the missions (AGN 1657). Significantly, both Jesuit reports as well as the testimony taken from civilians in 1638 clearly indicate that many Spanish or Jesuit "innovations" were of little consequence. All sources agree, for instance, that the Jesuit and their mission charges subsisted principally on maize, beans, squash, and other native cultigens (AGN 1657: 25–29; Hackett 1937: 97). It is also apparent that native, as opposed to Spanish, farming practices were employed by the Jesuits and their neophytes. In his report, Faría noted that the Jesuits had tried to use oxen and plows, but found that the oxen died from heat prostration and the plows created great dust storms (AGN 1657: 28). For a variety of reasons, but particularly because of the lack of suitable land and the heat, the Jesuits also had great difficulty growing wheat; most of the wheat that was consumed in the missions was in the form of communion wafers that were made from wheat raised on Spanish farms in the Valley of Santa Barbara and hauled to Sinaloa via Topia (AHH 1638; Hackett 1937: 98, 123, 125). Even in the late 1700s, after more than a century of experimentation, wheat was still difficult to raise in Sinaloa (Villa-Señor y Sánchez 1952: 383). More important is the fact that yields from maize were three to six times that of wheat (Nentvig 1980: 23; Treutlein 1949: 46). Not only was maize more productive, but it reportedly tasted better and was preferred over wheat by Indians as well as Sonorans and Mexican-born Spaniards (Treutlein 1949: 196).

In Faría's report, we learn that many other plants that the Jesuits had brought to the northern frontier were of little consequence during the early mission period. In 1657, for instance, there were only a few, scattered missions where the priests had been successful in establishing small orchards and vineyards. According to Faría, the "fruits" of the missions ordinarily were those that grew wild in the scrubland; most of the "wine" consumed in the missions was native (mescal), or was imported from Mexico (AGN 1657: 15, 25–29). The Jesuits also enjoyed limited success in their efforts to import artisans and farmers from Mexico to teach the Indians various trades. In 1638 the former Captain of the presidio and province of Sinaloa, Don Francisco de Bustamente, testified that the priests' houses and the churches in Sinaloa were built by the priests and the Indians, and that the priests had no other workmen or artisans (Hackett 1937: 94–117). This situation apparently changed only a little during the next 20 years. In Faría's report from 1657 he noted that, although the priests had endeavored to bring architects, mechanics, farmers, and others to the northern Frontier, there were only a small number of artisans scattered throughout the missions, such that one mission might have a carpenter, another a tailor, and so forth (AGN 1657: 15).

Of the many "innovations" introduced by the Jesuits and other Spaniards, cattle clearly had the most significant impact on aboriginal culture. The Jesuits introduced a large number and variety of domesticated animals (Bannon 1945: 195; Treutlein 1965: 177; Polzer 1972: 169), but it is doubtful that they constituted an "improvement" over deer and other wild game as a food resource. Many early observers, including the Jesuits, commented on the relative abundance of all types of wild game and fish in Sinaloa and Sonora (Hammond and Rey 1928: 87, 102, 257–259; Hedrick and Riley 1976: 45, 52; Pennington 1979: 207; Pérez de Ribas 1944: I, 134, II, 64, 123; Treutlein 1949: 106). There is little reason to believe that the number and variety of wild resources inhibited population growth and cultural development, or that they ever posed a threat to the economic well being of native peoples. The same cannot be said for cattle, which destroyed hundreds of thousands of acres of land in northwestern Mexico during historic and modern times. If cattle were, in fact, an "improvement" over wild game, perhaps it was because cows, sheep, and goats were a more readily available source of nourishment during epidemics. Indeed, most epidemics in northern New Spain as well as in other areas of Mexico (Cooper 1965) occurred during the fall and winter, when large mammals such as deer were hunted aboriginally. As Pérez de Ribas (Hackett 1937: 100) pointed out, were it not for the cattle introduced by the Jesuits, the Indian otherwise would have died during times of sickness.

If it is true that Jesuit "innovations" were of little consequence, what exactly precipitated and sustained native acceptance of missionization? Although it is difficult to infer what was in the minds of native peoples, particularly given the absence of native commentaries, it nevertheless is apparent that many natives petitioned for missionaries and baptism, believing that baptism and the priests provided a protection from and a cure for disease (AGN 1639a; Alegre 1958: 470; Decorme 1941: 360–361). There is also good reason to believe that many natives were motivated by the realization that the Jesuits pursued a policy of reconstituting native adaptive strategies that faltered or collapsed in the wake of Spanish-introduced diseases.

Because the Jesuits received only modest alms from the *Patronato Real*, each priest had to implement economic and organizational strategies that provided income for his assigned mission and its outlying *visitas* (Treutlein 1939: 289). In most cases, the local missionary served in a managerial capacity, much as "big-men" do in prestate societies (Harris 1979). Accordingly, the Jesuits organized the division of Indian labor as well as the production, exchange, and redistribution of goods. Indians living within a mission community generally were required to work three days a week on communal or church lands. These lands provided surpluses that were redistributed by the local missionary among members of the mission community, usually during feasts and times of hunger arising from crop failures. For four months in 1656, for example, food shortages prompted the resident priests at Raum and Potam to distribute over 6,000 daily food rations (AGN 1657: 30). Alternatively, food surpluses were sold by the missionary and the profits gained were used to buy church ornaments or items such as chocolate and rosary beads that were redistributed among the missionaries' loyal following (AGN 1657: 32–36). Among that following were *alcaldes, fiscales,* and Indian governors who assisted the Jesuits in the administration of the mission community (Polzer 1976; Spicer 1962; Treutlein 1939).

Although it has been suggested that the mission community with its requisite economic and social organization was "a new phenomenon of Indian life" (Spicer 1962: 292), archaeological and historical data suggest that, in many important respects, it was not. Before the advent of Old World diseases, and later, of the Jesuits, many native peoples in northern New Spain were living in towns and villages as well as small rancherías. Neither the idea nor the reality of living in nucleated settlements and building substantial houses of adobe were new to groups like the Acaxee, Cáhita, Opata, Pima Bajo, or the Tarahumara. Archaeological evidence as well as the explorers' accounts also indicate that many native peoples were quite adept at floodwater and irrigation agriculture, and were familiar with the production and management of crop surpluses. Aboriginally, surpluses frequently seem to have been controlled by what Pérez de Ribas (1944: I, 133) and other Jesuits termed "principal caciques." Although anthropologists traditionally have characterized native sociopolitical organization in terms of egalitarian and politically independent communities, the "principal chiefs" among groups like the Mayo, Yaqui, and Opata had thousands of followers in numerous villages (AGN 1614; Pérez de Ribas 1944: II, 66–83, 131; AGN 1610, 1620; Dunne 1940: 112–128, 148). There is good evidence that many principal chiefs were paramount heads of chiefdoms similar to those that existed in the southeastern United States (Hudson 1976). Pérez de Ribas (1944: I, 133) noted that the principal chiefs alone decided matters of war and peace, and "were like heads and captains of families and rancherias." Pérez de Ribas also observed that the principal chief hosted important war rituals and had the largest fields, which were cultivated with the assistance of his subordinates. In an apparent reference to the principal chiefs of the Opata of the Sonora Valley, Castañeda, who was with Coronado, noted that "the dignitaries of the pueblos stand on some terraces which they have for this purpose and remain there for one hour, calling like town criers, instructing the people in what they are to do. . ." (Hammond and Rey 1940: 250). Interestingly, the "terraces" referred to by Castañeda may be equated with two "court-platform" structures that recently were identified during archaeological excavations at two large villages in the Sonora Valley—villages that were abandoned before the Jesuits arrived in the Sonora Valley (Pailes 1980; Reff 1981).

In conclusion, it is argued that many of the rights and responsibilities of the principal chiefs were assumed by the Jesuits after Old World diseases had undermined the structure and functioning of native societies, including native sociopolitical organizations. Just as native caciques and their subordinates once directed native life from the tops of ramadas (Beals 1943: 56) or earth platforms, so each day the priest or his assistants appeared at the door of the mission church, "instructing the people in what they are to do" (Bannon 1955: 61). Similarly, through the practice and advocacy of Catholicism, the Jesuits filled a void left by the death or failure of native religious leaders to chart a course through uncertain and inexplicable times. Although few natives appreciated or grasped the meaning of their new faith (Bannon 1955: 59), the Jesuits cannot be faulted in this regard for failing to "revolutionize" aboriginal culture. Indeed, perhaps their greatest legacy is that they recognized the worth of many aspects of native life. Were it not for Old World diseases that the Jesuits unwittingly fostered, their efforts to protect and preserve native peoples undoubtedly would have proved more fruitful.

Acknowledgments. I wish to thank Dr. Charles W. Polzer, S.J., for providing encouragement, support, and access to the extensive computer bibliography and microfilm collection of the Documentary Relations of the Southwest Project, Arizona State Museum, University of Arizona, Tucson. In searching for documentary evidence of disease and related information, I was aided immeasurably by the computer bibliographies and staff of the DRSW. Thanks also are due Nancy Ettlinger for reading and commenting on several drafts of this paper.

Note. This chapter originally focused on the probable impact of Old World diseases on the Opata and their relations with the Jesuits during the 1600s. Since 1980, I have analyzed historical documents and archaeological data from northwestern Mexico and the American Southwest that provide the empirical evidence of disease discussed in this paper. Because of space limitations, it has not been possible to describe in detail individual disease episodes or how many documentary sources cited can be dated, assigned authorship, or otherwise interpreted. These topics and issues are discussed in a more detailed and comprehensive analysis of the demographic and cultural consequences of disease in the Greater Southwest (Reff 1985).

DOCUMENT REFERENCES

AGN (Archivo General de la Nacion, Mexico City)

n.d. *Misiones 25.* Puntos sacados de las relaciones de Antonio Ruíz, P. Martín Pérez, P. Vincente del Aguila, P. Gaspar Varela, Juan de Grixalva, Capitan Martinez, y otras.

1593 *Misiones 25.* Anua del año de mil quinientos de noventa y tres.

1594 *Historia 15.* Memoryas Para la Historia de la Provincia de Synaloa. Anua del año de mil quinientos noventa y quatro.

1601 *Historia 15.* Memoryas Para la Historia de la Provincia de Synaloa. Carta del Padre Juan Bautista Velasco de el año de mil seiscientos uno.

1602 *Historia 15.* Memoryas Para la Historia de la Provincia de Synaloa. Anua del año de mil seiscientos y dos.

1604 *Historia 15.* Memoryas Para la Historia de la Provincia de Synaloa. Anua del año de mil seiscientos quatro.

1610 *Historia 15.* Memoryas Para la Historia de la Provincia de Synaloa. Anua del año de mil seiscientos quatro.

1612 *Historia 15.* Memoryas Para la Historia de la Provincia de Synaloa. Anua del año de mil seiscientos doze.

1613 *Historia 15.* Memoryas Para la Historia de la Provincia de Synaloa. Anua del año de mil seiscientos trece.

1614 *Historia 15.* Memoryas Para la Historia de la Provincia de Synaloa. Anua del año de mil seiscientos catorce.

1615 *Historia 15.* Memoryas Para la Historia de la Provincia de Synaloa. Anua del año de mil seiscientos quinze.

1615 a *Historia 316.* Carta de Diego Martínez de Hurdaide al virrey, 10 de Abril de 1615.

1615 b *Historia 15.* Memoryas Para la Historia de la Provincia de Synaloa. Carta del Padre Diego de Guzmán al Padre Provincial de Septiembre de mil seiscientos veinte y nuebe [sic. 1615].

1616 *Historia 15.* Memoryas Para la Historia de la Provincia de Synaloa. Carta del Padre Martín Pérez, del año de mil seiscientos diez y seis.

1620 *Historia 15.* Memoryas Para la Historia de la Provincia de Synaloa. Anua del año de mil seiscientos y veinte.

1622 *Misiones 25.* Carta Annua de la Provincia de la Compañia de Jesús en Nueva España.

1623 *Misiones 25.* Carta annua de la Provincia de la Compañia de Jesús de Nueva España.

1624 *Misiones 25.* Carta Annua de la Provincia de la Compañia de Jesús de Nueva España.

1624a *Fondo Cossio II–7.* Catalogo de la Gente que tienen los partidos de la Provincia de Cinaloa fecho en 12 de henero de 1624.

1625 *Misiones 25.* Carta Annua de la Provincia de la Compañia de Jesús de Nueva España.

1626 *Misiones 25.* Carta Annua de la Provincia de la Compañia de Jesús de Nueva España.

1628 *Historia 15.* Memoryas Para la Historia de la Provincia de Synaloa. Missiones de San Ygnacio en Mayo, Yaqui, Nevomes, Chinipas, y Sisibotaris.

1638 *Misiones 25.* Copia de una carta del Padre Gaspar de Contreras para el Padre Provincial, Santiago Papasquiaro, 5 August 1638.

1639 *Misiones 25.* Puntos de Anua de la nueba mission de San Francisco Jabier, año de 1639.

1639a *Misiones 25.* Puntos de Anua de la nueba mission de San Francisco Jabier, año de 1639.

1647 *Misiones 25.* Letras Annuas de la Provincia de la Compañia de Jesús de Mexico, año 1647.

1647a *Misiones 25.* Carta de Marcos del Rio al Padre Visitador Pedro Pantoja etc., Guasabus, 4 April 1647.

1647b *Misiones 26.* Annua del Pueblo de Santa Catalina de Tepeguanes.

1649 *Misiones 26.* Carta annua De la Provincia De la Compañia De Jesús de Mexico; Del año de 1648 y [1]649, Andres Rada, 10 July 1650.

1653 *Misiones 26.* Puntos de annua del año de 1653 del collegio y misiones de Cinaloa.

1653a *Historia 15.* Memoryas Para la Historia de la Provincia de Synaloa. Carta Annua de la Mission de San Ygnacio de los Rios de Hiaqui y Mayo: año de mil seiscientos cincquenta y tres.

1656 *Historia 15.* Memoryas Para la Historia de la Provincia de Synaloa. Anua de la Mission de San Ygnacio del Rio de Mayo y Hiaqui: año de mil seiscientos cincuenta y seis.

1657 *Historia 316.* Apologetico Defensorio y Puntual Manifesto que los Padres de la Compañia de Jesús, Missioneros de las Provincias de Sinaloa y Sonora, Francisco Xavier de Faría, November 1657.

1678 *Misiones 26.* Relación de los Missiones que la Compañia tiene en el Reyno y Provincias de la Nueva Viscaya en la Nueva España echa el año de 1678 con ocasion de la Visita General dellas que por orden del Padre Provincial Thomas Altamirano hizo el Padre Visitador Juan Hortiz Zapata de la misma Compañia.

AHH (Archivo Historico de Hacienda, Mexico City)

1638 *Temporalidades 2009–1.* Memorial al Rey para que no se recenga la limosna de la missiones y consierva al

Senora Palafox en las relaciónes a la Compañia, 12 September 1638.

1666 *Temporalidades 1126–2*. Relación de lo sucedido en el pleito de la Compañia con los Religiossos de San Francisco.

DHM (Documentos para la Historia de Mexico), Cuarta Serie, Tomo III. Mexico, 1857.

1596 Del Anua Del Año De 1596.

1598 Del Anua Del Año De 1598.

1601 Carta del Padre Nicolas de Arnaya dirigida Al Padre Provincial Franciso Baez el año de 1601.

1607 Del Anua Del Año De 1607.

1608 Carta del Padre Luis de Ahumada, dirigida al Padre Martín Pelaez, Provincial de la Compañia De Jesús el 13 de Noviembre de 1608.

1645 Relación de los sucedido en este reino de la Vizcaya desde el año de 1644 hasta el de 45 acerca de los alzimientos, danos, robos, hurtos, muertos y lugares despoblados de que se saco un traslado para remitir al padre Francisco Calderon, provincial de la provincia de Mexico de la Compañia de Jesús . . . Nicolas de Zepeda, San Miguel de las Bocas, Abril 28 de 1645, mas addendum de 11 de septiembre de 1645.

1652 Noticias de las Misiones sacados de la anua del Padre Jose Pascual; año de 1651.

1653 Carta que escribe el Padre Gaspar De Contreras al Padre Provincial Francisco Calderon el año de 1653.

1658 Puntos de Annua, Año 1658, Mission de Nebomes de N.P.S. Francisco de Borja.

1662 Puntos de anua de estos diez años que he asistido en este partido de San Pablo, de la Mision de Taramuras y Tepehuanes (de unas y otras hay), desde el año de 1652 hasta este de 1662 sumariamente lo que ha pasado cuanto a lo espiritual.

1669 Patrocinio del glorioso apostol de las Indias S. Francisco Javier en el reino de la Nueva Vizcaya, año de 1669.

1730 Estado de la provincia de Sonora, con el catalogo de sus pueblos, iglesias, lenguas diversas que en ella se hablan y leguas en que se dilata; con una breve descripcion de la Sonora jesuitica, segun se halla por el mes de Julio de este año de 1730, escrito por un padre misionero de la provincia de Jesús de Nueva España.

HHB (Hubert H. Bancroft Collection, Bancroft Library, University of California, Berkeley)

1617 *Memorias Para la Historia de la Provincia de Sinaloa*. Carta del Padre Andres Pérez al Padre Provincial, Pueblo de Tesamo, 13 June 1617.

1633 *Mexican Manuscript 7*. Historia de las Missiones apostolicas, que los clerigos regulares de la Compañia de Jesús en echo en las indias occidentales del reyno de la Nueva Vizcaya, Juan de Albizuri.

Alegre 1956–1960
Arregui 1946
Ashburn 1947
Bakewell 1971
Bancroft 1886
Bannon 1945, 1955
Beals 1943
Bolton 1917, 1932, 1936
Borah and Cook 1963
Carrera Stampa 1955
Cloudsley-Thompson 1976
Cook and Simpson 1948
Cooper 1965
Cuidad Real 1976
Decorme 1941
Di Peso 1974
Dixon 1962
Dobyns 1963
Dunne 1940, 1944, 1948
Faust 1949
Florencia 1955
Fontana 1976
Friede 1967
Gibson 1964
Griffen 1979
Grijalva 1924
Hackett 1923, 1926, 1937
Hammond and Rey 1928, 1940
Harris 1979
Hedrick 1978
Hedrick and Riley 1974, 1976

Hu-DeHart 1981
Hudson 1976
Kitchens 1949
McNeill 1976
Mecham 1927
Mendieta 1945
Mota y Escobar 1940
Navarro García 1967
Nentvig 1980
Nuñez Cabeza de Vaca 1944
Ocaranza 1934
Pailes 1980
Pennington 1979
Pérez de Ribas 1896, 1944
Polzer 1972, 1976
Powell 1952
Reff 1981, 1985
Riley 1976, 1982
Sauer 1932, 1935
Sauer and Brand 1932
Shiels 1934
Shurkin 1979
Spicer 1962, 1980
Tello 1891
Treutlein 1939, 1949, 1965
Undreiner 1947
Villa-Señor y Sánchez 1952
West 1949
West and Parsons 1941
Zinsser 1934

CHAPTER TEN

The Renaissance of Anthropological Studies in Northwestern Mexico

Ralph L. Beals (University of California, Los Angeles)

The chapters in this volume show that a new generation of anthropologists is now utilizing the long-neglected potential for anthropological studies in northwestern Mexico. Despite claims that the discipline was universal, anthropologists for a long time were preoccupied with nonliterate and nonwestern societies. United States anthropologists particularly restricted their research to North American Indian studies. Even so, the Indians of northwestern Mexico were virtually unknown and unstudied by them. Some Mexican scholars of the 19th century dealt briefly with Indians but their work was almost entirely ethnohistorical and focused mainly on identifying tribes and languages in the area. This research was updated and made known to United States scholars through the work of Thomas and Swanton (1911). The most extensive sources of information in English, the neglected works of the historian Hubert Howe Bancroft (1875–1876), were virtually ignored by anthropologists.

CHRONOLOGY OF RESEARCH IN NORTHWESTERN MEXICO

Knowledge based on contemporary field studies began with the work of Carl Lumholtz in the 1890s. Lumholtz traversed the length of the Sierra Madre Occidental from Chihuahua to Michoacán, and his reports appeared in a series of notes and popular travelogs beginning with an article in Scribners Magazine in 1891 *(Explorations in the Sierra Madre)* and terminating with his *New Trails in Mexico* in 1912. Anthropologically, the most important publication was his two volume work, *Unknown Mexico* (1902a). The reports suffer from Lumholtz's lack of sophistication as well as his need to write to a paying popular audience, but his data seem accurate although centered on the more visible aspects of native life.

Published about the same time was *The Seri Indians* by McGee (1898). Close examination indicates that McGee spent only a brief time interviewing Seri who were working or visiting at a cattle estancia outside Seri territory. The work is so dominated by Morgan-style evolutionism that sometimes it becomes pure fantasy. McGee was so concerned with placing the Seri in their proper evolutionary niche that he either elicited or interpreted responses to fit his purpose.

Of far higher quality is the early research of Theodore Preuss (1912) with the Cora and Huichol. His published work deals largely with ritual objects and ceremonialism, and one limitation of it is a lack of social context for the ceremonialism and a tendency to interpret everything from a Valley of Mexico perspective. The major work is profusely illustrated and apparently quite reliable; when Elsie Clews Parsons and I showed the illustrations to Cora and Huichol we met in Tepic in 1932, they unhesitatingly identified the objects, describing the materials used, the method of manufacture, and their ritual or ceremonial purposes.

Beginning in 1898, Aleš Hrdlička published a number of notes and papers dealing with various peoples of northwestern Mexico. The most important is *Physiological and Medical Observations among the Indians of the Southwestern United States and Northern Mexico* (1908). Most of the papers report anthropometric data, but there are scattered comments on material culture and random observations about life ways or ceremonials. In some instances these do not refer to living Indians; his material on the Yaqui, for example, involves measurements taken on the corpses on the field of a recent battle between Yaqui and Federal troops, and his material culture objects were collected from the same location.

Before the 1920s, J. Alden Mason visited the Tepecano a number of times and published a series of short papers beginning in 1912. Some Mexican sources were available, especially Nicolas Leon's extensive series of brief papers dealing with the Tarascans. Although largely ethnohistorical, these reports do include some observations of contemporary Tarascan life. For the Yaqui, mention should be made of *Las Razas Indigenes de Sonora Y la Guerra del Yaqui* by Fortunato Hernández (1902). The nascent interest in Mexican research culminating in the establishment of the International Institute of Anthropology in Mexico City, a short-lived enterprise terminated by the Mexican Revolution, did not reach northwestern Mexico.

When United States anthropology in the 1920s began to free itself from its provincial concern with the ethnography of the United States and Canada, there was for most of Mexico (but especially the North), little knowledge of which Indian groups survived, where they were located, or any adequate idea of their cultures. With expanding interest, it was evident at the time that someone should supplement the linguistic mapping of the area by bringing together information about the cultures, both past and present. The first part of this task I undertook in my *Comparative Ethnology of Northern Mexico before 1750* (Beals 1932b), an early and somewhat incomplete attempt at what today is known as ethnohistory.

When I entered the University of California at Berkeley and began to study anthropology, I soon met with faculty members who were beginning to develop an interest in Mexico. Although I never had a formal course with him, one influential professor was the cultural geographer, Carl O. Sauer. When I first met him about 1926, he talked at length about a rather grandiose interdisciplinary program to study a cross section across the Sierra Madre Occidental along the proposed route of the Kansas City, Mexico, and Orient railway between Chihuahua and the Pacific, a plan modeled after the 19th century studies of the United States west of the 100th Meridian. The KCM&O had been acquired recently by the Santa Fe railway and there was talk of completing the line through the Sierras, skirting the Barranca de Cobre (a project completed much later by the Mexican government) and building a modern seaport at Topolobampo near the mouth of the Fuerte River. Topolobampo was the location of a proposed utopian cooperative colony, a project in which my parents had been much interested, although they always had the good sense not to invest any money in the various utopian schemes that attracted them. Sauer's project was predicated on the Santa Fe railway financing the enterprise to promote freight-producing development and as a publicity and public relations effort. An important part of the scheme was to use the friendship between the new President of the University, the astronomer William Wallace Campbell, and the new President of the Santa Fe railway, Mr. Story. The project foundered when Campbell, after much soul searching, decided he could not exploit his friendship to promote the enterprise.

Nevertheless, Sauer did a reconnaissance along the Pacific slope of the Sierra Madre, covering not only the coast but penetrating the Sierra along several of the major rivers (Sauer 1932, 1934, 1935). He and his students, most notably Donald Brand, did some more intensive surveys, particularly of the so-called Trincheras culture in northern Sonora (Sauer and Brand 1931; Brand 1935). He also stimulated A. L. Kroeber to make a survey from southern Sinaloa to the United States border. Kroeber located numerous groups of Mayo and Yaqui Indians. He also spent some time with Seri informants in the Barrio Seri of Hermosillo and collected a few texts and vocabularies from Yaqui informants, mostly in the same Barrio. The Seri material was published by the Southwest Museum (Kroeber 1931).

With Kroeber's encouragement and support, in 1930 I applied for and was awarded one of the new postdoctoral fellowships in the biological sciences offered by the National Research Council. The fellowship proposal was for an acculturation study among the Yaqui and Mayo. It may be of interest to historians of the discipline that the idea of acculturation was sufficiently current to be used in such an application, although the word had not yet been used generally in the literature. I recall Kroeber, somewhat sourly I thought, commented on an early draft of my application that he supposed fellowship applications always had to make use of the latest fad words. Fieldwork under the fellowship was carried out during the winter seasons of 1930 to 1932.

About this time Wendell Bennett and B. M. Zingg began their study among the Tarahumara. I do not know the source of their interest or financing, although most likely Robert Redfield's pioneering work in Tepoztlan had some influence on them, as did also the expanding horizons of United States anthropologists. In Bennett's case, his Tarahumara work led to a lifelong interest in Latin America. Although primarily known for his work in archaeology, Bennett once told me that he wanted first to be known as a social scientist, secondly as an anthropologist. He specialized in archaeology only because he enjoyed "playing with" the materials.

Bennett and Zingg did not get on well together. As the senior member of the pair, Bennett early sent Zingg into the barrancas, remaining himself in the sierra, and their joint work (Bennett and Zingg 1935) reflects this. Zingg (1938) also went on to study among the Huichol.

These beginnings in anthropological studies were not followed up immediately, possibly partly because the conditions of fieldwork were difficult, if not hazardous (see Chapter 1, Reflections). More significant, perhaps, were the relatively slow publication of the results and the "ethos" of fund granting agencies, then mostly foundations. Prolonged or repetitive studies were not favored. The Tarahumara, for example, were considered to have been "done" by Bennett and Zingg, despite the fact that they are the most numerous group north of the Valley of Mexico except for the Navajo, and the non-Christianized or "gentile" groups were unstudied. The inadequacy of early Cora-Huichol and Yaqui-Mayo studies is attested by the new riches provided by the papers in this volume.

As for publications, most of the important reports on this region did not appear for a decade or more after the field research. (In the overview above, a number of articles and marginal studies have been omitted.) An exception is the relatively prompt appearance of the report by Bennett and Zingg on the Tarahumara in 1935 and Zingg's study of the Huichol in 1938. Mason from time to time published short papers on the Tepecano. Of my own work, a short paper on "Aboriginal Survivals in Mayo Culture" appeared in the *American Anthropologist* in 1932, and in 1934 Elsie Clews Parsons and I published a more important paper on "The Sacred Clowns of the Pueblo and Mayo-Yaqui Indians." However, my two major monographs on the Yaqui and Mayo did not appear until 1943 and 1945. Edward Spicer's Pascua village study appeared in 1940, but his perhaps more significant study of Potam in the Yaqui valley did not appear until 1954. Farther south, the notes collected on the Cora and Huichol by Elsie Clews Parsons and myself were never published, although they were included in a volume of typescript essays presented to Robert H. Lowie around 1933.

Serious fieldwork among the Tarascans did not begin until my study of Cherán in 1940. Aside from articles, two monographs resulted (Beals, Carrasco, and McCorkle 1944 and Beals 1946). These were followed shortly by a report on Tzintzuntzan by Foster (1948) and one on Quiroga by Brand (1951). Two other geographers contributed importantly about the same time:

R. C. West published the *Cultural Geography of the Modern Tarascan Area* in 1948, and Dan Stanislawski contributed two short but seminal papers on Tarasco (1947) and Michoacán (1950). Other ethnographers such as Paul Friedrich (1957, 1958) provided some continuity with more contemporary research.

Follow-up work did not really begin until the 1950s, although Herbert Passin visited the Tarahumara about 1940 and published two brief notes and an article (1942). Jacob Fried made a more extended Tarahumara visit about 1950, producing an unpublished doctoral dissertation and two articles. His major printed contribution is in the *Handbook of Middle American Indians* (1969). In the 1960s, John G. Kennedy conducted extensive research among the non-Christianized Tarahumara and later made shorter studies elsewhere in the area. Aside from articles, the principal results are found in two monographs (Kennedy 1970; Kennedy and Lopez 1981). The Tepehuan and Tepecano have been studied by Elman R. Service and Carroll L. Riley, respectively; little has been published besides their *Handbook of Middle American Indians* summaries in 1969 (see below).

On the Pacific slope, Thomas B. Hinton and Roger Owen surveyed most of the Opata and other remnant groups (see especially Hinton 1959; Owen 1958, 1959). The next serious work among the Mayo was by Charles Erasmus, a study of the lower Mayo River, mainly reported in his 1961 book. Following that, and dating in the modern period, were important studies by the Crumrines. Thomas B. Hinton (1961, 1964) intensively studied the Cora of Jesus María. More comprehensive reviews and bibliographies may be found in the *Handbook of Middle American Indians* (1969), including a summary article for northwestern Mexico by Edward Spicer (1969b) and descriptive articles by Roger Owen, Thomas Hinton, Edward Spicer, Joseph A. Grimes and Thomas B. Hinton, Ralph L. Beals, Carroll L. Riley, Elman R. Service, and Jacob Fried.

Finally, most of the modern work is represented by the authors in this volume. They have made extended and problem oriented studies in depth through most of the area, mainly in the 1960s and early 1970s, and they are developing the kind of intellectual undertakings for which I had hoped my own exploratory studies might lay the groundwork. My own interests and career line went in different directions, but in a real personal sense this volume is a gratifying and rewarding outcome of my early interests in northwestern Mexico.

COMMENTARY ON ENCLAVEMENT RESEARCH

The chapters in this book all examine aspects of the concept of enclavement and, to a lesser degree, the ideas of "regions of refuge" advanced by Gonzalo Aguirre Beltrán (1967), for me the less satisfying of the two approaches. All the papers give substantive information about such matters as ethnohistory, Indian-mestizo relations, and the social organization of the groups studied, although not all treatments are equally weighted. The concept of enclavement emerges as one of great potential usefulness in a wide variety of cultural frameworks.

It also emerges as a complex phenomenon, with numerous situational and historical variables involved. And, as is characteristic of productive research, the papers raise many additional questions. I comment on what these chapters contribute to the understanding of enclavement and discuss at some length issues I believe they raise.

The original symposium paper by Daniel T. Reff was an excellent ethnohistorical study of the Opata, seeking to explain why they failed to survive as a significant ethnic group; instead they were almost completely assimilated by the rather special local mestizo culture of northeastern Sonora. He concluded that between the time of the first Spanish contacts and the period of missionization, the once town-dwelling Opata had been so decimated by Apachean raids and perhaps new Spanish introduced diseases that they were reduced to a scattered ranchería dwelling population. [This idea is explored in more detail in Chapter 9.] The mission policy of settling natives in towns thus was viewed by the Opata as restoring the basic Opata way of life, making them highly susceptible to new cultural influences and resulting in their almost complete assimilation as documented by Owen (1958, 1959) and Hinton (1959). The explanation is appealing but it is difficult to reconcile with the response to missionaries by the Cáhitians.

Why did the Cáhita groups, with few exceptions, accept missionaries as readily as did the Opata? They had no tradition of town dwelling but were primarily ranchería-dwelling farmers. There are hints of some larger tribal organization for the Yaqui and the Tehueco. Even the Sinaloa, the first group to receive missionaries, apparently could be treated as a unit. There were no Apachean raiders to scatter the Cáhitians, although introduced diseases probably were equally devastating. On the other hand, there were intergroup "wars," probably essentially massive raids, and the southern groups may have viewed the missionaries as protectors not only against these raids but also against Spanish slave raiders from the south. Cabeza de Vaca mentions encountering slavers from Culiacán north of the Sinaloa, but by the time the missions were established most Spanish settlements had withdrawn to the south. Permanent Spanish military forces in the area were established some years after the Sinaloa and upper Fuerte river missions were founded, and were used primarily to protect the Christianized Indians from raids by their gentile relatives. The major activities, punitive expeditions against the Tehueco and the Yaqui, were composed of a few Spanish soldiers—rarely were there more than 20 or 30 in the whole area—and large numbers of Indian auxiliaries.

Punitive raids against the Yaqui for their raids against their Christianized Mayo neighbors were all unsuccessful, and the largest narrowly escaped annihilation just as had the earliest expedition sent by the notorious Nuño de Guzmán. Yet ultimately the Yaqui, despite their military successes, finally requested voluntarily that missionaries be sent to them. The reason, according to the great Jesuit historian of the region, Andres Pérez de Ribas, was that they were tired of the constant turmoil and wished only to cultivate their fields in peace. The

Spanish found this explanation hard to believe, thus laying the foundation for centuries of mistrust.

The Yaqui and Mayo were not immediately enclaved in a meaningful sense of the concept. They continued to reside on ancestral lands and retained considerable autonomy throughout the Colonial period. Nor did this autonomy arise from any "refuge" situation. The populations remained in place, although concentrated in larger settlements. For many years, Spanish exploitation of local land was minimal. Efforts to secure Indian labor for the mines were both illegal and actively opposed by the missionaries. The main Spanish settlements were in mining areas in the mountains and foothills. Their communication lines were along the foothills or through interior lateral valleys such as those of the Alamos and Cedros rivers, away from the main Cáhita settlements. The main exception in late Colonial and Republican times was the route from the port of Agiabampo near the mouth of the Mayo River to Alamos, the distributing and administrative center for a rich mining area and for a time the capital of the early state of Ostimuri, which comprised most of modern Sonora and Sinaloa. But generally north-south travel was easier through the interior valleys and foothills than in the dense thorn forests of the coastal plains.

Although forced labor was forbidden, many Indians, especially the Yaqui, voluntarily became wage workers in the mines, and the Yaqui soon became enterprising prospectors on their own. Tradition attributes the discovery of many of the more important mining centers of Sonora to Yaqui prospectors. In addition, the coastal area provided most of the food for the Spanish settlements. The Yaqui also built large cattle herds and were exempted from government monopolies for tobacco and salt, the latter produced in lagoons near the mouth of the Yaqui River. Attempts after Independence to infringe on these rights, especially the salt trade, broke the long period of Colonial peace (except for the "strange revolt of 1740"). Spicer (1980) has treated Yaqui history in some detail. He makes clear the rather unusual nationalism, both in a territorial sense with strong sacred meanings and in a sense of the Yaqui as a people, characteristics reflected in their development of political institutions and activism vis-a-vis the Spanish, the missionaries, and the hacendados of the 19th century.

In their resistance to encroachments, the Yaqui perhaps differed from the Mayo and other peoples only in the vigor of their resistance. In the late 19th century, during the Diaz regime, this resistance led finally to the *diaspora*, either flight to the United States or deportation of many to Yucatan or the Valle Nacional in Oaxaca. The ability of the Yaqui to survive and to reconstitute their tribal activities after the start of the revolution in 1910 is remarkable. For much of the period between 1910 and 1920 they militarily dominated the coastal and foothill region from Hermosillo south to the Fuerte River or beyond, systematically destroying haciendas and confining mestizos to a series of strongholds, mostly in the towns, and to a few precarious communication routes, mainly along the railroad. During the 1920s, Yaqui troops formed the backbone of General Alvaro Obregón's military following.

Local folklore, I suspect carefully fostered by the Obregón family, attributes a Mayo Indian grandmother to the General, although the family estates were on the south bank of the Yaqui River. Obregón certainly spoke reasonably fluent Yaqui. In the late 1920s, Arthur Hofmann traveled in a train, to which Obregón's private car was attached, when the train was stopped by some 400 Yaqui warriors who had burned a wooden culvert on the line. As only two or three months earlier the Yaqui had stopped and burned a passenger train, killing all but one or two of the passengers, the situation was tense. According to Hofmann, Obregón stood on the back platform of his car and harangued the Yaqui in their own tongue for some two hours until they finally abandoned the train and allowed the construction of a shoo-fly about the burned culvert (an operation for which Sud Pacífico trains at the time were usually equipped).

The point of this somewhat rambling discourse is to underscore the unique character of Yaqui resistance to outside domination. It is questionable whether they represent an example of enclavement before the present development of the large water control systems by the Federal government. Although the Yaqui had wrested from the government a special status for their lands unique in Mexico, the nature of the agricultural opportunities offered by large scale irrigation, with its requirement of extensive capital investment for land preparation and equipment, led to leasing of large tracts of Yaqui land and a curtailment of Yaqui opportunities for subsistence farming. The Yaqui thus appear on the one hand to be landlords receiving rents from agribusinesses, and on the other being wage workers for their own tenants. As yet they have maintained some territorial integrity and autonomy, but these are increasingly undermined by a growing number of mestizos in their area.

A key variable in the different adaptations of Opata and Yaqui may be that the Opata dwelt not on extensive coastal plains but in a series of mountain basins in the midst of what became an active mining area. A better comparison for the Opata, therefore, may be the mountain or foothill peoples of southern Sonora and Sinaloa, including such vanished groups as the Chinipa and Acaxee or the Tahue of the coasts in the southern half of Sinaloa. But whether viewed from the perspective of the Opata or of the Yaqui, the enclavement of the Mayo appears unique.

Many years ago I remarked that I expected the Yaqui to survive as a culturally distinct group, but that the Mayo probably soon would disappear because they had lost the boundary maintaining mechanism of the civil wing of the civil-religious hierarchy. Crumrine shows quite clearly that I was wrong, and an active complex ritual life requiring extensive participation and the maintenance of some competence in the native language are enough to permit survival of an ethnic unit without territorial boundaries or political power. Spicer often averred that the Yaqui as an ethnic group would disappear when so many individual Yaqui defected that there were too few to maintain the ritual system; it seems likely that the same is true for the Mayo.

The chapters by Crumrine and Carlos deal with two different

groups of Mayo, those of the Mayo River valley and those of the Fuerte. Crumrine focuses on the Mayo resort to religious revivalism and the elaboration of ritual and symbolism to maintain their identity. Thus far they are succeeding despite loss of territoriality, political power, and most of their independent economic base. In material culture and life styles, Crumrine's Mayo can easily become mestizos of the lowest economic stratum and many of them do; all that is necessary is to abandon the use of the house cross and to cease to participate in rituals or to speak Mayo.

In contrast, Carlos emphasizes the operation of socioeconomic and political factors as distinct from what he calls "cultural" factors. How political and socioeconomic factors cease to be cultural eludes me, but clearly there is a considerable difference between the approaches of Crumrine and Carlos. Crumrine views the modern enclaves as primarily the result of Mayo efforts to preserve their cultural identity, whereas Carlos considers enclavement as the result of systematic discriminatory efforts by the government and the economically advantaged mestizos.

That external forces emanating from the government and social characteristics of the dominant society contribute to the creation of ethnic enclaves is unarguable, but I have difficulty with many aspects of the analysis by Carlos. For one thing, he gives too little attention to assimilation, both as a potential solution for the Mayo and as a policy goal of the dominant society. I doubt that there is any official government policy to create Mayo enclaves; in fact, a major slogan since the revolution of 1910–1920 has been "the incorporation of the Indian." Because of mestizo attitudes toward the "inferiority" of the Indian and, in part, through inferior education and lack of adaptive skills on the part of many Mayo, "incorporation" means assimilation into the least privileged class of labor, a fact that worries government planners and theorists very little. It is relevant to the soundness of some of his arguments that, as Carlos himself points out, assimilated or partially assimilated Mayos are economically better off than their more traditional counterparts.

Another set of objections arises from undocumented historical assertions. Carlos ignores the problem of the origin of the Fuerte River Mayo. Historically, the Fuerte River valley was inhabited by a number of distinct Cáhitian speaking tribes. These people either became Mayoized or were replaced or absorbed by Mayo immigrants from the north, changes that may have relevance for current enclavement processes. In contrast to the apparent aboriginal homogeneity of the Mayo River group, the Fuerte tribes were often involved in intertribal warfare. The Cáhita were not brought under mission control until the late 16th and early 17th century. A Spanish settlement was founded by Ibarra on the upper Fuerte in 1564; it was soon moved southward to the Sinaloa River and when the first Cáhita mission was established on the Sinaloa, it had dwindled to five Spanish residents. Missions were established on the Fuerte beginning in 1604, on the Mayo in 1616, and on the Yaqui in 1620. None of these missions was established by military force as Carlos seems to imply. Regular military presence in Cáhita territory began with the establishment of the Fuerte de Montesclaros, giving the River its present name. Its main function was to protect missionized groups against raids by gentile neighbors, at first mainly protecting the Sinaloa and converted Fuerte tribes against the bellicose Tehueco and Ahome, and later protecting the Mayo against Yaqui raids. The number of Spanish troops was small, at times dwindling to some 20, and most punitive expeditions were composed mainly of Indian allies. Even so, punitive expeditions against the Yaqui were all soundly defeated at considerable cost to expeditionary forces.

When the Yaqui voluntarily requested missionaries, they laid down conditions regarding the entry of other Spaniards into their territory. These conditions were rather scrupulously observed by the military, who took great pains to avoid any show of force in their few visits to Yaqui territory. This situation is well documented by Spicer (1980). In the light of these facts, Carlos seems to overemphasize the effects of military coercion.

Most of the pressures placed on the Sinaloa Mayos as described by Carlos actually were exerted in the 19th and 20th centuries. Throughout most of the Colonial period, secular Spanish settlements were confined to the foothills and mountains, the mining regions, as noted above. Independence brought "full citizenship" to the Indians and the abandonment of all Spanish protective legislation. While this led to some encroachment on Indian territories, including both farming haciendas in valleys and cattle estancias between the rivers, not until the Reform laws of the 1850s did this encroachment become serious from the Indian viewpoint. Even so, the cattle raising enterprises may have been primarily Indian undertakings in the 1800s; certainly the Yaqui were the major cattle raisers in the Northwest until the Diaz regime. The picture, incidentally, of abundant game animals in aboriginal times is almost certainly false; although the vegetation might have supported a fair game population, the arid interriverine lands lacked adequate water supplies for many animals. Vegetable resources such as the mesquite bean were far more important. The mesquite bean is still largely available to the Mayo, but even aboriginally it was not highly prized and was sought only in famines. As late as 1928, during periods of warfare the Yaqui were able to subsist for many months hidden in the thorn forests, relying mainly on wild vegetable products. In any case, the use of military force on any considerable scale did not occur until after Independence. And as a final query, I wonder what differences between the Fuerte River and Mayo River groups may be accounted for by the historical and perhaps environmental forces that led to large-scale sugar cane production in the Fuerte valley but not in the Mayo?

I have reviewed these thoughts in detail because Carlos has weakened his important contribution by focusing his research on the modern political and economic power structures in Mexico without adequately considering the historical realities, and by his dedication to some concepts developed for other parts of Mexico. Even in using these rather dogmatic frameworks of analysis, he tends to overstate his position. For instance, he seems to say that the agrarian land distribution program began with President Lázaro Cárdenas. While this fits his explanations, it is not correct. The land distribution program began before 1920. While its initial stages were slow, it acquired considerable momentum until it languished under Cárdenas's immediate predecessor. Under Cárdenas it accelerated enormously, but it did not originate with him.

Moving to the south, other pictures emerge. Shadow, in a somewhat different approach, also uses multiple causation in his interpretation of a Tepecano area, relating production modes, agrarian conflicts, and social identity to enclavement processes. The Tepecano situation is complex, for despite historic marginalization and exploitative contacts with mestizo cultures, the main conflicts currently are between two Tepecano groups who have opted for (or would Castile say "were forced into"?) different patterns of land accessibility. The conflict is thus between ejiditarios and comuneros. The first group seems oriented toward assimilation, the second toward perpetuation of enclave status. Both groups are responding to what they perceive as their best economic interests with ideology playing little part.

Weigand and Ron Siordia bring significant new dimensions to enclavement in their study of the ejidos in an irrigation district of Jalisco. The groups involved are mestizo rather than Indian, and the study suggests that economic marginalization does not produce enclavement in the ordinary sense under these conditions. Rather, class differences within the mestizo culture seem involved, although some parallels with the ejiditario group among the Tepecano are suggested. Certainly the chapter invites speculation about how the results might differ if ethnic Indian groups had been involved.

Weigand's previous research (1978) on the Nayarita and Huichol shows that the history of tribal movements is much more complex and indicates more diversity in culture within the larger units such as the Huicholes than previous students have suggested. In a sense, the populations of the area appear to have been territorially compressed by outside pressures, but many of them have been in place for a very long time, probably long before Spanish contacts. Except for the relatively small number of immigrants, then, they have not sought a "region of refuge"; in a sense, they have always occupied one. The various groups illustrate that the operation of external pressures as well as the efforts to preserve ethnic identities thus far have contributed heavily to the enclavement process, assisted until recent years by geographic isolation and poor communications. In modern times, commercialization of ethnic arts not only has debased the corpus of Nayarit folk art, but it has afforded many individuals the means to move out of the enclavement situation into urban settings. Weigand's research strongly suggests that ethnic identity and its preservation are necessary for the occurrence of enclavement rather than the formation of subclass distinctions as is illustrated in the Weigand and Ron Siordia ejido study.

Castile focuses on an important new factor, the meaning of "choice," in his attempt to explain the persistence of Cherán's "Tarascanness." In his initial discussion he makes a number of cogent observations on some widely used cliches, pointing out the often ideological overtones to the use of such expressions as "the culture of repression" or "exploitation" without adequate definition of meaning and context.

Castile is irked by the idea of choice as portrayed in *A Village that Chose Progress: Chan Kom Revisited* (Redfield 1950), and argues that the only real choice is between alternatives offered by the dominant culture within the limits set by political, social, and economic pressures over which the group has no control. In this, his views are not widely dissimilar to those of Carlos. But I think he has made both too much and too little of parts of his argument: too much in selecting his Cherán facts to meet his concept of choice, too little because he has not explored adequately the full implications of this important concept for the process of enclavement.

"Choice" is an individual phenomenon. Groups make choices only in the sense that their members reach some consensus or at least accept or accede to a decision made by some internal power or leadership mechanism. Moreover, choice always is limited. Individuals make or accept or reject only those choices they perceive. They do not have an infinite array of possibilities and the perceptive creativeness of most humans is strictly limited; they borrow or adapt rather than discover or invent. Contact with a different culture may vastly expand the range of choices. Even though overt or covert pressures may be exerted by a dominant culture, the possibility of rejection exists. Cherán residents in 1940, for example, were well aware of the consequences of mestizo penetration and often cited the fate of San Juan Parangaricutiro in contrast to exclusive Angahuan (see Nolan's paper). One had permitted mestizo residents, the other had not, and the Cherán residents I talked with wanted no part of the mestizos in Cherán.

Cherán residents also had their own experiences to support this opinion. Before the Revolution, there were some foreign residents and land owners in Cherán. Indeed, the isolation of Cherán was only relative, a myth that I once tended to accept and probably helped perpetuate. Cherán obviously was once under substantial mission influence in the 16th and 17th centuries and, as Castile notes, was once part of the encomienda of Sevina. The important colonial salt route from Colima to Mexico City passed through Cherán lands and although purely a mule trail, it can still be traced through the malapais west and south of Cherán. I doubt if only visual contacts occurred between the muleteers and the residents. One of my older friends in Cherán in 1940 claimed to have seen the Empress Carlotta when he was a boy. Apparently there were no true haciendas in the closed highland basin drainage in which Cherán is located, but the reason for this is not, as Castile supposes, that the area available was too small. In this conclusion evidently he has fallen into the common trap of viewing the hacienda in terms of the stereotype equating the hacienda in Mexico with the great cattle estancias of the northern highlands. By Oaxaca standards, for example, the drainage about Cherán would have supported at least half a dozen agricultural haciendas.

In the 19th century, Cherán was near the center of the extensive lumbering industry that brought the first railroad into the Tarascan highlands. Nahuatzen, but a short walk from Cherán, was founded as a lumber company town, although in 1940 it seemed to be thoroughly Tarascan, a center of native costume and of the production of the cross-stitched bands widely used for decorating traditional blouses and petticoats. During the Revolution after 1910, Cherán twice was burned completely to the ground in the bitter struggle between Cristeros and Agraristas. Cherán residents lived in the woods, died, or emigrated, mainly to the United States. If one could get together enough tortillas for a week and thirty pesos, one could walk to the Mexican National Railway line at Celaya and travel to Ciudad Juárez. The border was essentially open, and by walking into the hills back of El Paso one could find the Coyoteros for the Santa Fe Railroad and be shipped out to track maintenance crews anywhere from Chicago to Los Angeles. Indeed, some accounts suggest recruiters operated in Michoacán. Many stayed in California, Utah, or Colorado, shifting to agricultural work; others became workers in the steel mills in Gary, Indiana, or the sugar beet fields of Michigan. One even became the leader of a dance band in one of the main hotels in Houston. In 1940 I met Cheranese with all these histories, either home simply to visit, or returning to reclaim lands after 20 or 30 years. Following the Revolution and until the mid-1930s, Cherán was administered by a military governor supported by a detachment of troops (Beals 1946).

My reason for reviewing the Cherán data is twofold. They challenge, I think, the view that Cherán had no choices except those imposed by outside forces or their occupancy of a "region of refuge." They were not pushed into the region; they had occupied it for centuries. And they were not isolated or without awareness of the outside world. They accepted and reworked European cultural elements to the extent that little identifiable aboriginal culture remains. Primarily the Tarascan culture of 1940 was colonial Spanish with adaptations characteristically Tarascan. In this adaptive process, the Cheranese (and the Tarascans rather generally) were undergoing acculturation in the original meaning of the term, that is, as an accommodation and adaptation of a culture or social system in contact with another in contrast to its current bowdlerized use to mean essentially the assimilation of individuals.

At the same time, Castile reaches the conclusion that Cherán will maintain its enclavement status only if both the Cheranese and the members of the non-Tarascan culture around them continue to insist on it. Nevertheless, I doubt that outside influence will be effective so long as enough Cheranese cling to the symbols of status embodied in los costumbres. But this adherence, I suspect, will not continue for long; even in 1940 children playing in the street spoke Spanish. Many individuals have already shifted to the values of mestizo culture and abandoned the traditional symbols. Since 1940 in Cherán women's native dress apparently has been all but abandoned—in a collection trip the Museum of Cultural History at UCLA was able to get only one or two examples, treasured heirlooms at fantastic prices. Many people in 1940 were refusing the ritual obligations and contributed to their support only through collection commissions backed by civil authority. Altar societies were being successfully promoted by the church as a substitute for the rituals of the mayordomias. Once the rituals are gone and the costly wedding and funerary services abandoned, there will be little left of Tarascanness.

Actually, Castile probably has hit on the real reason for the termination of Cherán enclavement—the outside world has not so much been forced upon them as it has been opened up to them. Many from Cherán have chosen to compete in the outside "game," and many of them are winning. For them, abandoning enclavement status does not mean becoming a rural proletariat or city ghetto-dweller, but offers attainable rewards within the new system. Among more visible examples, all the good guitar makers and wood carvers of nearby Paracho now live in Mexico City or Guadalajara, where the most customers are, much like the Huichol craftsmen described by Weigand.

Nolan's chapter deals with the process of disenclavement among the Tarascans, focusing on the five villages most affected by the forcible relocations and adjustments after the volcanic eruption of Parícutin. She finds two main assimilative processes at work: migration to cities, and the penetration of the villages by the culture of the cities. Her discussion is preceded by a competent and penetrating review of relevant historical events leading to the original enclavement. Her methodology also is concrete, focusing on a detailed analysis of family groups through time. The sample size is small but the results, although tentative, are persuasive. Like Castile, Nolan is impressed by the adequacy of the assimilative adaptations made by many Tarascans; unlike Castile, however, she apparently recognizes (and is impressed with) the availability of rational choices among numerous alternatives rather than attributes the adaptations to pressures of the dominant culture. Among such people, Tarascanness no longer is viewed as a liability as it is among many economically marginal or former Tarascans. An exception is Angahuan, where the tourist trade makes "Tarascanness" a commercial asset. But this is a new Tarascanness, idealizing a past that never existed wherein individuals and families find roots of which they can be proud. This is a very different sort of enclavement than that of the Mayo, for example, and perhaps has more bearing on ethnic enclaves in industrial nations.

Comparison of the Castile and Nolan chapters reveals a difference of interpretation of the concept of choice. Castile seems to feel that if the only new alternatives are created by exogenous factors in the surrounding dominant culture, there can be no real choice involved. The community is essentially "forced" into new situations rather than exercising a choice. Nolan, in contrast, sees the exogenous factors as widening the opportunities for individual choices, and, as I pointed out earlier, possibly giving rise to a community consensus for the adoption of a particular strategy. In other words, Castile sees the Tarascans as pawns pushed about by external forces, while Nolan sees these same external forces as opening up a wider field of choices.

UNDERSTANDING ENCLAVEMENT

Most of the preceding remarks have tended to be critical of specific details and interpretations or have been intended to supplement the data and raise additional questions. This approach may obscure the very positive value of these chapters and their contribution to the understanding of enclavement and the shaping of more sophisticated theories for the formation and persistence of ethnic enclaves as well as for the alternative process of assimilation.

At first reading this contribution may not be obvious, for the chapters indicate much variation in the kinds of enclavement described and suggest many different causal factors. In fact, they are making unusually clear the complexities inherent in most social phenomena. Life notoriously is not simple, and social phenomena are even more complex. The authors thus show that enclavement may take many forms and that similar results may be the product of complex or different causal factors. Thus, in many ways, the Opata, Yaqui, and Mayo exhibit similar historical pressures, yet the end results are strikingly different in each case. The Nayaritas and Tarascans, at first sight both "west central highlanders," each retaining a strong sense of identity, actually occupy different terrains and have markedly different histories of isolation and external pressures. Among Nayaritas, substantial aboriginal elements have survived in recent cultures. Among Tarascans, aboriginal culture has been replaced almost completely by modified colonial-Indian elements, while subtly retaining a unique pattern. Tarascanness is hard to define, yet it is readily apparent and may be consciously used to exploit tourists and mestizo neighbors.

The significance of these results and interpretations is that they not only help us to understand segments of northwestern Mexican society, but they also have relevance for the understanding of ethnic enclaves everywhere, a point supported by the Weigand and Ron Siordia chapter on Jalisco mestizo ejidos. The goal to which this collection contributes is not just a theory for this limited area but one that can embrace similar groups elsewhere.

This connection between the problems of enclavement and the rapidly growing literature on ethnicity thus far has not been explored, yet it seems to me to cry out for a larger synthesis. Even the older literature with which I am familiar suggests that the collection of papers in this volume, with its multi-dimensional treatment of enclavement and even without the development of its full theoretical potential, has relevance for understanding such groups in the United States as the Amish, the Italians of New York and San Francisco, the Blacks of Brooklyn, the Chicanos of the Southwest, and many others. Each of these groups in varied ways and for quite different reasons has found satisfaction in the assertion of ethnic identity, often involving the search for roots that never existed or have ceased to exist. Examples are the Danes of Solvang (California) who, after World War II, idealized a prewar royalist Denmark that never was, and the Aztec Nationalist movement among the Chicanos that has tried to create the myth of an Aztec past, idealizing the most widely hated pre-Spanish group of Mexico. In some cases, the primary causative factor appears to be external pressure or the need for self-defense. In others, there is need for a common identity to create a sense of worth in precarious social situations. Perhaps in some instances these factors may be enough, but there also appears as a necessary precondition adherence to a common set of symbols—common language, shared religious beliefs and rituals, identifiable distinct value-sets, common historical origins—before other factors may operate. Or is it possible that the pressures may at times create the symbols providing identity?

It may be that this hope for a larger synthesis is a personal and utopian aspiration. A call to action in which others must do the hard work if a sound theoretical structure is to be developed is necessarily suspect. More modestly, I know these chapters have provided me with new insights into the persistence of ethnic cultures and identities everywhere.

Aguirre Beltrán 1967
Bancroft 1875–1876
Beals 1932b, 1943, 1945, 1946, 1969
Beals, Carrasco, and McCorkle 1944
Bennett and Zingg 1935
Brand 1935, 1951
Foster 1948
Fried 1969
Friedrich 1957, 1958
Grimes and Hinton 1969
Hernández 1902
Hinton 1959, 1961, 1964
Hrdlička 1908
Kennedy 1970
Kennedy and Lopez 1981
Kroeber 1931
Lumholtz 1902a, 1912
McGee 1898
Owen 1958, 1959, 1969
Parsons and Beals 1934
Passin 1942
Preuss 1912
Redfield 1950
Riley 1969
Sauer 1932, 1934, 1935
Sauer and Brand 1931
Service 1969
Spicer 1940, 1954, 1969b, 1980, 1984
Stanislawski 1947, 1950
Thomas and Swanton 1911
Weigand 1978
West 1948
Zingg 1938

References

Aberle, D. F., A. K. Cohen, A. K. Davis, M. J. Levy, Jr., and F. X. Sutton
    1950   The functional prerequisites of a society. *Ethics* 60(2): 100–111.

Aguirre Beltrán, Gonzalo
    1942   *El trabajo del indio comparado con el del negro en Nueva España*. Mexico: Mexico Agrario.
    1952   Problemas de la población indígena de la cuenca del Tepalcatepec. *Memorias de la Instituto Nacional Indigenista* 3. Mexico.
    1958   *Cuijla: esbozo etnográfico de un pueblo negro*. Mexico: Fondo de Cultura Económica.
    1967   Regiones de refugio: el desarrollo de la communidad y el proceso dominical en mestizo América. *Ediciones Especiales* 46. Mexico: Instituto Indigenista Interamericano.
    1970a   Review of *Guatemala: una interpretación histórico-social*, by Carlos Guzman Bockler and Jean-Loup Herbert. Siglo XXI Editores: 307–322. Mexico.
    1970b   Los símbolos étnicos de la identidad nacional. *Annuario Indigenista*: 101–140. Mexico: Instituto Indigenista Interamericano.
    1977   Los olvidados. *La Revista Interamericana Visión* 48(5): 6–10.

Alegre, P. Francisco Xavier
    1956–1960   *Historia de la provincia de la compañia de Jesús de Nueva España (1780)*. 4 Vols. New edition by Ernest J. Burrus and Felix Zubillaga, editors. Rome: Bibliotheca Instituti Historici S. J.

Arregui, Domingo Lázaro de
    1946   *Descripción de la Nueva Galicia (1621)*. New edition by François Chevalier. Sevilla: Escuela de Estudios Hispano Americanos de la Universidad de Sevilla.

Ashburn, P. M.
    1947   *The Ranks of Death*. New York: Coward-McCann.

Bakewell, P. J.
    1971   *Silver Mining And Society In Colonial Mexico: Zacatecas 1546–1700*. Cambridge: Cambridge University Press.

Balan, Jorge, Harley L. Browning, and Elizabeth Jelin
    1973   Men in a Developing Society. *Latin American Monographs* 30. Institute of Latin American Studies. Austin: University of Texas Press.

Bancroft, Hubert H.
    1875–1876   *The Native Races of the Pacific States of North America*. 5 Vols. San Francisco and New York.
    1886   *The Works of Hubert Howe Bancroft*. Vol. 10, *History of Mexico, Covering the Years 1521–1600*. San Francisco: The History Company.

Bannon, John F., S.J.
    1945   Pioneer Jesuit Missionaries on the Pacific Slope of New Spain. In *Greater America, Essays In Honor of Herbert Eugene Bolton*, pp. 181–197. Berkeley: University of California Press.
    1955   The Mission Frontier in Sonora, 1620–1687. *Monograph Series* 26. New York: United States Catholic Historical Society.

Barbosa, A. R., and Sergio Maturana
    1972   *El arrendamiento de tierras ejidales: un estudio en tierra caliente, Michoacán*. Mexico: Centro de Investigaciones Agrarias.

Bartell, Gilbert
    1964   Directed Culture Change among the Sonoran Yaqui. MS, doctoral dissertation, University of Arizona, Tucson.

Barth, Fredrik
    1969   Introduction. In *Ethnic Groups and Boundaries: The Social Organization of Culture Difference*, edited by Fredrik Barth. Boston: Little, Brown.

Bartra, Roger
    1974   *Estructura agraria y clases sociales en México*. Mexico: Serie Popular Era.

Beals, Ralph L.
    1932a   Aboriginal survivals in Mayo culture. *American Anthropologist* 34(1): 28–39.
    1932b   The comparative ethnology of northern Mexico before 1750. *Ibero-Americana* 2. Berkeley: University of California Press.
    1943   The aboriginal culture of the Cáhita Indians. *Ibero-Americana* 19. Berkeley: University of California Press.
    1945   The contemporary culture of the Cáhita Indians. *Bureau of American Ethnology, Bulletin* 142. Smithsonian Institution. Washington.
    1946   Cherán: a Sierra Tarascan village. *Institute of Social Anthropology Publication* 2. Smithsonian Institution. Washington.
    1953a   Acculturation. In *Anthropology Today*, edited by Alfred L. Kroeber, pp. 621–641. Chicago: University of Chicago Press.
    1953b   Social stratification in Latin America. *American Journal of Sociology* 58: 327–339.
    1969   The Tarascans. In *Handbook of Middle American Indians*, Vol. 8 (General editor, Robert Wauchope), *Ethnology*, Vol. 2, edited by Evon Z. Vogt, pp. 725–773. Austin: University of Texas Press.

Beals, Ralph L., Pedro Carrasco, and Thomas McCorkle
    1944   Houses and house use of the Sierra Tarascans. *Institute of Social Anthropology Publication* 1. Smithsonian Institution. Washington.

Bennett, Wendell C., and R. M. Zingg
    1935   *The Tarahumara: an Inland Tribe of Northern Mexico*. Chicago: University of Chicago Press.

Berdichewsky, Bernardo
    1979   Anthropology and the peasant mode of production. In *Anthropology and Social Change in Rural Areas*, edited by Bernardo Berdichewsky. The Hague: Mouton Publishers.

Berrin, Kathleen, editor
    1978   *Art of the Huichol Indians*. Fine Arts Museums of San Francisco. New York: Harry N. Abrams.

Bolton, Herbert E.
　1917　The mission as a frontier institution in the Spanish-American colonies. *American Historical Review* 23: 42–61.
　1932　*The Padre on Horseback: A Sketch of Eusebio Francisco Kino, S.J.* San Francisco: Sonora Press.
　1936　*Rim of Christendom, A Biography of Eusebio Francisco Kino, Pacific Coast Pioneer.* New York: Macmillan Company.

Borah, Woodrow W., and Sherburne F. Cook
　1963　The aboriginal population of central Mexico on the eve of the Spanish conquest. *Ibero-Americana* 45. Berkeley: University of California Press.

Brand, Donald D.
　1935　The distribution of pottery types in northwest Mexico. *American Anthropologist* 37: 287–305.
　1951　Quiroga: a Mexican municipio. *Institute of Social Anthropology Publication* 11. Smithsonian Institution. Washington.

Braybrooke, George
　1980　Ethnology in China. *Current Anthropology* 21(2): 264–266.

Broom, Leonard, Bernard J. Siegel, Evon Z. Vogt, and James B. Watson
　1954　Acculturation: an exploratory formulation. *American Anthropologist* 56(6): 973–1000.

Butterworth, Douglas
　1970　From royalty to poverty: the decline of a rural Mexican community. *Human Organization* 29: 5–31.

Carrera Stampa, Manuel, editor and annotator
　1955　*Memoria de los servicios que había hecho Nuño de Guzmán, desde que fue nombrado gobernador de Panuco en 1525.* Mexico: José Porrua e Hijos.

Castile, George P.
　1974　Cherán: la adaptación de una communidad tradicional de Michoacán. *Serie De Anthropología Social* 26. Mexico: Instituto Nacional Indigenista.
　1975　An unethical ethic: self-determination and the anthropological conscience. *Human Organization* 34(1): 35–40.
　1979　*North American Indians: An Introduction to the Chichimeca.* New York: McGraw-Hill.
　1981　On the Tarascanness of the Tarascans and the Indianness of the Indians. In *Persistent Peoples: Cultural Enclaves in Perspective,* edited by George P. Castile and Gilbert Kushner, pp. 171–191. Tucson: University of Arizona Press.

CETENAL (Comisión de Estudios del Territorio Nacional)
　1974　*Cartas de climatología.* Mexico.

Cloudsley-Thompson, J. L.
　1976　*Insects and History.* New York: St. Martin's Press.

Cook, Sherburne F., and Lesley B. Simpson
　1948　The population of central Mexico in the sixteenth century. *Ibero-Americana* 31. Berkeley: University of California Press.

Cooper, Donald B.
　1965　*Epidemic Disease in Mexico City, 1761–1813.* Austin: University of Texas Press.

Crumrine, N. Ross
　1964　The House Cross of the Mayo Indians of Sonora, Mexico: A Symbol in Ethnic Identity. *Anthropological Papers of the University of Arizona* 8. Tucson: University of Arizona Press.
　1975　A new Mayo Indian religious movement in northwest Mexico. *Journal of Latin American Lore* 1(2): 127–145.
　1977　*The Mayo Indians of Sonora: A People Who Refuse to Die.* Tucson: University of Arizona Press.
　1981　The ritual of the cultural enclave process: the dramatization of oppositions among the Mayo Indians of northwest Mexico. In *Persistent Peoples: Cultural Enclaves in Perspective,* edited by George P. Castile and Gilbert Kushner, pp. 109–131. Tucson: University of Arizona Press.

Cuidad Real, Antonio de
　1976　*Tratado Curioso y Docto de las Grandezas de la Nueva España.* (Relación breve y verdadera de algunas cosas de las muchas que sucedieron al Padre Fray Alonso Ponce en las provincias de la Nueva España siendo Comisario General de aquellas partes). 2 Vols. Josefina Garcias Quintana and Victor M. Castillo Farreras, editors and annotators. Mexico: Instituto de Investigaciones Históricas, Universidad Nacional Autónoma de México.

Dabdoub, Claudio
　1965　*Historia de el valle de Yaqui.* Mexico City: Librería de Manuel Porrua, S.A.

Decorme, Gerard, S.J.
　1941　*La obra de los Jesuítas Mexicanos durante la época colonial, 1572–1767.* 2 Vols. Mexico: Jose Porrua e Hijos.

Diener, Paul
　1978　The tears of St. Anthony: ritual and revolution in eastern Guatemala. *Latin American Perspectives* 5(3): 92–116.

Di Peso, Charles C.
　1974　Casas Grandes, A Fallen Trading Center of the Gran Chichimeca. 8 Vols. *Amerind Foundation Publication* 9. Dragoon, Arizona: Amerind Foundation, and Flagstaff: Northland Press.

Dirección General de Estadística, Mexico
　1972　*Noveno censo general de población, 1970.* Mexico.

Dixon, C. W.
　1962　*Smallpox.* London: J. and A. Churchill.

Dobyns, Henry F.
　1963　Indian extinction in the middle Santa Cruz River Valley, Arizona. *New Mexico Historical Review* 38(2): 163–181.

Dunne, Peter M., S.J.
　1940　*Pioneer Black Robes on the West Coast.* Berkeley: University of California Press.
　1944　*Pioneer Jesuits in Northern Mexico.* Berkeley: University of California Press.
　1948　*Early Jesuit Missions in Tarahumara.* Berkeley: University of California Press.

Eckstein, S.
　1966　*El ejido colectivo en México.* Mexico City: Fondo de Cultura Económica.

Erasmus, Charles J.
　1961　*Man Takes Control: Cultural Development and American Aid.* Minneapolis: University of Minnesota Press.
　1967　Culture change in northwest Mexico. In *Contemporary Change in Traditional Societies,* Vol. 3, Mexican and Peruvian Communities, edited by Julian H. Steward, pp. 3–131. Urbana: University of Illinois Press.
　1968　Community development and the encogido syndrome. *Human Organization* 27(1): 65–74.
　1970　Comment on Huizer. *Human Organization* 29(4): 314–320.

Fabila, Alfonso
　1940　*Las tribus Yaquis de Sonora: su cultura y anhelada autodeterminación.* Mexico: Depto. Asuntos Indígenas.

Faust, Ernest Carroll
　1949　Malaria incidence in North America. In *Malariology,* edited by Mark F. Boyd, Vol. 1, pp. 749–763. Philadelphia: W. B. Saunders.

Florencia, Francisco de, S.J.
　1955　*Historia de la provincia de la Compañía de Jesús de Nueva España (1694).* Mexico: Editorial Academia Literaria.

Flores, Edmundo
　1961　*Tratado de economía agrícola.* Mexico City: Fondo de Cultura Económica.

Fontana, Bernard L.
1976 The faces and forces of Pimería Alta. In *Voices from the Southwest, A Gathering in Honor of Lawrence Clark Powell*, edited by D. C. Dickinson, W. D. Laird, and M. F. Maxwell, pp. 45–54. Flagstaff: Northland Press.

Foster, George
1948 Empire's children: the people of Tzintzuntzan. *Institute of Social Anthropology Publication* 6. Smithsonian Institution. Washington.
1967 *Tzintzuntzan: Mexican Peasants in a Changing World*. Boston: Little, Brown.
1970 Comment on Huizer. *Human Organization* 29(4): 313–314.

Fried, Jacob
1969 The Tarahumara. In *Handbook of Middle American Indians*, Vol. 8 (General editor, Robert Wauchope), *Ethnology*, Vol. 2, edited by Evon Z. Vogt, pp. 846–870. Austin: University of Texas Press.

Friede, Juan
1967 Demographic change in the mining community of Muzo after the plague of 1629. *Hispanic American Historical Review* 47: 338–343.

Friedrich, Paul
1957 Community Study of a Tarascan Community. MS, doctoral dissertation, Yale University, New Haven.
1958 A Tarascan cacicazgo: structure and function. In Systems of Political Control and Bureaucracy in Human Societies, edited by V. F. Ray, pp. 23–29. *Proceedings of the 1958 Annual Spring Meeting of the American Ethnological Society*.

Fromm, Erich, and Michael Maccoby
1970 *Social Character in a Mexican Village*. New Jersey: Prentice-Hall.

Gámez García, Ernesto
1955 *El valle del Fuerte: historia y geografía*. Sinaloa, Mexico.
1985 *Historia antigua de Sinaloa del Mocorito al Zuaque, Culiacán*. Sinaloa: Universidad de Sinaloa.

Gibson, Charles
1964 *The Aztecs Under Spanish Rule: A History of the Indians of the Valley of Mexico, 1519–1810*. Stanford: Stanford University Press.

Gilbert, Alan
1974 *Latin American Development: A Geographical Perspective*. Middlesex, England: Penguin Books.

González Casanova, Pablo
1967 *La democracia en México*. Mexico City: Era.

González Cosío, Arturo
1961 Clases y estratos sociales. In *Mexico: cincuenta años de revolución*, Vol. 2. Mexico: Fondo de Cultura Económica.

Griffen, William B.
1979 Indian Assimilation in the Franciscan Area of Nueva Vizcaya. *Anthropological Papers of the University of Arizona* 33. Tucson: University of Arizona Press.

Grijalva, Juan de
1924 *Crónica de la orden de N.P.S. Augustin en las provincias de la Nueva España. . . de 1533 hasta el de 1592 (1624)*. Mexico: Imprenta Victoria.

Grimes, Joseph E., and Thomas B. Hinton.
1969 The Huicol and Cora. In *Handbook of Middle American Indians*, Vol. 8 (General editor, Robert Wauchope), *Ethnology*, Vol. 2, edited by Evon Z. Vogt, pp. 792–813. Austin: University of Texas Press.

Grindle, Merilee S.
1977 *Bureaucrats, Politicians, and Peasants in Mexico*. Berkeley: University of California Press.

Gutelman, Michel
1971 *Capitalismo y reforma agraria*. Mexico: Ediciones Era.

Hackenberg, Robert
1970 The social observatory: time series data for health and behavioral research. *Social Science and Medicine* 4: 343–357.

Hackett, Charles
1923– Historical Documents Relating to New Mexico, Nueva Vizcaya, and Approaches Thereto, to 1773. Collected by
1937 Adolph F. A. Bandelier and Fanny R. Bandelier. 3 Vols. *Carnegie Institution of Washington Publication* 330. Washington.

Hagen, E. E.
1962 *On the Theory of Social Change: How Economic Growth Begins*. Homewood, Illinois: Dorsey Press.

Hammond, George, and Agapito Rey, editors, translators, and annotators
1928 *Obregón's History of 16th Century Explorations in Western America*. Los Angeles: Wetzel.
1940 Narratives of the Coronado Expedition, 1540–1542. *Coronado Cuarto Centennial Publication*, Vol. 2. Albuquerque: University of New Mexico Press.

Harris, Marvin
1974 Why a perfect knowledge of all the rules one must know to act like a native cannot lead to the knowledge of how natives act. *Journal of Anthropological Research* 30(4): 242–251.
1979 *Cultural Materialism and the Struggle for a Science of Culture*. New York: Random House.

Hedrick, Basil C.
1978 The location of Corazones. In *Across the Chichimec Sea*, edited by Carroll L. Riley and B. Hedrick, pp. 228–232. Carbondale: University of Southern Illinois Press.

Hedrick, Basil C., and Carroll L. Riley, translators
1974 The Journey of the Vaca Party. *University Museum Studies* 2. Carbondale: Southern Illinois University Museum.
1976 Documents Ancillary to the Vaca Journey. *University Museum Studies* 5. Carbondale: Southern Illinois University Museum.

Hernández, Fortunato
1902 *Las razas indígenas de Sonora y la guerra del Yaqui*. Mexico: Editorial J. de Elizalde.

Herskovits, Melville J.
1938 *Acculturation: The Study of Culture Contact*. New York: J. J. Augustin.

Hewitt de Alcantara, Cynthia
1976 Modernizing Mexican agriculture: socio-economic implications of technological change 1940–1970. *Studies on the Green Revolution* 11. Geneva: United Nations Research Institute for Social Development.

Hinton, Thomas B.
1959 A Survey of Indian Assimilation in Eastern Sonora. *Anthropological Papers of the University of Arizona* 4. Tucson: University of Arizona Press.
1961 The Village Hierarchy as a Factor in Cora Indian Acculturation. MS, doctoral dissertation, University of California, Los Angeles.
1964 The Cora village: a civil-religious hierarchy in northern Mexico. In *Culture Change and Stability: Essays in Memory of Olive Ruth Barker and George C. Barker, Jr.*, edited by Ralph L. Beals, pp. 44–62. Los Angeles: University of California Press.

Hinton, Thomas B., and Phil C. Weigand, editors
1981 Themes of Indigenous Acculturation in Northwest Mexico. *Anthropological Papers of the University of Arizona* 38. Tucson: University of Arizona Press.

Howard, Michael C.
1982 Aboriginal brokerage and political development in southwest Australia. In *Aboriginal Power in Australian Society*,

edited by Michael C. Howard, pp. 159–183. Honolulu: University of Hawaii Press.

Hrdlička, Aleš
1903 The Chichimecs and their ancient culture. *American Anthropologist* 6: 51–89.
1908 Physiological and medical observations among the Indians of southwestern United States and northern Mexico. *Bureau of American Ethnology, Bulletin* 34. Smithsonian Institution. Washington.

Hu-DeHart, Evelyn
1981 *Missionaries, Miners, and Indians: Spanish Contact With the Yaqui Nation of Northwestern New Spain, 1533–1820.* Tucson: University of Arizona Press.
1984 *Yaqui Resistance and Survival: The Struggle for Land and Autonomy, 1821–1910.* Madison: University of Wisconsin Press.

Hudson, Charles
1976 *The Southeastern Indians.* Knoxville: University of Tennessee Press.

Huizer, Gerrit
1970 "Resistance to Change" and radical peasant mobilization: Foster and Erasmus reconsidered. *Human Organization* 29(4): 303–322.
1973 *El potencial revolucionario de campesino en América Latina.* Mexico City: Siglo XXI.

Hunt, Robert C.
1979 Introduction. In Regions of Refuge. *Society for Applied Anthropology Monograph Series* 1: 1–3.

Iwánska, Alicja
1971 *Purgatory and Utopia: a Mazahua Indian Village of Mexico.* Cambridge: Schenkman.

Jalisco, El Estado de
1969 Vol. 239, No. 26, 21 de octubre. Guadalajara.

Jansen, William H., II
1973 The applied man's burden: the problem of ethics and applied anthropology. *Human Organization* 32(3): 325–329.

Jones, J. A.
1962 Tepecano house types. *The Kiva* 27(4): 24–27.

Kaplan, Bernice A.
1965 Mechanization in Paracho, a craft community. In *Contemporary Cultures and Societies of Latin America*, edited by C. B. Heath and Richard N. Adams. New York: Random House.

Keesing, Felix M.
1953 Culture Change: An Analysis and Bibliography of Anthropological Sources to 1952. *Stanford Anthropological Series* 1. Stanford: Stanford University Press.

Kennedy, John M.
1970 *Inapuchi.* Mexico: Instituto Indigenista Interamericana.

Kennedy, John M., and Raul A. Lopez
1981 Semana Santa in the Sierra Tarahumara. A Comparative Study in Three Communities. *Museum of Cultural History, Occasional Papers* 4. Los Angeles: University of California.

Kitchens, S. F.
1949 Quartan Malaria. In *Malariology* 2: 1017–1026. Philadelphia: W. B. Saunders.

Kluckhohn, Clyde
1951 Values and value orientations in the theory of action. In *Toward a General Theory of Action*, edited by Talcott Parsons and Edward A. Shils, pp. 388–433. Cambridge: Harvard University Press.

Kluckhohn, Florence
1950 Dominant and substitute profiles of cultural orientations. *Social Forces* 28(4): 376–393.

Kroeber, Alfred L.
1931 The Seri. *Southwest Museum Papers* 6.

Lewis, Oscar
1952 Urbanization without breakdown: a case study. *The Scientific Monthly* 75: 31–41.
1961 *The Children of Sánchez.* New York: Random House.
1963 *Life in a Mexican Village: Tepoztlán Restudied.* Urbana: University of Illinois Press.
1966 The culture of poverty. *Scientific American* 215(4): 19–25.

Ley Federal de Reforma Agraria
1971 Mexico: Editorial Porrua, S.A.

Linton, Ralph, editor
1940 *Acculturation in Seven American Indian Tribes.* New York: Appleton-Century-Crofts.

Lumholtz, Carl
1891 Explorations in the Sierra Madre. *Scribner's Magazine* 10(5): 531–548.
1902a *Unknown Mexico.* 2 Vols. New York: Charles Scribner.
1902b *El Mexico desconocido.* 2 Vols. Mexico: Editora Nacional (1970).
1912 *New Trails in Mexico.* New York.

Lutes, Steven V.
1977 Alcohol-use Among the Yaqui Indians of Potam, Sonora, Mexico. MS, doctoral dissertation, University of Kansas, Lawrence.
1983 The mask and magic of the Yaqui Paskola clowns. In *The Power of Symbols: Masks and Masquerade in the Americas*, edited by N. Ross Crumrine and Marjorie Halpin, pp. 81–92. Vancouver: University of British Columbia Press.

Malinowski, Bronislaw
1938 (Editor) Methods of study of culture contact in Africa. *International Institute of African Languages and Cultures Memorandum* 15. London.
1945 *The Dynamics of Culture Change.* New Haven: Yale University Press.

Margolies, Luise
1969 The rural elite in a Mexican municipality. *Anthropological Quarterly* 42: 343–353.

Martínez, Miguel
1963 El alcohol en la salud individual y colectiva. *Higiens* 4: 343–357.

Mason, J. Alden
1912a The fiesta of the pinole at Azqueltán. *The Museum Journal* 3: 44–50. Philadelphia.
1912b Four Mexican-Spanish fairy-tales from Azqueltán, Jalisco. *Journal of American Folk-Lore* 25(92): 191–198.
1912c Los Indios Tepehuanes de Azqueltán. *Report of the Escuela Internacional de Arqueología e Etnología Americanas*, pp. 19–20.
1913 The Tepehuan Indians of Azqueltán. *Proceedings, 18th International Congress of Americanists*, pp. 344–351. London.
1948 The Tepehuan and other aborigines of the Mexican Sierra Madre Occidental. *América Indígena* 8(4): 289–301.
1952 Notes and observations on the Tepehuan. *América Indígena* 12: 33–53.
1981 The ceremonialism of the Tepecan Indians of Azqueltán, Jalisco. MS edited and with footnotes by Phil C. Weigand. In *Themes of Indigenous Acculturation in Northwest Mexico*, edited by Thomas B. Hinton and Phil C. Weigand, pp. 62–76. *Anthropological Papers of the University of Arizona* 38. Tucson: University of Arizona Press.

Mason, J. Alden, and George Agogino
1972 The Ceremonialism of the Tepecano. *Eastern New Mexico University Contributions in Anthropology* 4(1). Portales: Eastern New Mexico University.

McClelland, David C.
1961 *The Achieving Society*. Princeton: Van Nostrand.
McGee, W J
1898 The Seri Indians. *Bureau of American Ethnology, 17th Annual Report, 1895–96*. Smithsonian Institution. Washington.
McNeill, William H.
1976 *Plagues and Peoples*. Garden City: Anchor Press-Doubleday.
Mecham, John Lloyd
1927 *Francisco de Ibarra and Nueva Vizcaya*. Durham: Duke University Press.
Mendieta, Fray Gerónimo de
1945 *Historia Eclesiástica Indiana*. Mexico.
Miller, Frank C.
1973 *Old Villages and a New Town: Industrialization in Mexico*. Menlo Park: Cummings Press.
Moone, Janet R.
1969 Tarascan Development: National Integration in Western Mexico. MS, doctoral dissertation, University of Arizona, Tucson.
Morenos Sánchez, Manual
1960 *Política ejidal*. Mexico: U.N.A.M.
Mota y Escobar, Alonso de la
1940 *Descripción Geográfica de los Reinos de Nueva Galicia, Nueva Viscaya y Nuevo León (1605)*. Mexico: Editorial Pedro Robredo.
Nash, Manning
1955 The reaction of a civil-religious hierarchy to a factory in Guatemala. *Human Organization* 13(4): 26–28.
1958 Machine Age Maya: the Industrialization of a Guatemalan Community. *American Anthropological Association Memoir* 87.
Navarrette, Ifigenia M. de
1970 La distribución del ingreso en México: tendencias y perspectivas. In *El Perfil de México en 1980*, Vol. 1. Mexico City: Siglo XXI.
Navarro García, Luis
1967 *Sonora y Sinaloa en el siglo XVII*. Sevilla: Escuela de Estudios Hispano-Americanos.
Nentvig, Juan, S.J.
1980 *Rudo Ensayo: A Description of Sonora and Arizona in 1764*. Translated, clarified, and annotated by Alberto F. Pradeau and Robert R. Rasmussen. Tucson: University of Arizona Press.
Nolan, Mary Lee
1973 *The Towns of the Volcano: A Study of the Human Consequences of the Eruption of Parícutin Volcano*. Doctoral dissertation, Texas A and M University. Ann Arbor: University Microfilms.
1979 Impact of Parícutin on five communities. In *Volcanic Activity and Human Ecology*, edited by Payson D. Sheets and Donald K. Grayson, pp. 293–338. New York: Academic Press.
Nolan, Mary Lee, and Sidney Nolan
1979 The five towns of Parícutin. *The Geographical Magazine* 51: 338–344.
Nuñez Cabeza de Vaca, Alvar
1944 *Relación de los naufragios y comentarios. Tomo I*. Collección de libros y documentos referentes a la historia de América. Madrid: Librería General de Victoriano Suarez (1906). Also in *Naufragios de Alvar Nuñez Cabeza de Vaca*. Páginas para la historia de Sinaloa y Sonora, Vol. 1, pp. 7–74. Mexico: Editorial Layac.
Ocaranza, Fernando
1934 *Historia de la Medicina en México*. Mexico.

O'Connor, Mary I.
1980 Ethnicity and Economics: The Mayos of Sonora, Mexico. MS, doctoral dissertation, University of California, Santa Barbara.
Owen, Roger C.
1958 Easter ceremonies among Opata descendants of northern Sonora, Mexico. *The Kiva* 23(4): 1–11.
1959 Marobavi: A Study of an Assimilated Group in Northern Sonora. *Anthropological Papers of the University of Arizona* 3. Tucson: University of Arizona Press.
1969 Contemporary ethnography of Baja California, Mexico. In *Handbook of Middle American Indians*, Vol. 8 (General editor, Robert Wauchope), *Ethnology*, Vol. 2, edited by Evon Z. Vogt, pp. 871–878. Austin: University of Texas Press.
Pailes, Richard A.
1980 The upper Rio Sonora Valley in prehistoric trade. In New Frontiers in the Archaeology and Ethnohistory of the Greater Southwest, edited by Carroll L. Riley and Basil C. Hedrick. *Transactions of the Illinois State Academy of Science* 72: 20–39.
Palerm, Angel
1967 Agricultural systems and food production. In *Handbook of Middle American Indians* (General editor, Robert Wauchope), Vol. 6, edited by Manning Nash, pp. 26–52. Austin: University of Texas Press.
Parsons, Elsie Clews, and Ralph L. Beals
1934 The sacred clowns of the Pueblo and Mayo-Yaqui Indians. *American Anthropologist* 36: 491–514.
Passin, Herbert
1942 Tarahumara prevarication: a problem in field method. *American Anthropologist* 44: 235–247.
Pennington, Campbell W.
1969 *The Tepehuan of Chihuahua: Their Material Culture*. Salt Lake City: University of Utah Press.
1979 *The Pima Bajo of Central Sonora, Mexico, Their Material Culture*, Vol. I. Salt Lake City: University of Utah Press.
Pérez de Ribas, Andrés
1896 *Crónica y historia religiosa de la provincia de la Compañía de Jesús de México en Nueva España (1655)*. 2 Vols. Mexico: Sagrado Corazón.
1944 *Historia de los triumphos de nuestra santa fee entre gentes las más bárbaras y fieras del nueve orbe (1645)*. 3 Vols. Edited by Luis Alvarez y Alvarez de Cadena. Mexico: Editorial Layac.
1968 *My Life among the Savage Nations of New Spain* (original, 1644). Los Angeles: Ward Ritchie Press.
Pesqueira Olea, Eduardo
1985 Sonora: pronta ayuda a los agricultores damnificados por las inesperadas lluvias. *Tiempo (Hispano)* 86(2228): 27–28.
Polzer, Charles W., S.J.
1972 The Franciscan entrada into Sonora, 1645–1652, a Jesuit chronicle. *Arizona and the West* 14(3): 253–278.
1976 *Rules and Precepts of the Jesuit Missions of Northwestern New Spain, 1600–1767*. Tucson: University of Arizona Press.
Powell, Philip Wayne
1952 *Soldiers, Indians, and Silver: The Northward Advance of New Spain, 1550–1600*. Berkeley: University of California Press.
Preuss, K. T.
1912 Die Nayarit-Expedition, Textaufnahmen und Beobachtungen unter mexikanischen Indianern. Band 1. *Die Religion der Cora Indianer*. Leipzig.

Redfield, Robert
  1950 *A Village that Chose Progress: Chan Kom Revisited.* Chicago: University of Chicago Press.
Redfield, R., R. Linton, and M. J. Herskovits
  1936 Memorandum for the study of acculturation. *American Anthropologist* 38(1): 149–152.
Reff, Daniel T.
  1981 The location of Corazones and Señora: archaeological evidence from the Rio Sonora Valley, Mexico. In The Protohistoric Period in the North American Southwest, A.D. 1450–1700, edited by David R. Wilcox and W. Bruce Masse, pp. 94–112. *Arizona State Anthropological Research Papers* 24. Tempe: Arizona State University.
  1985 The Demographic and Cultural Consequences of Old World Diseases in the Greater Southwest, 1519–1660. MS, doctoral dissertation, University of Oklahoma, Norman.
Riley, Carroll L.
  1969 The Southern Tepehuan and Tepecano. In *Handbook of Middle American Indians,* Vol. 8 (General editor, Robert Wauchope), *Ethnology,* Vol. 2, edited by Evon Z. Vogt, pp. 814–821. Austin: University of Texas Press.
  1976 Sixteenth Century Trade in the Greater Southwest. *Southern Illinois University Museum Research Records* 10. Carbondale: Southern Illinois University.
  1982 The Frontier People: The Greater Southwest in the Protohistoric Period. *Center for Archaeological Investigations Occasional Paper* 1. Carbondale: Southern Illinois University.
Rollwagen, Jack
  1974 Mediation and rural-urban migration in Mexico: a proposal and case study. In *Latin American Urban Research, Anthropological Perspectives on Latin American Urbanization,* Vol. 4, edited by Wayne A. Cornelius and Felicity M. Trueblood. Beverly Hills: Sage.
Sauer, Carl O.
  1932 The road to Cibola. *Ibero-Americana* 3. Berkeley: University of California Press.
  1934 The distribution of aboriginal tribes and languages in northwestern Mexico. *Ibero-Americana* 5. Berkeley: University of California Press.
  1935 Aboriginal population of northwestern Mexico. *Ibero-Americana* 10. Berkeley: University of California Press.
Sauer, Carl O., and Donald D. Brand
  1931 Prehistoric settlements of Sonora with special reference to Cerros de Trincheras. *University of California Publications in Geography* 5: 67–148.
  1932 Aztatlán: prehistoric Mexican frontier on the Pacific Coast. *Ibero-Americana* 1. Berkeley: University of California Press.
Seevers, Maurice
  1971 Psychopharmacology of alcohol dependence. In Alcoholism and Drug Dependence. *Proceedings of the 29th International Congress.* Sydney: Butterworths Press.
Service, Elman R.
  1969 The Northern Tepehuan. In *Handbook of Middle American Indians,* Vol. 8 (General editor, Robert Wauchope), *Ethnology,* Vol. 2, edited by Evon Z. Vogt, pp. 822–829. Austin: University of Texas Press.
Shadow, Robert D.
  1978 Land, Labor and Cattle: The Agrarian Economy of a West Mexican Municipio. MS, doctoral dissertation, State University of New York, Stony Brook.
Shiels, W. Eugene, S.J.
  1934 *Gonzalo de Tapia (1561–1594), Founder of the First Permanent Jesuit Mission in North America.* New York: United States Catholic Historical Society.
Shurkin, Joel N.
  1979 *The Invisible Fire.* New York: G. P. Putnam and Sons.
Silva Herzog, Jesus
  1959 *El agrarismo Mexicano y la reforma agraria.* Mexico: Fondo de Cultura Mexicana.
Spicer, Edward H.
  1940 *Pascua: a Yaqui Village in Arizona.* Chicago: University of Chicago Press. (See also Spicer 1984 reprint.)
  1954 Potam: a Yaqui village in Sonora. *American Anthropological Association Memoirs* 77.
  1961 Yaqui. In *Perspectives in American Indian Culture Change,* edited by Edward H. Spicer, pp. 7–93. Chicago: University of Chicago Press.
  1962 *Cycles of Conquest: The Impact of Spain, Mexico, and the United States on Indians of the Southwest, 1533–1960.* Tucson: University of Arizona Press.
  1964 El Mestizaje cultural en el suroeste de Estados Unidos y noroeste de Mexico. *Revista de Indias* 24(95–96): 1–26. Madrid.
  1966 The process of cultural enclavement in Middle America. *35th International Congress of Americanists* 3: 267–279. Seville.
  1969a Political incorporation and cultural change in New Spain: a study in Spanish-Indian relations. In *Attitudes of Colonial Powers Toward the American Indian,* edited by Howard Peckham and Charles Gibson, pp. 107–135. Salt Lake City: University of Utah Press.
  1969b The Yaqui and Mayo. In *Handbook of Middle American Indians,* Vol. 8 (General editor, Robert Wauchope), *Ethnology,* Vol. 2, edited by Evon Z. Vogt, pp. 830–845. Austin: University of Texas Press.
  1971 Persistent cultural systems: a comparative study of identity systems that can adapt to contrasting environments. *Science* 174: 795–800.
  1976 The Yaquis: A Persistent Identity System. Paper presented at the Singer Symposium, 75th Annual Meeting of the American Anthropological Association, Washington.
  1980 *The Yaquis: A Cultural History.* Tucson: University of Arizona Press.
  1984 *Pascua: a Yaqui Village in Arizona.* Tucson: University of Arizona Press (reprint).
Stanislawski, Dan
  1947 Tarascan political geography. *American Anthropologist* 49: 46–55.
  1950 The anatomy of eleven towns in Michoacán. *Institute of Latin American Studies Publication* 10. Austin: University of Texas Press.
Stavenhagen, Rodolfo
  1966 Aspectos sociales de la estructura agraria en México. *América Indígena* 9(1): 3–19.
  1969a Marginalidad y participación en la reforma agraria Mexicana. *Revista Latinoamericana de Sociología* 5(2): 249–275. Buenos Aires: Centro de Investigaciones Económicas, Instituto Torcuato di Tella.
  1969b *Las clases sociales en las sociedades agrarias.* Mexico: Siglo XXI.
  1970a Classes, Colonialism and Acculturation. In *Comparative Perspectives in Stratification,* edited by Joseph Kahl. Boston: Little, Brown.
  1970b Social aspects of agrarian structure in Mexico. In *Agrarian Problems and Peasant Movements in Latin America,* edited by Rodolfo Stavenhagen. New York: Doubleday.

1971 Decolonializing applied social science. *Human Organization* 30(4): 333–344.
1975 *Social Classes in Agrarian Societies.* New York: Anchor.

Tannenbaum, Frank
1929 *The Mexican Agrarian Revolution.* New York: Anchor Books (1968).

Tello, Fray Antonio
1891 *Libro segundo de la crónica miscelanea de la Santa Provincia de Xalisco. . . .* Guadalajara: La República Literaria.

Thomas, C., and J. R. Swanton
1911 Indian languages of Mexico and Central America and their geographical distribution. *Bureau of American Ethnology, Bulletin* 44. Smithsonian Institution. Washington.

Treutlein, Theodore E.
1939 The economic regime of the Jesuit missions in the eighteenth century. *Pacific Historical Review* 8: 284–300.
1949 (Translator and annotator.) *Sonora, A Description of the Province, by Ignaz Pfefferkorn.* Albuquerque: University of New Mexico Press.
1965 (Translator and annotator.) *Missionary in Sonora, The Travel Reports of Joseph Och, S.J., 1755–1767.* San Francisco: California Historical Society.

Undreiner, George J.
1947 Fray Marcos de Niza and his journey to Cibola. *The Americas* 3: 415–486.

Vargas Montero, Guadalupe
1978 Los Yaquis de Sonora. *México Indígena, Supplement* 3.

Velázquez Chávez, María del Carmen
1961 *Colotlán: doble frontera contra los bárbaros.* Mexico: U.N.A.M.

Villa-Señor y Sánchez, Joseph Antonio de
1952 *Theatro Americano, descripción general de los reynos, y provincias de la Nueva-España, y sus jurisdicciones* (1748). Mexico: Editora Nacional.

Warman, Arturo
1976 *Y venimos a contradecir: los campesinos de Morelos y el estado nacional.* Mexico: Ediciones de las Casa de la Chata.
1978 Los indigenistas y el modelo de país. *Nexos* (Febrero), pp. 3–6.

Warren, Kay B.
1978 *The Symbolism of Subordination.* Austin: University of Texas Press.

Weigand, Phil C.
1969 The role of an indianized mestizo in the 1950 Huichol revolt, Jalisco, Mexico. Latin American Institute, *Specialia* 1, *Interamericana* 1. Carbondale: Southern Illinois University.
1972 Co-operative labor groups in the subsistence activities among the Huichol Indians of the gubernancia of San Sebastián Teponahuastlan, municipio of Mezquitic, Jalisco, Mexico. *Mesoamerican Studies* 7. Carbondale: Southern Illinois University Museum.
1976 The Role of the Huichol Indians in the Revolutions of Western Mexico. Paper presented to the Pacific Coast Council on Latin American Studies.
1977 Ethnoarchaeology of the Highlands of Western Mexico. Paper presented to the 42nd Annual Meeting of the Society for American Archaeology.
1978 Contemporary social and economic structure among the Huichol Indians. In *Art of the Huichol,* edited by Kathleen Berrin, pp. 101–115. San Francisco: Fine Arts Museum of San Francisco, Harry N. Abrams.

Weigand, Phil C., and Celia García de Weigand
1974 Migrations and the formation of the new barrios of the Villa de Etzatlán, Jalisco, Mexico. *Stony Brook Anthropologist* 1(1): 1–12. Stony Brook, New York.

West, Robert C.
1948 Cultural geography of the modern Tarascan area. *Institute of Social Anthropology Publication* 7. Smithsonian Institution. Washington.
1949 The mining community in northern New Spain: the Parral mining district. *Ibero-Americana* 30: 131–147. Berkeley: University of California Press.

West, Robert C., and James J. Parsons
1941 The Topia road: a trans-sierran trail of colonial Mexico. *The Geographical Review* 31: 406–413.

Whiteford, Andrew H.
1964 *Two Cities of Latin America.* Garden City: Doubleday.

Wilkie, Raymond
1971 *San Miguel: A Mexican Collective Ejido.* Stanford: Stanford University Press.

Williams, Glyn
1978 Industrialization and ethnic change in the lower Chubut Valley, Argentina. *American Ethnologist* 5(3): 618–631.

Wilson, G., and Monica Wilson
1945 *The Analysis of Social Change Based on Observations in Central Africa.* Cambridge: Cambridge University Press.

Wolf, Eric
1955 The Mexican Bajío in the Eighteenth Century. *Middle American Research Institute Publication* 17. New Orleans: Tulane University Press.
1959 *Sons of the Shaking Earth: The People of Mexico and Guatemala: Their Land, History, and Culture.* Chicago: University of Chicago Press.
1967 Closed corporate peasant communities in Meso-America and central Java. In *Peasant Society,* edited by Jack M. Putter, pp. 230–246. Boston: Little, Brown.

Yoneyama, T.
1967 Kaminosho: a farm village suburban to Osaka in south central Japan. In *Contemporary Change in Traditional Societies,* edited by Julian H. Steward, Vol. 2, pp. 187–257. Urbana and Chicago: University of Illinois Press.

Zantwijk, Rudolf A. M. van
1967 *Servants of the Saints: The Social and Cultural Identity of a Tarascan Community in Mexico.* Assen, The Netherlands: Royal Van Gorcum.

Zingg, R. M.
1938 The Huichols: Primitive Artists. *University of Denver Contributions to Ethnography* 1. Denver.

Zinsser, Hans
1934 *Rats, Lice, and History.* Boston: Little, Brown.

Index

Acaxee Indians, 87, 88, 89, 92, 98
Accommodation, 11, 14, 16, 17, 53, 101. *See also* Acculturation; Assimilation
Acculturation, 8, 35, 36, 39–45, 85, 96, 101. *See also* Accommodation; Assimilation
Agiabampo, 35, 98
Agrarian bank. *See* Banks
Agrarian Code, 42–44. *See also* Land reform
Agricultural machinery, 4, 23, 48, 51, 52. *See also* Agriculture, business development of
Agriculture
  business development of, ix, 4, 5, 13, 14, 15, 17, 20, 21–24, 34, 46–55, 74, 98
  coamil (swidden), 41, 44, 50
  floodwater, 12, 24
  irrigation, 21, 22, 23, 26, 34, 35, 40, 46–55, 85, 90, 92, 98, 100
  plow, 23, 41, 44, 47, 58, 59, 85, 91
  subsistence, 15, 17, 18, 33, 35, 36, 40, 41, 48, 52, 55, 60–71, 76, 81, 82, 90, 97, 98. *See also* Farming; Gardens
Aguirre Beltrán, Gonzalo, ix, x, 9, 21, 33, 73, 74, 79, 97
Ahome Indians, 35, 36, 99
Ahualulco Basin, 47, 49
Alamos, 2, 98
Alcohol abuse, 18, 31, 59. *See also* Beer; Fiestas; Mescal
Alcoholic beverages. *See* Beer; Mescal
Altos de Jalisco, 48
Angahuan, Michoacán, 60–71, 100, 101
Apache raids, 97
Archaeology, in the Sonora Valley, 92
Arriba, Manos, 3
Arrows, 1, 31
Assimilation, ix–x, 10, 11, 14, 15, 16, 19–20, 21, 23, 25, 33, 36, 39, 57, 74, 78, 80, 97, 99, 100, 101, 102. *See also* Accommodation; Acculturation
Augustinian monastery, friars, 59, 61
Azqueltán, 39–45
Aztatlán, 85

Bahi Mariam, Bahi Reyesim, 7
Baja California, 52, 85
Banditry. *See* Robbery
Bands, musical, 59
Banks, agrarian or ejido, 4, 14, 17, 23, 31
Baptism, of Indians, 85–92
Basilio, Father Tomás, 88
Beals, Ralph, ix, x, 1–3, 14, 73, 76, 79, 80, 81, 95–102
Beans, 31, 40, 41, 59, 91. *See also* Garbanzo cultivation
Beer, 18
Bennett, Wendell, 3, 96
Berdichewsky, Bernardo, 9
Beteta, Ramón, 1
Bilateral kindred, 14, 15, 24. *See also* Kin, kinship
Bilingualism, 36, 59, 61, 63, 64, 68, 69, 70, 101
Boas, Franz, 8

Boats, 22
Bolaños canyon, 39, 40, 41
Bolaños River, 40, 43
Bolton, Herbert E., 90, 91
Boundary Maintenance, 11, 15, 33, 34, 45, 74, 98
Bows and arrows, 1, 31
Brand, Donald, 96
Burial, mass, 87
Bustamente, Don Francisco de, 91

Cabeza de Vaca. *See* Nuñez Cabeza de Vaca
Cáhita Indians, x, 2, 14, 89, 91, 92, 97, 98, 99
Cáhitan language, 12, 99
Cahuemetos Indians, 87
Cajeme. *See* Ciudad Obregón
Cakchiquel Indians, 81
Calpulli, pre-Hispanic, 44
Calzontzin, Michoacán, 63, 67, 70, 71
Camino Real de la tierra adentro, 86
Cantel, Guatemala, 31
Cárdenas, Lázaro, President, 12, 13, 23, 55, 100
Cargo system, 45, 81
Cártamo, 17, 23
Cattle, 14, 22, 34, 35, 40, 41, 42, 45, 50, 53, 58, 67, 85, 90, 91, 92, 95, 98, 99, 100
Ceremonial goods, 1, 12, 45, 60, 95. *See also* Ritual life
Cerros de Tancitaro, 58, 60
Charles III, 85
Cherán, Michoacán, x, 73–83, 96, 100, 101
Chicorato Indians, 87
Chihuahua, 87, 95, 96
Chiles, 59
Chinipa Indians, 88, 98
Choice, availability of, 73–83, 101–102
Churches, 5, 7, 36, 40, 60, 73, 92, 101. *See also* Missionaries
Ciudad Obregón, 1, 2, 4, 8, 12, 14, 19, 23
Civil-religious hierarchy. *See* Government, Indian
Classes, social (class system), 9, 21, 23, 25, 100
Climate, in Sierra Tarasca, 58
Closed corporate community, 73, 74, 81, 82
Coffee, 4, 5, 6
Colonial era. *See* Colonization; Contact period, Spanish
Colonization, 9, 12, 13, 19, 35, 39, 58–59, 76, 99
Compadrazgo, compadres, 14, 15, 17, 28, 73, 81
Comunidad agraria, 40–45
Comunidad indígena, 40–45
Congregación, 40
Consanguineal kin, 58. *See also* Kin, kinship
Contact, conditions of, 8, 9, 10
Contact period, Spanish, 11, 12, 24–25, 34–35, 39, 40, 41, 47, 58–59, 73–76, 78, 85–92, 97, 98, 99. *See also* Missionaries
Cora area, 3
Cora Indians, 39, 40, 95, 96, 97
Corn, 5, 17, 23, 31, 40, 41, 47–55, 58, 59, 71, 76, 91. *See also* Agriculture
Coronado, 92
Cortez, Hernán, 58
"Costumbres," 73, 74, 80, 81, 101

Cotton, 23, 31
Coyote skin headdress, 1
Craft production, specialization, 40, 59, 65, 67, 76, 85, 90
Creole immigrants, 40
Cristero Revolt, 48
Crops. *See* Agriculture; and by specific name
Cross, crucifix, 7, 24, 25, 28, 29–30, 99. *See also* Ritual life
Cruz, Father Diego de la, 88
Culiacán, 86, 97
Cultic movements, 18–19, 74
Cultivation machinery. *See* Agricultural machinery
Culture change, role of choice in, 73–83. *See also* Accommodation; Acculturation; Assimilation; Enclavement; Integration; Regions of refuge
"Culture of repression," 76
Curing, curers, 26, 27, 29, 31

Dances, 24, 28, 29, 59, 70. *See also* Fiestas
De jure entitlement, 48
Díaz, Porfirio, 12, 13, 25, 31, 98, 99
Dingfelder, Gus, 1
Diseases, x, 1, 2, 3, 11, 39, 58, 73, 74, 85–93, 97
Domestic animals, 12, 22, 50, 59, 90, 91, 92. *See also* by specific name
Domestic plants, 12, 59. *See also* by specific name
Donkeys, 50
Drought, 87, 88
Drums, war, 1
Durango, 85, 86, 87
Dysentery, 86, 88, 89

Earnings. *See* Income; Labor, wage
Economy, economic activities, 11, 14, 15, 17, 18, 21–23, 30, 31, 33, 34, 35–37, 39, 42, 43, 44, 45, 57, 59, 60–71, 81, 85, 86, 90, 91, 92, 98, 99, 100, 101
Education, 11, 13, 17, 21, 36, 40, 52, 57, 61–71, 81, 99
El Fuerte, 2, 34
Embedded groups, x, 8, 10, 21, 31. *See also* Enclavement
Empalme, 12
Enclavement, ix–x, 8, 9, 10, 11–20, 21–31, 33–37, 59, 63, 70, 73–83, 97–102. *See also* Regions of refuge
"Encogido syndrome," 75
Endogamy, 59, 61, 63, 64, 67–69. *See also* Marriage
"Enduring people." *See* Persistent cultural systems
Epidemics, 85–92. *See also* Diseases
Espinosa, Father Juan Augustín de, 87
Estación Vicam, 2, 3, 12
Etcheverría, President, x
Etchoja, 4
Ethnohistory, 95
Etzatlán, Jalisco, 46–55

111

Index

Exchange systems, 12, 14–15, 30, 34, 35, 59, 61, 86, 90, 91, 92, 98, 100. *See also* Market economy

Family
 extended, 15
 lineages, 57–72
 nuclear, 15
Faría, Father Francisco Xavier de, 91
Farming, 12, 14, 15, 22, 23, 24, 26, 33–37, 39, 40, 41, 46–55, 58, 71, 76, 85, 90, 91, 92, 97, 98, 99, 101. *See also* Agriculture, subsistence; Gardens
Fertilizers, 21, 23, 41, 47, 51, 52, 55
Fiestas, 16, 18, 29, 36, 45, 59, 60, 61, 63, 70. *See also* Ritual life
Fish, 12, 22, 35, 40, 86, 91
Fishing cooperatives, 14, 22
Flores, General Angel, 1
Fonte, Father Juan, 88
Foods, 3, 4, 5, 6, 7, 18, 21, 22, 23, 35, 59, 86, 91, 92, 98, 99. *See also* Agriculture, subsistence; Farming; and by specific name
Fuerte River, 2, 12, 21, 33, 34, 35, 87, 96, 97, 98, 99

Garbanzo cultivation, 47–55
Gardens, subsistence, 17, 18, 23. *See also* Agriculture, subsistence; Foods
Gathering, 24, 35
Genocide, 12
Goats, 22, 92
God, Saints, 5, 21, 24, 25, 27, 28, 29, 31, 59, 60, 81. *See also* Ritual life
Government
 federal, 12, 13–14, 15, 17, 20, 24–25, 34–35, 42, 44, 55, 82. *See also* Policies, state and national
 Indian civil-religious, 13, 14, 15, 17, 45, 73, 98. *See also* Mayordomia system
 state and local, 12, 13, 14, 24–25, 44, 76–83. *See* also Policies, state and national
Granaries, 58
"Great Matlazahuatl," 86
Guadalajara, 48, 52, 76, 86, 101
Guasave Indians, 88, 91
Guaymas, 12, 16
Gulf of California, 21
Guzmán, Nuño de, 58, 59, 73, 85, 97

Haciendas, 34, 35, 36, 43, 53, 61, 63, 74, 98, 99, 100, 101
Haro, Pedro de, 42
Harvests, 47–55. *See also* Agriculture
Headdresses, 1
Health care, 13, 21, 23, 81. *See also* Diseases
Herbicides, 47
Hermosillo, 96, 98
Hernández, Fortunato, 95
Herskovits, Melville, 8
Hofmann, Arthur and Mona, 1, 2, 98
Horses, 22, 50
Housing, 1, 4, 5, 16, 17, 40, 58, 60, 70, 85, 91, 92
Hrdlička, Aleš, 95
Huatabampo, 23, 31
Huichol area, ix
Huichol Indians, 3, 39, 40, 42, 95, 96, 100, 101
Hunting, 12, 24, 31, 35

Ibarra expedition, 86, 90, 99
Identity, Indian, 9, 21, 25–28, 33, 36–37, 39, 40, 42, 45, 59, 70, 73–82, 99, 100, 101, 102
Ihuatzio, 78, 79, 81

Illness, 29. *See also* Diseases
Immigrants, 40, 44, 100. *See also* Migration
Income, 15, 17, 50, 51, 52. *See also* Labor, wage
Indigenismo, 76
Infant mortality, 81. *See also* Diseases
Influenza, 86, 88
Inheritance. *See* Land, inheritance of
I.N.I. Regional Coordinating Center, 76, 78, 81, 82
Insecticides, 21, 23, 52
Insistence, 76, 78, 79, 80
Instituto Nacional Indigenista, 9
Integration, integrative agencies, 7, 8, 10, 11, 14, 15, 17, 19, 20, 73–83. *See also* Assimilation
Intermarriage. *See* Marriage
International Institute of Anthropology, 95
Intoxication. *See* Alcohol abuse
Irrigation projects, 76, 77. *See also* Agriculture, irrigation
Irritila Indians, 87, 88, 89
Izolta, 40, 43

Jalisco, x, 39–45, 100, 102
Jesus María, 97
Júpare, 5, 7, 24

Kelly, Isabel, 3
Kin, kinship, 12, 14, 15, 17, 20, 24, 57–71, 81
Konti, 5, 7. *See also* Ritual life
Kroeber, Alfred, 1, 96

La Florida, 36
La Gúasima, 40, 43, 44
La Joya, Jalisco, 54
La Piedad, Michoacán, 48
Labor
 division of, 15, 41, 92
 wage, 17, 18, 22, 23, 35, 36, 44, 53, 57, 63–71, 76, 98, 101
Ladinos, 45, 79. *See also* Mestizos
Laguna region, 87
Lagunero Indians, 89
Lake Cuitzeo, 58
Lake Pátzcuaro, 58
Land reform, 9, 14, 17, 19, 23, 24, 30, 31, 34, 35, 36, 40–45. *See also* Lands
Lands
 church, 92
 communal, x, 39–45, 59, 61, 92
 ejido, 4, 14, 18, 20, 21, 22, 23, 24, 31, 34–37, 39–45, 46–55, 65–67, 70–71, 77, 100, 102
 inheritance of, 23, 24, 44, 50, 65, 67, 70–71
 privately owned, 48–55, 59, 61, 64–70, 100
 renting of (leasing), 21, 36, 43, 44, 50, 67, 98
 selling rights to, 21, 44
Leon, Nicolas, 95
Ley fuga, 3
Leyes de Desamortización, 41, 42
"Limited good," 75, 83
Linseed, 23
Linton, Ralph, 8
Livestock. *See* Cattle; Donkeys; Goats; Horses; Oxen; Sheep
Lorencio, Father Juan, 88
Los Amoles, 44
Los Angeles, California, 52, 64, 101
Los Reyes, Michoacán, 60
Lumber company, 101
Lumholtz, Carl, 73, 79, 95

Machinery, *See* Agricultural machinery
Magdelena, Jalisco, 40, 46–55
Magdalena-Etzatlán basin, x, 46–55

Maize. *See* Corn
Malaria, 85, 86, 89
Malinowski, Bronislaw, 8
Malnutrition, 87
Marginality, marginalization, ix, 11, 18, 33, 34, 36, 37, 42, 47–55, 71
Market economy, 14, 15, 17, 23, 34, 42, 45, 86. *See also* Economy; Merchants
Marriage, intermarriage, 12, 15, 59, 61, 64, 67, 68, 69
Mason, J. Alden, 95, 96
Mayan Cult of the Talking Cross, 74
Mayo Indians, ix, x, 1–8, 11–20, 21–31, 33–37, 77, 88, 89, 92, 96, 97, 98, 99, 102
Mayo River, 2, 4, 21, 25, 26, 76, 77, 88, 97, 98, 99
Mayo-Yaqui contrasts, ix–x, 18
Mayordomia system, 59–60, 61, 63, 101
Measles, 86, 87
Medical treatment, modern, 23. *See also* Health care
Méndez, Father Pedro, 88
Merchants, 65–70, 86. *See also* Market economy
Mescal, 91
"Mestizaje," 74
Mestizos, ix–x, 2, 5, 10, 11, 12, 13, 14, 15, 16, 17, 18, 25–31, 47–55, 61, 68, 69, 74, 76–83, 97, 98, 99, 100, 101, 102
Mexico City, 14, 76, 82, 86, 100, 101
Mezquitic, 44
Michoacán, 48, 57–72, 73–83, 86, 95, 97, 101
Migration, x, 12, 15, 40, 48, 52, 55, 57, 63, 64, 65, 66, 67, 70, 81, 98, 101
Miguel Silva, Michoacán 63
Military conquest, 12, 17, 18, 19, 25, 34, 48, 58, 73, 76, 85, 97, 98. *See also* Contact period, Spanish; Wars
Mines, mining, 41, 61, 74, 86, 98, 99
Minifundia, minifundistas, 36, 53, 81. *See also* Land reform
Missionaries, 59, 60, 61, 97
 Franciscan, 73, 74
 Jesuit, x, 12, 21, 24, 34, 85–94
Mitla, 3
Mixton War, 74
Mochicahui, 35, 36
Mocorito, 87
Modernization, ix, 3, 4, 5, 20, 21–31, 55, 57, 63, 68, 70, 76–83, 91, 101
Morelia, Michoacán, 58, 76
Mule strings, mules, 50, 59, 61, 86, 100
Music, 26, 29, 59

National Indian Institute, 5
Navojoa, 2, 3, 4, 5, 12, 16, 23
Nayarit, 3, 39, 86, 87, 100, 101
Nebome Indians, 88
Negro populations, 9
Nueva Galicia, 58, 85, 86, 87
Nueva Vizcaya, 86, 91
Nuevo Obelatos, 48
Nuñez Cabeza de Vaca, Alvar, 97

Oaxaca, 3, 98, 101
Obregón, Alvaro, 98
Obregón, Baltasar, 86, 90
Obreros, 14
Occupations, of Indians, 17, 18, 58–71, 81
Ocoroni, 87
Ocotlan, 88
Once Pueblos, 58
Opata Indians, ix, x, 88, 89, 92, 97, 98, 102
"Oppositional process," 77, 78

Orchards, 91
Oxen, 91

Pahkom, 4, 5. *See also* Ritual life
Panaleros, 79
Paracho, Michoacán, 60–71
Parícutin (town), 61
Parícutin volcano, x, 57, 61, 63, 64, 70, 101
Pariseros, 5, 7
Parrot feather headdress, 1
Parsons, Elsie Clews, 2, 3, 95, 96
Particulares, 14
Pascua Village, Tucson, 1, 2, 31, 96
Passin, Herbert, 97
Pasturage. *See* Cattle
Patron saint. *See* God, Saints
Peas, 23
Peasants, 9, 45, 75, 78
Pérez, Father Martín, 85, 87, 91
Pérez de Ribas, Andres, 87, 88, 89, 91, 92, 97
Persistent cultural systems, 73, 75, 76, 77, 78, 79, 80, 102
Personality traits, 28
Pesticides, 47
Pima Bajo Indians, 12, 88, 89, 92
Pistoleros, 20
Plants. *See* Domestic plants; and by specific name
Platform structures, 92
Playas, 47
Plows. *See* Agriculture, plow
Pluralism, 11, 20
Pneumonia, 88
Policies, state and national, 11, 13, 18, 19, 20, 23, 24–25, 33–37, 40–45, 57, 74, 76–83, 85, 92, 98, 99, 101
Political organization, power, 11, 12, 13, 18, 21, 23, 24, 29, 31, 34, 36, 42, 44, 45, 58, 76, 90, 91, 92, 99. *See also* Government
Population figures, 12, 40, 42, 43, 67, 85–92
Porfirio, Don, 76. *See also* Díaz, Porfirio
Potam, 1, 2, 13, 18, 19, 96
Poverty, ix, 18, 68, 70, 75, 81, 83
Precipitation. *See* Rainfall
Preuss, Theodore, 95
Produce, marketing of, 51. *See also* Exchange systems; Market economy
Puig Cassauranc, José Manuel, 1
Punishment, 18, 28
Purepeachas. *See* Tarascan Indians

Quiroga, Vasco de, 58–59, 73

Radin, Paul, 3
Raids. *See* Wars
Railroads, 61, 96, 98, 101. *See also* Train travel
Rainfall, amounts of, 40, 47–55, 58, 87
Ramírez, Father Gerónimo, 87
Rancherías, 12, 24, 35–37, 85, 88, 90, 91, 92, 97. *See also* Settlement patterns
Redfield, Robert, 3, 8, 96
Reducción, 12, 40. *See also* Land reform
Regions of refuge, ix, x, 8, 9, 10, 21, 33, 35, 36, 39, 74, 76, 97–102
Residence patterns, 15, 28. *See also* Housing; Settlement patterns
Revitalization movements, ix, 1, 18–19, 21
Revolution, Mexican, 1–3, 12, 23, 25, 31, 35, 42, 43, 76, 95, 98, 99, 100, 101

Rio Culiacán, 87
Rio Grande de Santiago, 40
Ritual life, Indian, 1, 4, 5, 7, 12, 15, 16, 18, 21, 24–29, 33, 35, 36, 37, 45, 59, 81, 98–99, 101
Roads, 3, 30, 55, 61, 76
Robbery, theft, 3, 18
Rosenberg, Max, 1

Saenz, Moisés, 1
San Blas, 35
San Felipe, 85, 88
San Ignacio Rio Muerte, 19
San Isidro, 40
San Juan Parangaricutiro, 60–71, 100
San Juanito, Jalisco, 47, 53, 54
San Miguel, 35, 36
San Pedro, Jalisco, 53
Santiago, Jalisco, 54
Sauer, Carl, 1, 85, 96
Sayula Valley, Jalisco, 48
Schools. *See* Education
Schoolteachers, 61, 65, 66, 68, 69, 82. *See also* Education
Seri Indians, 12, 95, 96
Serpents, in religion, 5
Sesame, 23
Settlement patterns, 12, 15, 21, 29, 35, 36, 40, 57–71, 85, 90, 91, 92, 97, 98, 99. *See also* Rancherías
Sevina, Michoacán, 73
Sheep, 22, 90, 92
Shipping ports, 35
Sierra de Ameca, 47
Sierra de Bacatete, 1, 2
Sierra Madre, 21, 22, 34, 39, 40, 42, 85–92, 95, 96
Sierra Tarasca, 57–71, 73–83
Silver mines, 41, 86
Sinaloa, Mexico, ix, x, 1, 33–37, 85–93, 96, 98
Sinaloa River, 2, 85, 87, 97, 99
Slave raiders, 97
Smallpox, 85, 87, 88, 89, 90
Social classes. *See* Classes
Social Science Research Council, 8
Socioeconomic categories, Cosio's, 68. *See also* Economy
Socios, sociedades, 14
Soil fertility, 47
Sorghum, 47–55
Spanish contact. *See* Colonization; Contact period, Spanish; Missionaries
Spicer, Edward H., ix, x, 8, 9, 15, 24, 31, 73, 75, 76, 77, 78, 80, 81, 91, 96, 97, 98, 99
Squash, 31, 40, 41, 91
State policies. *See* Policies, state and national
Students. *See* Education
Subsistence patterns, 12. *See also* Agriculture, subsistence; Farming; Fishing cooperatives; Gathering; Hunting
Sud Pacífico train, 1, 98
Sugarcane, 49, 99

Tahue Indians, 98
Tapia, Father Gonzalo de, 85, 87, 91
Tarahumara Indians, 3, 88, 89, 92, 96, 97
Tarascan area, ix

Tarascan Indians, x, 57–72, 95, 96–97, 100, 101, 102
Tarasco, 97
Taxation, 20, 44, 52. *See also* Tribute, paying of
Tehueco Indians, 24, 97, 99
Tenochtitlán, 58
Tepecano Indians, x, 39–45, 95, 96, 97, 100
Tepehuan Indians, 87, 88, 89, 97
Tepic, 3, 95
Tepotzlan, 74, 96
Thorn forests, 3, 21, 98, 99
Topia, 86, 87, 88, 91
Topia Road, 86
Topolobampo, 35, 96
Tourism, tourists, 63–64, 70, 81, 101, 102
Trade. *See* Exchange systems; Market economy
Train travel, 1–3, 98. *See also* Railroads
Tribal organization, 13, 24, 58, 59, 97. *See also* Government, Indian
Tribute, paying of, 34–35, 73, 74. *See also* Taxation
Trincheras culture, 96
Tylor, Edward, 8
Typhoid, 86, 87, 88, 89
Tzintzuntzan, 58, 77–78, 80, 83, 96

Unified Yaqui Tribe, 13. *See also* Yaqui Indians
Unión de Ejidos, 51
United States, migration to, 52, 63, 64, 65, 66, 67, 70, 76, 98, 101
Uruapan, Michoacán, 57, 60, 63, 66, 70, 76

Velasco, Juan Bautista de, 87
Vicam Estación. *See* Estación Vicam
Vicam Pueblo, 13
Villa Guerrero, 39, 40, 41, 42, 43, 44
Vineyards, 91
Violence, fighting (individual), 18, 19, 20, 47–48.
Volcán de Tequila, 47
Volcanoes, x, 47, 57, 61, 63, 64, 70, 101

Wage labor. *See* Labor, wage
Wars, warfare, 1–3, 12, 74, 97, 98, 99. *See also* Contact period, Spanish; Military conquest
Water supplies, 12, 22, 23, 30, 31, 34, 36, 46–55, 58, 98, 99. *See also* Agriculture, irrigation
Wheat, 4, 17, 21, 23, 47–55, 85, 91
White, Leslie, 3
Witchcraft, 18, 79

Xixime Indians, 88

Yaqui Indians, ix, 1–3, 12–20, 24, 25, 31, 75, 79, 80, 88, 89, 90, 92, 95, 96, 97, 98, 99, 102
Yaqui Indigenous Community, 12–14, 17
Yaqui-Mayo area, ix-x, 1–8
Yaqui River, 1, 12, 21, 76, 88, 98, 99
Yucatan, 25, 74, 98

Zacan, Michoacán, 60–71
Zacatecas, 48, 86
Zacateco Indians, 87, 88, 89
Zamora, Michoacán, 58, 61, 76
Zapata, Father Juan Ortiz, 89
Zapotec Indians, 3
Zinacantan, 74
Zingg, B. M., 3, 96
Zirosto, Michoacán, 59, 60–71